Fiscal Federalism in the European Union and Its Countries

A Confrontation between Theories and Facts

P.I.E. Peter Lang

Bruxelles · Bern · Berlin · Frankfurt am Main · New York · Oxford · Wien

Clément VANEECLOO, Augusta BADRIOTTI
& Margherita FORNASINI

Fiscal Federalism in the European Union and Its Countries

A Confrontation between Theories and Facts

"International Financial Relations"
No.2

The authors would like to thank the *Fondation Internationale Triffin* of Louvain-La-Neuve, the *Compagnia di San Paolo* of Turin and the *Centro Studi sul Federalismo* of Moncalieri (Turin), institutions without which this book would not have seen the light of day.

© P.I.E. PETER LANG s.a.
Éditions scientifiques internationales
Brussels, 2006
1 avenue Maurice, B-1050 Brussels, Belgium
info@peterlang.com; www.peterlang.com

Printed in Germany

ISSN 1377-5669
ISBN 13 : 978-90-5201-044-1
ISBN 10 : 90-5201-044-7
US ISBN 13 : 978-0-8204-6689-7
D/2006/5678/53

CIP available from the British Library, GB and the Library of Congress, USA.

Bibliographic information published by "Die Deutsche Bibliothek"

"Die Deutsche Bibliothek" lists this publication in the "Deutsche Nationalbibliografie"; detailed bibliographic data is available in the Internet at <http://dnb.ddb.de>.

Table of Contents

List of Tables and Graphs

Acronyms

CAP	Common Agricultural Policy
CEECs	Central and Eastern European Countries
CI	Cohesion Index
COR	Committee of Regions
DM	Deutsche Mark
EAGGF	European Agricultural Guidance and Guarantee Fund
EC	European Commission
ECB	European Central Bank
EMU	Economic and Monetary Union
ERDF	European Regional Development Fund
ESF	European Social Fund
EU	European Union
FABs	Fiscal Auditing Boards
FDI	Fiscal Decentralisation Index
FF	Fiscal Federalism
FPC	Fiscal Policy Council
FPs	Financial Perspectives
FRG	Federal Republic of Germany
GDP	Gross Domestic Product
GDR	German Democratic Republic
GNI/GNP	Gross National Income/Product
IMF	International Monetary Fund
MS	Member States
NMS/OMS	New/Old Member States
NUTS	Nomenclature des Unités Territoriales Statistiques
OECD	Organisation for Economic Cooperation and Development
PDI	Political Decentralisation Index
PPS	Purchasing Power Standard
QMV	Qualified Majority Voting

SGP	Stability and Growth Pact
THA	Treuhandanstalt
VAT	Value added Tax

Acknowledgements

This work would not have been possible without the nascent co-operation and the substantial financial support of the *Compagnia di San Paolo* (Italy) – operating through the *Centro Studi sul Federalismo* in Turin (Italy) – and the *Fondation Internationale Triffin* in Louvain-la-Neuve (Belgium). Moreover, the three authors are grateful for the opportunity given by both Research Centres to stay in quiet and enriching research environments and for the very rich exchange experience it triggered. This contribution is thus a joint product at both institutional and personal scales.

Although this book is the result of the three main authors common reflections and discussions, each made at least one special contribution from her/his field of expertise.

Common discussions improved our understanding of a very difficult subject: Fiscal Federalism, the EU and its Member states.

We want to express our special thanks to many scholars and colleagues for their comments and feedbacks. We would also like to thank a number of people for useful discussions, guidance to the literature and specific comments. We wish to thank in particular for their support all the staff of CSF (especially P. Caraffini) at the Fondazione Collegio Carlo Alberto in Moncalieri and FIT at the European Studies Department of the Catholic University of Louvain. N. Bednar, G. Brosio, M. Dumoulin, A. Lamfalussy, A. Majocchi, U. Morelli, A. Padoa Schioppa and Ph. Rollet deserve particular thanks for their useful comments. Mistakes and imperfections remain our exclusive responsibility and usual disclaim applies.

April 2006

Forewords

Alexandre LAMFALUSSY

President of the Triffin International Foundation

These are challenging times for all of us who in the midst of the constitutional Treaty *débâcle* refuse to despair, but instead are determined to lend their support to the emergence from this severe trial of a stronger, better structured Europe. One of the preconditions for this happening is to instil clarity, intellectual honesty, rigorous analysis and a fair dose of humility into the political debate – much of which was missing from the emotionally overheated and often distorted debate surrounding the ratification process.

This book offers a timely and constructive help to comply with this precondition. It addresses one precise, but undoubtedly key governance issue which has to be dealt with in any event. The authors start from the assumption that fiscal policy (very broadly defined) covers three main functions: macroeconomic stabilisation, redistribution and the provision of public goods and services. They then ask the question: can we take it for granted that in a federal, or quasi-federal organisation, the two first functions have to be assumed by the central level of government, while the third should be handled at the level of decentralised authorities? And: could these distinctions be useful in helping us to decide what should be allocated to which level of government in the case of the European Union?

The originality of their approach resides in the skilful and careful confrontation of abstract (both theoretical and normative) reasoning with empirical evidence – and by empirical evidence they mean not only econometric testing, but also a thorough historical, political and institutional analysis. It is by using this method that they have a lot to say on two specific fiscal policy issues in the European Union: on Cohesion policy, which performs a redistribution function, and on the Growth and Stability Pact, which can be seen as a specific EU attempt to provide a framework for implementing a macroeconomic stabilisation policy. They also demonstrate their interest in history by drawing on the lessons that can (or should have been) derived from the German unification for the enlargement process, and by learning from the great diversity of the national fiscal experiences.

I found particularly stimulating Chapter 6, which sums up their recommendations on how to try to respond to their initial queries: well, instead of making a heroic (and probably futile) attempt at allocating the three core functions of fiscal policy to the various levels of government in the EU, they suggest attributing policy-making responsibility of specific *area* – rather than functions. And, most important, they insist on taking into account the historical, political and institutional features of both the EU and its member countries.

May I strike here a rather personal note? I have been on record of repeatedly stressing the need to strengthen the E-leg of EMU in order to have a policy tool which would enable us to have an optimal macroeconomic policy mix for the euro area. I still believe that this is an important policy objective without which there is not much chance of carrying out a rational Euroland-wide stabilisation policy. But with Euroland's dismal growth performance and with unemployment rates that are ethically unacceptable, socially disruptive and which amount in economic terms to a stupid waste of resources, the full implementation of the Lisbon agenda should receive priority treatment. The greater part of what this agenda contains falls under the heading of "provision of public goods and services", for which conventional wisdom suggests a "decentralised" approach. Well, much of this is likely to be so, but given the urgency of implementing the agenda and its vast cross-border implications, I would suggest avoiding the risk of getting lost in an a-priori ideological debate about who should be in charge. The decision should be made on a case-by-case basis, by keeping in mind the subtle analysis of Chapter 6.

I would strongly recommend to our policy makers to read this book. It does not make easy reading, but the effort would be worthwhile. They may disagree on a number of points – so do I – but not on the political relevance of the points made by the authors.

I would like to thank warmly the Compagnia di San Paolo whose financial and moral support made it possible to carry out this ambitious research project, and welcome this fruitful cooperation between the Centro di Studi sul Federalismo and the Triffin International Foundation.

*

Alberto MAJOCCHI

*Member of the Board of directors of
the Centro Studi sul Federalismo (CSF)
President of the Institute for Studies and Economic Analyses (ISAE)*

The title of the last paragraph of this important contribution to the theory – and practice – of fiscal federalism is enlightening: "Europe, once again at a turning point", and the conclusion of the book puts forward a proposal regarding the budget, the fiscal setting and the political organisation of the European Union that seems particularly relevant in this delicate phase of the European unification process. This proposal comes at the end of an in-depth analysis of fiscal federalism, starting from the remark that, while in the literature fiscal federalism is generally considered to postulate that a central government decentralises some of its powers to lower levels of government, the context of the European Union shows exactly the opposite, since actually its Member States are centralising some of their traditional functions upwards to the central level; and the distribution of economic competencies between different tiers of government does not correspond exactly to that foreseen in the Musgrave-Oates model. Hence, the European experience is from many points of view relatively new, and a comprehensive reappraisal of the existing theory is needed if we want theory to match reality. And this book provides a good contribution in this direction.

But this is not the only merit of the book, that provides an overview of the main problems that arise in devising an optimal fiscal setting for the Union, moving from an analysis of the Stability and Growth Pact to the Cohesion Policy and to the lessons learned from the experience of German unification. As a matter of fact, the role of fiscal policy seems particularly relevant in the present difficult circumstances, after the no in the French and Dutch referendums and the deadlock in the negotiations about the Financial Perspectives 2007-2013 emerged in the Brussels European Council. In this framework, my personal view is that, on the one hand, if one wants to guarantee the compliance with the Maastricht Treaty constraints by each Member State and, at the same time, finance the Lisbon Agenda, it is unavoidable – given the limited size of the European budget and the difficulty to change its structure – that additional resources be found at the European level, outside of its budget; on the other hand, it seems convenient to exploit the strength of the euro and import capitals from the rest of the world to supplement the largely available domestic funds in financing a European Growth Plan. From a political point of view, my basic idea is that, taking into account the difficulty to proceed towards a federal solution in the framework of a European Union of 25 Member States, a two-speed Europe seems to be the only way out. And this implies that, if the financing of the Lisbon Agenda could only be guaranteed in the present conditions through the emission of Union bonds, the political framework where this decision could be taken is that of the euro-zone. The boost given by a successful economic growth process in Europe will also create the climate of confidence necessary to support any further advance in the institutional field.

As a matter of fact, after the launch of the Monetary Union, Europe is involved in a cyclical downturn and the gap with the American economy is widening: per capita income in the euro zone is stuck at only 70 per cent of the corresponding American value, and the US economy is recording growth levels far superior to the European ones. Talk of Europe's decline is once again rife. An in-depth analysis of these phenomena is contained in the Sapir Report, which sets out to define the political agenda that must be followed in order to revamp Europe's economic growth.

In the decade 1981-90 the growth rate of the American economy was already half a point higher than that of the European economy, but afterwards the gap widened to almost a point. The picture changes a bit if one considers GDP-per-capita growth: indeed, whereas in the first of the last three decades growth in the euro zone was slightly higher than in America, in the following period the reverse has been true. A large share of the difference in growth rate measured in this way, *i.e.* on the basis of GDP, is thus attributable to the increase in population.

If we want to understand more in depth the factors that have influenced the growth-rate differentials, we have to consider how increased hourly productivity contributed to reducing the income gap between Europe and the United States: the euro zone was recording a higher level as against the US in the average of the period 1979-2000, a trend dramatically reversed from 2000 to 2003, which saw American productivity shooting up and European productivity falling sharply to one point lower. In particular, the productivity growth rate in Europe is lower than that in the United States after 1995. But, leaving aside this long-term trend of increased productivity, the factor that really seems to account for the persistence of the disparity in per capita income is labour utilisation, that in 2003 was 28 per cent lower in Europe than in the United States. In particular, EU employees were working 15 per cent fewer hours than their US counterpart, thus accounting for about one half of the gap in labour utilisation.

Even if this fact, as Olivier Blanchard believes, reflects a different system of preferences between the US and Europe, the central point in the discussion about the poor performance of the European economy during the 1990s remains its modest rate of productivity growth compared to the United States. This factor seems to be able to explain as well the lack of competitiveness of European exports in the globalised world market. But while the existence of this gap is unquestionable, it is important to analyse more in depth which are the main factors explaining this relative productivity drop in Europe during the last period of time.

A significant contribution to the explanation of the origin of the different productivity patterns has been recently provided by a study carried out by O'Mahoney and van Ark, that allows to trace the evolution of productivity in different industrial sectors, subdivided in ICT-producing, ICT-using and non-ICT industries. According to this study there has been no productivity increase in the US industries that are classified as neither ICT-producing, nor ICT-using. The core of the US success story appears to have been the ICT-using industries, *i.e.* retail, wholesale and security trading industries: all the productivity growth differential of the US over Europe in the late 1990s came from these three sectors, with retail contributing for about 55 per cent of the differential, wholesale for 24 per cent and security trade for 20 per cent.

America is now almost universally acknowledged to have leapt to the top in most of the ICT industries, not just in computer hardware, but more broadly in software, pharmaceuticals and biotech. The literature points to peculiar national characteristics that help explain why particular inventions and industries are dominated by particular countries. Perhaps the one generalization that is applicable to most industries is the role of the product cycle, since technology eventually diffuses from the leading nations to other nations that may have lower labour costs. Among the traditional factors of the US competitive edge, it is usual to include educational attainment levels and university research, government-funded military and civilian research, efficiency of the capital market, language and immigration. There is no doubt that the growing American dominance in the field of innovation in ICT, biotech and pharmaceuticals reflects the fruitful collaboration of government funding of research, world-leader private universities, innovative private firms and a dynamic capital market.

In Europe, creating a successful knowledge-based economy involves both enhancing the EU's capacity to invent, implement and export a series of world-class innovative technologies, and creating an environment conducive to the imitation and absorption of externally available know-how. This implies that Europe needs to shift the emphasis in its present economic model towards more innovation, by embracing an open-economy- and innovation-based model which emphasises the importance of world-class educational establishments; higher levels of R&D, excellence-driven and better targeted; more market-based financing systems; and more flexible regulations and institutions delivering a more dynamic and competitive business environment. This is the challenge that Europe has decided to take up when it defined its new growth strategy in the European Council held in Lisbon in March 2000.

Why have the results of the Lisbon Strategy been so poor thus far, as has been recently recognised by the Kok Report? We have to go back to the main causes of Europe's relative failure after the launch of the Monetary Union in 1999. In most of the literature, this failure is usually explained by two factors: first, the crisis of public finance in many European States. The Maastricht Treaty has considered the risk of external diseconomies coming from excessive deficit in a Member State of the Monetary Union and has set down rules for avoiding this risk. With a lot of difficulties, consolidation of public finance has taken place, but the positive impact of this on the rate of economic growth is difficult to see. The second explanation lies in the failed completion of the EU internal market, especially in the services sector, where the most significant gap with the US lies with regard to productivity-growth rates. Some progress has been achieved, but with no clear impact on growth. Thus, we have probably to consider another factor for explaining the gap between Europe and the US, that is, the different efficacy of economic policies. In the US an expansionary monetary policy has been backed by a growing deficit in the federal budget: in fiscal year 2000 there has been a surplus equal to 1.6 per cent of GDP, while in 2004 the budget balance has been reversed, with a net borrowing that equals 4.4 per cent of GDP. In Europe too there has been a worsening of fiscal balances during the last years, but with no expansionary impact on domestic economies, due to the uncoordinated efforts by each Member State to promote its own policy, disregarding what was being done by the others.

In principle, the implementation of the Lisbon strategy at the level of each Member State seems to require two different fiscal policy measures: one supporting domestic demand, and the other bringing about the unavoidable reforms on the supply side. But supporting domestic demand through fiscal policy measures is difficult for two main reasons: the first is linked to the constraints imposed by the Maastricht Treaty, that limits to a maximum of 3 per cent of GDP the deficit in national budgets; the second, and probably equally important, is the limited impact on national income of an increase of expenditures or tax cuts, since the marginal propensity to import goods in the economy of the Monetary Union's Member States is very high, hence the multiplier effects are low. As usual, when there are external benefits, the production of the public good "stabilisation" is less than optimal.

But equally relevant are the limits of measures impacting the supply side of national economies, since many reforms, even if they will improve the budget balance in the long run, have a negative impact in the short run. This is true, for instance, of political measures implemented to reform the pensions structure, moving towards a capitalisation system of the same. In conclusion, at the level of each Member State it is quite difficult to implement the Lisbon agenda and the recent reform of the Stability Pact seems unable to cope with these difficulties and could ultimately further worsen the perspectives of economic growth within the Monetary Union; indeed, the only result could well be the stiffening of the European Central Bank's policy, should it fear a further deterioration of public finance balances due to the larger flexibility allowed by the new Pact.

The only possible way out seems to lie in implementing the Lisbon agenda at the European level. This means increasing the EU expenditures for completing the TENs programme, promoting R&D in order to raise the competitiveness of European goods, supporting the adoption of advanced technologies in the industrial sector, financing improvements in the EU systems of higher education and the conservation of natural and cultural richness. But also in this case there are a lot of constraints, as it has been shown by the difficulty to reach an agreement on the Financial Perspectives 2007-2013, among them the shift from agricultural expenditures towards the new pattern of expenditures sketched in the Sapir Report.

All in all, if the Lisbon agenda could not be fulfilled neither at the national level, due to the constraints of the Maastricht Treaty and the Stability Pact, nor through the European budget, due to the limited size of the budget itself and to the political unwillingness by the Member States to increase their contributions, the only way that remains open is to implement the "golden rule" at the European level, *i.e.* financing the expenditures required by the Lisbon strategy through the emission of Union bonds. This way of funding the Lisbon strategy could also be supplemented by private investments. The emission of Union bonds could be placed on the international market, exploiting the strength of the euro and thus balancing the negative effects of an overvalued EU currency on European exports.

A revamping of growth within the European economy seems to be the best answer to the stop in the process of ratification of the Constitutional Treaty following the no in the French and Dutch referendums. The euro-scepticism must and can be overcome through a political initiative showing that the completion of the European unification process will improve the welfare of European citizens. But a political willingness to accept a federation as the final goal of this process is required too. This was the original goal of Monnet and Spinelli, the founding fathers; but not all the 25 Member States of the European Union share this view. If Europe has to go on, the six countries that have launched the European Economic Community in 1957 and probably most of the countries of the euro zone sharing the goal of a federal conclusion of the process of European unification should take the initiative of a new round of institutional reforms, targeted at the establishment of a "hard core" with a federal structure, in the framework of a larger Union enjoying the existing institutions and exploiting all the *acquis communautaire.*

This is my approach to the relaunching of the process of European unification. But any step forward seems unlikely in the present conditions, due to the lack of confidence in the public opinion and the weakening of the political class, both at the European and the national level. In this difficult context, what could be the role of a think-tank like the *Centro Studi sul Federalismo*? In my view, we have to reject the idea of an unavoidable European decline and on the contrary we have to carry out in-depth studies with the aim of providing proposals and suggestions useful to support a positive development of the process of European unification. This is exactly the task of this book, that combines new ideas with a fresh analysis of the main facts regarding the current developments of fiscal federalism in Europe. And the *Centro Studi sul Federalismo* should be grateful to the authors and to the Triffin International Foundation for their important contribution to the shaping up of a new approach to the fiscal problems of the European Union.

CHAPTER 1

Fiscal Federalism Perspective(s) and the European Union

Introductory Framework

Clément VANEECLOO

When dealing with Fiscal Federalism, it is sometimes difficult to comply with the academic tradition of surveying the literature before presenting one's own added value, either theoretical or empirical. Indeed, Fiscal Federalism literature seems to be inherently ill-defined and its research areas are by definition numerous, if not infinite.[1] As we will argue, this may blur one's understanding of the application of this theoretical framework, especially when applied to the European Union (EU).

The aim of this chapter is to recall some basic features of the Fiscal Federalism theoretical perspective, by stressing its relative advantages in understanding the EU. Additionally, this chapter points out briefly usual flaws of Fiscal Federalism. Our perspective is original as it insists on the distinction and interactions between, on the one hand, *Fiscal Federalism* as a theory, and, on the other hand, *fiscal settings* as the numerous 'Fiscal Federalism' practices encountered in reality. Our aim is not to write a conventional survey, as this task has already been done elsewhere.[2] Alternatively, we here try to clarify some ontological fundamentals of Fiscal Federalism (*i.e.* the literature's perception of the very nature of the world). We also assess the relevance of these fundamentals. We show that this perspective can easily be used to understand European reality and realities. Finally, we show how a renovated and more positive Fiscal Federalism perspective, based on a 'politically-minded and policy-making conscious' analysis of real-world European

---

[1] Fiscal Federalism deals with all the traditional issues in the field of public finance, multiplied by the average number of levels of government (say three), plus the interactions between these levels.

[2] See for instance Oates (1999), Inman and Rubinfeld (1998), Padoa-Schioppa (1987), Gramlich (1987a) or Deschamps (ed.) (1994).

fiscal settings, may improve the assumptions usually made by the Fiscal Federalist perspective and, ultimately, our understanding of the EU.

Section 1.1 introduces Fiscal Federalism: what it is, where it comes from, and what it tells us. Section 1.2 assesses its potential relevance for the understanding of the EU and its countries. Finally, it also presents the main motives and the 'loose' framework underpinning the rest of our analysis.

1.1. Introducing Fiscal Federalism and the European Union

1.1.1. What Is Fiscal Federalism?

The terminology of 'Fiscal Federalism' is generally used to identify different things.[3] Fiscal Federalism both refers to facts: the actual – vertical and horizontal – organisation of the public sector in a given country (later labelled as Fiscal Settings), and to theoretical analysis: the normative and positive ways in which economists understand the latter. In other words, Fiscal Federalism can be defined both as the relationships between the various levels of governments composing a given territory and as the – sometimes heavily theoretical – economic literature which studies these relationships.

What is Fiscal Federalism then? Is it reality or is it the depiction of this reality? In the latter case, is Fiscal Federalism a theory, a model, a framework, or is it just a combination of theses elements? As often is the case, there are in fact no easy answers to these questions. The simplest way to define the Fiscal Federalism literature is to highlight its object of analysis.[4] Namely, Fiscal Federalism studies countries or political entities where there is more than one level of government. As often stated in the literature, Fiscal Federalism is supposed to apply to both federal and unitary States because both kinds are actually composed of different levels of governments. Moreover, owing to the growing number of contributions using Fiscal Federalism insights to apply them to the EU considered as a single economic entity (Breuss and Eller, 2003; Buti and Nova, 2003; Stehn, 2002; Tabellini, 2002), it can

---

[3]   The terminological debate about Fiscal Federalism actually seems more intense in the French-speaking academic community. For example, authors disagree on whether *Fiscal Federalism* should be translated by *fédéralisme financier*, *fédéralisme budgétaire* or *fédéralisme fiscal*.

[4]   It should be noted that Oates (1972, 1991, 1992 and 1999), makes an extensive use of the term "literature" when referring to Fiscal Federalism, strengthening our belief that it is less than clear whether it refers to a theory, a model, a reality or a set of different realities or fragments of each and every one.

be asserted that Fiscal Federalism more generally analyses the way(s) different levels of government interact on a given territory.

Fiscal Federalism, thus, studies all the means of coordination (and sometimes competition) between different levels of government and between governments at the same level but ruling over different jurisdictions. It tries to determine both horizontally and vertically an optimal allocation of public finances. The spectrum of analysis here is clearly one of centralisation *versus* decentralisation. Drawing on Musgrave (1959), and his functional decomposition of the economic role of the State, Fiscal Federalism therefore tries to determine in terms of equity and efficiency which function(s) – stabilisation, (re)distribution, allocation – should be assigned to which level of government. For example, it gives advice on whether the distribution function should be centralised or not; on whether it would be *a priori* more efficient and/or equitable to leave employment policy, defence, primary schooling, health services or street lamps to the local, regional or central level; or on ways to help less developed territories catch-up the richer ones. This last example illustrates our previous point. Indeed, this question can be asked both at the European (*e.g.* Chapter 2 about Cohesion Policy) and at the Member States level (*e.g.* Chapter 4 about unification of Germany).

Most revealing about the sheer number of meanings attributed to Fiscal Federalism and the intrinsically heteroclite nature of the field lies in the definition given by Derycke:

> Fiscal Federalism, it is all in once: the territorial organisation of a country; the principles underlying repartition of powers, competencies, public revenues and expenditures between hierarchical levels of government; and the degree of territorial centralisation/decentralisation of territorial administration. It is thus a set of precepts underlying the conduct of public actions in more or less decentralised states.[5]

Although the debate about the definition and the theoretical status of the literature on Fiscal Federalism would deserve more attention, our contribution does not seek to pioneer a complex epistemological polemic. Going forward, we will only focus on such issues as long as this ill-defined status is relevant for our understanding of i) the relationships between the theory of Fiscal Federalism and the European Union (EU), ii) fiscal settings of the EU and its Member States (MS). Great care will be taken in order to stick to a single terminology. We will thus make recurrent discursive distinctions between fiscal settings and Fiscal Federalism. Fiscal settings are the various means of coordination and cooperation, fiscal or not, in a multi-level government structure.

---

[5] Derycke, in Deschamps *et al.* (1994), p. 19.

These means refer to the real-world: all of them are actually encountered in reality. Fiscal Federalism, on the other hand, is constituted by the set of theories, which aim at enlightening public choices about fiscal settings *ex-ante* and explaining them *ex-post*. Fiscal Federalism here clearly refers to the theoretical perspectives, which tend to be more and more normative (but not solely), whereas fiscal (federalism) settings refer to the practice of actual fiscal systems.

Another important and more traditional distinction will be made between the central level of government as the highest level of government, *i.e.* the one ruling the biggest territory, not necessarily yielding the biggest power (*cf.* the EU), and sub-central levels of government referring to the regional (*e.g. Länder* in Germany, *Communidad* in Spain) or local levels of government. Some states have more than one regional (*e.g.* the *Régions* and the *Départements* in France) or even local (*e.g. Communautés de Communes* and *Communes* in France) levels of government, in which case we will explicitly precise it.

When dealing with the EU as a whole, we will refer to the European (*i.e.* central) level on the one hand, and to national or regional (*i.e.* sub-central) levels on the other hand. This will avoid confusions triggered by the changing scales of analysis we successively endorse.

One of the principles of Fiscal Federalism is that sub-national governments should have the means of their ambitions. Taxes should thus follow responsibilities. As various problems of tax collection may arise, either related to effectiveness, political or practical matters, there are usually various indirect systems to achieve this financing requirement. As a given role distribution does not generally neatly suit the institutional and historical fiscal traditions, 'fiscal coordination' is needed. The means of coordination are numerous, but the most important ones are fiscal settings (including interjurisdictional grants) and regulations. The following chapters highlight the huge variety of potential means of coordination, which actually compose a given fiscal setting. Hence, Fiscal Federalism is not just about financial and budgetary matters, although finance may be one of the most important coordination mechanisms of the public sector and for sure the most debated one.

As it is well-known, there can only be educated guesses in terms of paternity. However, it is worth trying to trace back to the theoretical sources of this fairly recent literature. Even though pioneered in the fifties, in a context of general acceptance of the Beveridgean doctrine of Welfare State and of acute trust in public intervention, Fiscal Federalism seems to be the offspring of two influential fathers. Firstly, Fiscal Federalism clearly tries to express the political theory of Federalism in economic terms. Thus, most of the normative prescriptions presented hereafter were already intuitively mentioned by authors like Kant,

Hamilton or Tocqueville, which saw Federalism as the best way to combine the respective advantages of big and small nations: closer accountability to people, inter-jurisdictional checks and balance, power-sharing, accountability and heterogeneity mindedness, better access to information and to people's preferences, etc. The other influential genitor of Fiscal Federalism is public economics. This is confirmed by Oates (1991) when he asserts that Fiscal Federalism is 'public finance with several levels of government'.[6] The seminal works of Musgrave (1959), Tiebout (1957), Buchanan (1955) and the textbook written by Oates (1972) are famous contributions in the field of public economics. The most salient issues in public finances are also at the core of Fiscal Federalism: the distinction between equity and efficiency, strong emphasis on public goods, on problems related to their provision and financing or on preferences and their disclosures.

Nevertheless, Fiscal Federalism has apparently emancipated itself from these influent genitors in two important ways. With respect to the political theory of Federalism, Fiscal Federalism differs in the sense that it rests on the assumption that the advantages of Federalism can be achieved even in unitary states or in a hybrid political structure such as the EU, and thus without the constitutional need to write federalist principles in marble. Moreover, apart from 'constitutional Fiscal Federalism', Fiscal Federalism clearly focuses on economic matters and has a normative nature. With respect to public finances, Fiscal Federalism has dramatically widened the range of issues deserving attention. To name but a few, we can cite secessionism, laboratory Federalism, the flypaper effect or other elaborated concerns related to the grant system, or issues of coordination. Moreover the Fiscal Federalism literature is rather heterogeneous (some may say heteroclite), welcoming many different theories and broader strands of the economic literature, more or less compatible among themselves, but decisively compatible with the fiscal federalist perspective of understanding public finances in a multi-level polity. For instance, Fiscal Federalism specialists can be either Keynesian or neo-classical, as are for instance followers of Tiebout.

Last but not least, by its very nature, the Fiscal Federalism literature is highly empirically-minded. Indeed, the number of case studies under scrutiny is huge. These case studies most of the time focus on federations in the political sense of the term. For instance, the United States (US), Canada, Australia, Switzerland and Germany have given rise to many useful analysis, some of which we will pay respect to later on (*cf.* Chapter 4). However, in the last few years, studies about unitary states and about the EU have burgeoned. Most often detailed and precise, this

---

[6] Once again, it is less than clear whether Oates refers to theory, facts or both.

literature takes great care in understanding fiscal mechanisms and coordination, which in turn gives rise to many typologies or 'fiscal settings *idéaux-types*' (see for instance Inman and Rubinfeld, 1997; Guihéry, 1999; Aubin and Léonard, 2000; and Brosio, 1995). These numerous contributions try to put order into the empirical complexity by classifying various settings on the basis of their common features.

To conclude, we would like to make clear that the Fiscal Federalism literature comprises of different theoretical corpus and that 'Fiscal Federalism' settings are of various types. The best way to clarify this may well be to label it as a 'perspective', *i.e.* a lens/spectrum through which to see problems. Fiscal Federalism just tries to address usual problems related to the public sector by taking into account the fact that the latter is always composed of more than one level of government. Adopting this perspective automatically renders problems more complex and solutions less clear-cut or easy to implement, but it also makes economic thinking more realistic.

1.1.2. What Does Fiscal Federalism Tell Us?

The literature exhibits some kind of consensus about the way the above-mentioned Musgravian functions should be assigned to different levels of government. Put differently, Fiscal Federalism analysts more or less agree on what in theory constitutes the optimal fiscal setting. The basic guideline they usually prescribe is the following one. Redistribution and stabilisation should be provided by the central level of government, whereas allocation of the different public goods and services should follow an 'assign where it hits' principle (decentralisation principle). The way this guideline should influence decision-makers is not unanimously uncontroversial. It is defended with more or less confidence depending on the author. For example, there is a huge gap between the confidence with which Gramlich (1987a) prescribes it and the great rhetoric care with which Oates (1999) speaks about it. Nevertheless, most authors would agree that such a guideline is by no way rigid: it should not be blindly referred to in a dogmatic manner when applied to a given country and should take into account historical and institutional features. This should be kept in mind in the European context. Still, this guideline can fairly be labelled as the common wisdom within the field.

Although some of these issues are extensively tackled in the following chapters, it is worth explaining briefly the rationale(s) behind this guideline. We take these three functions in turn, explaining why the balance bends in a particular direction and trying to pay respect to the buoyant debates in the literature, by highlighting the basic pros and cons of decentralisation, or, conversely, of centralisation.

By far, the most debated function is allocation. Public goods and services should be allocated to the most appropriate level of government. Put differently, decentralised governments should provide goods and services whose consumption is limited to their specific jurisdiction. In contrast, the principal argument in favour of a centralised allocation of a given good is the extent to which it exhibits economies of scale or a high degree of inter-jurisdictional spillovers/externalities. For instance defence, legal systems, provision of money, highways or postal services often enter into this category. They should, thus, typically be centrally financed and provided public goods. Generally, though, most public goods and services would be more efficiently provided by sub-central (regional or local) levels of government. This includes fields as 'important' as education, local security, or health, and as 'trivial' as public lighting or sports facilities. Indeed, decentralised governments are seen as being closer to people, economic conditions and problems of their own jurisdiction. They are as such often perceived as aware of local preferences, people's willingness to pay, and cost conditions better than would a central agency. In the same vein, faster and more accurate responses to local preferences and increased financial accountability of election-focused politicians may also enhance efficiency, thus calling for a decentralised system. Decentralisation is sometimes also seen as a means to introduce supply-side efficiency in the public sector. Allowing experimental Federalism would allow for the identification, selection and generalisation of the best local practices. Other pro-decentralisation arguments are more contested. For example, some authors claim that the introduction of competition among jurisdiction would also be Pareto-efficient (this is a translation – from the market to the public sector – of the neo-classical core conclusions) or will even be a means of revealing people's preferences as they would move from one jurisdiction to another in a footloose manner to select their preferred fiscal package, *i.e.* their 'menu' of taxes and public goods (this is the voting with one's feet argument of Tiebout, 1957).

However, many others fear a harmful fiscal race-to-the-bottom (see Oates, 1999). In this context, decentralisation can imply system unsustainability, triggered by tax-free jurisdictions. Another argument against decentralisation is that heightened corruption may be the opposite face of the accountability coin. Greater accessibility to decision-makers may also mean easier bribing in 'clientelist' localities or regions. All in all, this mixed record shows that the provision of a given good or service at a given level is not straightforward. It depends on more than one trade-off: along with the traditional one opposing efficiency/equity, other trade-offs such as the ones opposing corruption/accountability or mobility/cohesion need to be considered. Political in essence, these factors are, as we will show, hardly truly taken into account by Fiscal Federalism contributions. Moreover, many other 'non-fiscal' factors, as diverse as market and networks size or as the weather, actually have to be considered.

Stabilisation should be provided by the central level of government. Why is it so? When the economic conjuncture is bad, it usually affects most of the country. In which case, there is a national need for stabilisation. This national need could also be fulfilled independently by all sub-central levels of government. However, crucial questions here are the means and efficiency of such a decentralised stabilisation policy. If a shock affects the entire country, then the central government is likely to act more efficiently (as it controls the main stabilisation tools) in order to control and manage the shock either 'using' automatic stabilisers or discretionary fiscal policies. The possibility to control fiscal policy is generally higher at the national level, which can decide on the most suitable regulatory or budgetary measures to maintain the growth pace of the economy.

If the shock affects one part of a given country, the question is: how can the affected area deal with it? If it has fiscal powers, it can decide to adopt a counter-cyclical fiscal policy. If it has no autonomy, it could create deficits to cover the losses of the shocks, but this is likely to lead this level of government to insolvency problems and bankruptcy. Even worse, theory suggests that with a higher degree of openness and economic proximity of regions within a single currency area like the euro-zone, regional economies will tend to move together. Any shock in one region will rapidly be transmitted to the other regions, jeopardising the stability of the whole area (Ackrill, 1998). Referring back to Optimal Currency Area arguments,[7] if Mundell's (1961) currency-area membership criteria of factor mobility and price flexibility are not adequately satisfied, there are alternative ways to ensure stabilisation in a single currency area in case of asymmetric shocks. Namely, the centralisation of budgetary powers can help to improve macro-economic management.

As shown in Chapter 3, debates about stabilisation are vivid both at national and European level. The question is for instance at the centre of most debates about the EMU and the Stability and Growth Pact (SGP). Among other issues, this chapter also discusses in length the SGP and proclaims that this fiscal arrangement is not the most appropriate instrument to reach stabilisation in the EU.

It is often argued that redistribution should remain the exclusive task of the central government (Brown and Oates, 1985; Wildasin, 1990;

---

[7] According to Mundell and McKinnon a currency area is optimal when it is possible to obtain simultaneously a balanced budget, price stability and full employment.

Musgrave, 1976; Oates, 1999; and for an opposite view, see Pauly, 1973 or Gramlich, 1987b). This strong presumption both stems from externalities and from households' mobility, leading to unsustainable decentralised redistribution systems. Indeed, a differentiated redistribution scheme among territories means that 'generous' jurisdictions will have to bear a double burden: redistribution spending will increase as poorer households are attracted, while redistribution revenues may drop as richer households emigrate in order not to bear the extra fiscal burden. Moreover, even in an economic entity where labour and capital mobility are initially low, differentiating redistribution may well trigger mobility. Unless a jurisdiction pursues a segregation policy (politically undesirable, if not unfeasible), there is no way to escape this adverse selection phenomenon. Of course, real-world so-called 'frictions' may allow to undertake decentralised redistribution schemes, as it is often the case in the US. Still, the extent and the financial modalities of this redistribution seems to confirm theory. The case for European redistribution and its practical design are discussed in length in Chapter 2.

This elusive presentation of the Fiscal Federalism common wisdom, however controversial it may be, shows that such factors as mobility, preferences, cost conditions, information, accountability, system efficiency, fiscal capacities, and inter-jurisdictional interactions have to be taken into account when analysing or reforming a given fiscal setting. All these issues are also at the centre of the most buoyant debates in the European Union. This naturally converts Fiscal Federalism to being a good candidate for descriptive and prescriptive interpretations of the EU.

1.2. Assessing the Relevance of Fiscal Federalism for the Study of the EU and Its Countries

1.2.1. *Comparative Advantages of Fiscal Federalism in Understanding the EU and Its Countries*

As argued before, Fiscal Federalism shows that when economists take into account the fact that most States are not just 'one' but are composed of multiple levels of government, *i.e.* that authority is dispersed, the traditional story becomes more complex. Consequently, Fiscal Federalism is *a priori* a more realistic *perspective*. The fact that the way authority is territorially dispersed and divided may matter constitutes a breakdown with traditional public economics. The implicit question here is the one of the 'effectiveness of public intervention' (Oates, 1992).

Owing to its comparative advantage, Fiscal Federalism has been mobilised to understand Europe in two different ways. First, theory has been used to advise policy-makers in national arenas about the internal restructuring of their public sector. The main arguments in favour of decentralisation have already been presented in the previous section. As most European countries have recently experienced an unprecedented wave of decentralisation (see Chapter 5), it is fair to say that national decision-makers have been very sensitive to these pro-decentralisation arguments. The extent to which such decentralisation have been backboned with Fiscal Federalism economical insights or with other political justifications remains however unclear. More generally, Fiscal Federalism also advises policy-makers in the day-to-day management of their fiscal settings or when they have to face extraordinary circumstances. For instance, Chapter 4 provides a thorough analysis of German unification. Second, such a theoretical perspective has also been used to advise European policy-makers – most of them being also in charge of the decentralisation process at the national level – about the way the EU as a single economic entity works or should work. As the first way to mobilise Fiscal Federalism is already well-documented, we concentrate on the reasons which make Fiscal Federalism potentially highly relevant for the understanding and reform of the EU.

In this context, the EU can indeed be seen as a multi-level polity, where the European level of 'government' is assimilated to the central level of government, and where the national levels are seen as sub-central levels of government. The Fiscal Federalism agenda apparently fits with the most salient economic issues concerning the European Union, which suffices to make its programme legitimate. Indeed, the Fiscal Federalist literature typically asks 'who should do what in the EU?' (Breuss and Eller, 2003; Stehn, 2002; Tabellini, 2002; Théret, 2001; Aubin and Léonard, 2000; Costello, 1993; EC, 1993).

For instance, the EMU is a *de facto* transfer of the monetary policy to the central level. The related issue of the Stability and Growth Pact focuses on the question of whether one should consequently centralise fiscal policy, either under the form of an increased budget or of increased coordination between national fiscal policies (the SGP being a minimal form of coordination and, as many point out, a rather unbinding one). Chapter 3 analyses this issue further. This debate can be reformulated as follows: should stabilisation be centralised and which form should this stabilisation take?

Competitiveness, employment, growth, and social Europe are related issues. Should they be tackled at the European level? Once again, the form matters as it is unclear whether they should be tackled on the basis of a greater budget or of greater legal and fiscal regulated coordination.

Is there any risk of social dumping? On the other hand, would social harmonisation hamper the development of the poorest European countries, as they claim? Another related issue indirectly deals with national contexts. Are national trends of decentralisation threatening national social or redistributive policies,[8] and are social or cohesion policies supposed to replace them? Should there be a European economic and social model or not? If yes, should this model take the form of convergence of national policies *via* harmonisation and minimal standards or should it be achieved through a bigger budget and a more complicated European fiscal setting?

Another issue, which was widely seen as solved in June 2004 in Brussels, but has been seriously undermined after the May/June 2005 failed referenda in France and Holland, is the European Constitution (or Constitutive Treaty).

Although most of it just confirms pre-established treaties and solves (vote-weighting related) political issues, the problems debated here were also of an economic nature. The voting issue is crucial. The decision to leave fiscal issues under unanimity, for instance, can be seen as the willingness of European countries (the most obvious one being the UK, but not only) to keep the reins of the European budget and fiscal settings.

As shown in Chapters 2 and 4, enlargement, development of backward regions and the reform of Cohesion Policy (often presented as the European distribution function), which are deeply intertwined issues, can also be viewed in terms of Fiscal Federalism.

All these – highly debated – issues about the future of the EU are for sure interrelated, in turn rendering the analysis more difficult. However, the main point remains clear. A fiscal federalist perspective, with its central concern for authority dispersion among different jurisdictions and for the optimal assignment of functions between them, mirrors most debates on the economic role of the EU.

Fiscal Federalism is therefore potentially highly attractive for one who wishes to understand and/or reform it. This strand of the economic literature, admittedly, is the one which takes best into account the interactions of jurisdictions which belong to the same economic system.

---

[8]   Once again, Chapter 4 exemplifies rising pressures made by rich German *Länder* on the Federal government to decrease inter-regional solidarity. The same could be said about Belgium.

1.2.2. The Flaws of Fiscal Federalism

The acknowledged criticisms directed at Fiscal Federalism are both empirical and theoretical and, in point of fact, it is not always easy to distinguish between these two kinds of criticisms. Moreover, much criticism tends to derive from a misunderstanding of the Fiscal Federalism project. As this literature embraces different schools of thought, it is not often clear whether such criticism applies to the overall perspective or to one of the theories within this perspective. For instance, many commentators fail to acknowledge the diversity of theories represented in the fiscal federalist perspective and generalise criticism to the entire field, where it in fact should only apply to one particular theory within the field (Théret, 2001). In fact, the only valid criticism one can take from this kind of dispute is that the theoretical status of Fiscal Federalism may be ill-defined: it is not always clear whether one particular author follows a normative or positive approach, an empirical, theoretical or mixed one, and to which *Grand Theory* (Keynesian, neo-classical, etc.) he pays respect to. Consequently, the same concepts or phenomena (for instance mobility, preferences, competition) have different meanings according to different authors. It is sometimes unclear whether these concepts are to be viewed as a means or an end. In addition, they are perceived as being more or less positive ones depending on the contributions. Moreover, it is also sometimes hard to find a coherent order in the range of case studies, which easily leads one to conclude that there is no regularity among different countries. Real comparative studies are therefore found to be rare and typologies too 'flexible'. The rest of our contribution, which, among other things, stresses general criticism before exemplifying them with the European case(s), tries to avoid these mistakes as much as possible.

As agreed by most fiscal federalist specialists (see Oates, 1999 or Musgrave, 1976) the working basis of Fiscal Federalism is imprecise. Indeed, the decomposition of functions is problematic as in practice it is difficult to state whether a given good or service, or whether a given fiscal setting enters into the category of redistribution, stabilisation or allocation. The categories are permeable, which makes policy comprehension imperfect and policy choices uneasy. Many stabilisation and allocation measures are highly distributive in nature. For instance, Cohesion policy, which is a European policy undertaken with the cooperation of different levels of government, combines a bit of all three (*cf.* Chapter 2). Moreover, the interpersonal feature of redistribution in the Musgravian decomposition of functions is actually quite remote from its actual form in many States, where redistribution is often inter-territorial (the subject matter of grant economics), which theory only sees as a second-best. Finally, the real-world permeability of this functional decomposition raises doubts about the usefulness of the above-mentioned guideline as this contested decomposition structures the way most specialists of Fiscal Federalism think. The fact that this decomposition has purposively been built to allow one to distinguish between equity (redistribution) and efficiency (stabilisation, allocation) criterion makes the criticism even more meaningful. As argued notably by Derycke and Gilbert (1988) or Walsh (1993), in practice, Fiscal settings are just not as neat and a-contextual – *i.e.* a-historical, a-constitutional and a-political – as the traditional fiscal federalist perspective predicts. This makes comparative analysis uneasy. This also makes the most theoretical strand of the Fiscal Federalism literature somewhat questionable.

Another important criticism relates to the lack of theoretical differences between centralisation of a given function and coordination. Cooperation between levels of governments and governments at the same level can be achieved through various means: regulation, fiscal coordination (including harmonisation), a bigger common budget or a complex system of various grants. However, Fiscal Federalism's main focus relates to the differences between various types of grants. It does not for instance inform us of the practical differences (and sometimes superiority) between these diverse forms of cooperation. Put differently, fiscal coordination (*e.g.* minimal tax harmonisation through minimal tax rates on labour in sub-central regions) is often seen as strictly equivalent to a common fiscal setting (*e.g.* a unique tax on labour collected by the central level) in achieving the same goal (*e.g.* avoiding a race to the bottom between sub-central governments to attract companies). This is not in fact true, because power and tax collection or spending are clearly interrelated. However, current debates on the Stability and Growth Pact (SGP), and the spectacular dead-end in which European governments decision has plunged it, clearly show that all forms of coordination are not equivalent, and that some may be more efficient, effective or credible in order to achieve a given goal (in this case, stabilising the EU economy, or at least preventing EMU participants from free-riding by undertaking an inflationist fiscal policy).

The most problematic feature of Fiscal Federalism relates to its political assumptions. Although Fiscal Federalism is supposed to apply to all kinds of political structures, unitary, federal and 'EU type' states, it makes contradictory implicit assumptions about the nature of the political system. As argued by Walsh (1993), most Fiscal Federalism contributions still make implicit assumptions about the political system their analysis is supposed to apply to. According to him, this implicit political assumption is that the political system is a democratic system, with a benevolent and representative government and a federal structure in the political sense of the term *i.e.* the US (*sic*). The extent to which the EU corresponds to this model will be discussed throughout the rest of our contribution. Additionally, as argued by Vaneecloo (2003), this literature disregards an (the most?) important characteristic of European integration process: its dynamics. While Fiscal Federalism generally claims that a central government decentralises some of its powers to sub-central levels of government, the context of the EU is exactly the opposite. Sub-central levels of government (Member States) actually 'supra-centralise' some of their functions to the central level (the EU) as shown by table 1.1. The real political dynamic of European integration is completely different from the theoretical assumption regarding the mode of creation of fiscal settings. In this respect, the fiscal federalist postulate is misleading in that it does not address the feasibility issue of its prescriptions regarding the assignation of economic roles in the EU. It completely ignores important political factors, which are of crucial importance.[9]

Table 1.1: Fiscal Federalism Theories and the EU:
a Misleading Political Assumption

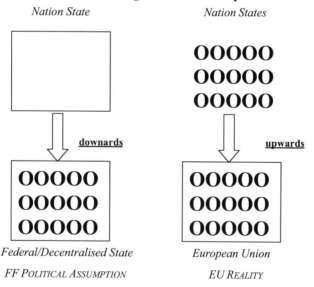

Source: author

---

[9] The political theories of European integration all make this point clear (see Rosamond, 2000 for a review of these theories).

As we will show in the following chapters, these political factors have to be taken into account explicitly if the Fiscal Federalism perspective wants to be really applicable to the EU. In other words, too little attention is paid to the dynamics of change from one fiscal setting to another, which is at the core of all the above-mentioned European debates. This may be seen as an insignificant issue where most changes are efficiency-induced and take place in a mature State. It is not so in the EU case, as shown by Chapters 2 and 3. Chapter 4 also shows that Fiscal Federalism even underestimates the importance of these political factors in the case of the biggest European federal state: Germany. The example of unification just illustrates it perfectly. Disregarding such political factors probably constitutes the main flaw of Fiscal Federalism because they happen to be very important when, in reality, policy-makers choose among various 'fiscal setting options'. Adapting Fiscal Federalism for it to include a European-like integration process is necessary. For instance, this process, determined by both supranational and inter-governmental factors, is surely the main explication for the current small size of the EU budget. This minimalist budget forbids the creation of any ambitious Fiscal setting at the European scale. This state of affairs contrasts with the conclusions of most Fiscal Federalism contributors, which would probably argue for a bigger budget (*cf.* above-mentioned guideline).

As in the case of the Musgravian decomposition of functions with public finances, Fiscal Federalism thus suffers from atavism as it makes political assumption, which correspond to mature and Federal States. The essence of the previous criticism is that one may simply have to reconsider fiscal federalist assumptions to make it fully applicable to the reform and the understanding of the EU. The following approach tries to meet the challenge by avoiding the above-mentioned flaws of Fiscal Federalism.

1.2.3. Our Approach: a Loose Research Agenda

How to save Fiscal Federalism and how to make it fully applicable to the EU? This voluntary provocative question may seem quite strange to one aware of the relative popularity of this framework. This book is both an anthology and a critique of Fiscal Federalism. It argues that it is not possible to understand the economics of the EU without taking into account the fact that it is a multi-level polity, where (notably fiscal) interactions between the various States on one hand, and between them and the EU on the other hand, are complicated. However, it is also important to admit that Fiscal Federalism is, at best, ill-defined. Owing to our previous criticisms, Fiscal Federalism as such only vaguely applies to the European case. The next chapters of this book will recurrently make this point clear. However, criticising is not enough. It is also necessary to look for ways in which this applicability could be improved. A basic Popperian argument claims that for a theory to be valid, it needs to take reality into account. Conversely, as long as it is intrinsically coherent and that it has not been challenged by real trends, then a theory should be taken as truth. Our analysis thus proposes, on the basis of a double emphasis, one on policy issues, and the other on empirical lessons, a change in the way Fiscal Federalists see the EU. This, it is argued, will allow this valuable literature to be relevant for the EU, and not only for mature Federal States.

There are indeed various dimensions related to the theme of Fiscal Federalism and the EU. For instance, simply disentangling facts (Fiscal settings) and theory allows to identify five dimensions of this relationship. One can ask what are the lessons 1) from national experiences for the EU and conversely,[10] 2) from national experiences for the theory of FF, 3) from the EU for the FF theory, 4) from FF for the EU, 5) from FF for individual Member States. This is shown in table 1.2 below.

Traditionally, the most frequently treated dimensions are relations 4 and 5. Our work takes a quite different perspective. Hence, the three following chapters insist more on relations 1, 2 and 3. They assume the EU and its countries are Fiscal settings, in various ways, financial or not. They identify some key policy issues in relation to the EU. For instance, Chapter 2 looks at dimension 3 and 4. It studies carefully European Cohesion Policy by stressing the above-mentioned criticisms. It also insists on the fact that political issues are to be considered as central if one wants Fiscal Federalism to inform us properly about this policy, under dimension 3. Chapter 3 does the same job with stabilisation in the Economic and Monetary Union (EMU). Additionally, its analysis of domestic pacts illustrates dimensions 1 and 2. Chapter 4 looks at dimension 1, and by extension at dimension 2, using the German case as a yardstick. Its analysis of the German unification and the comparison it makes with the European enlargement teaches us many useful things for the EU and the Fiscal Federalist perspective.

Referring to the various dimensions of this loose framework, our aim is to identify ways in which the study of various fiscal settings could help to improve the applicability of the Fiscal Federalism perspective to the EU. From this, we notably insist on the flaws of traditional political economy assumptions Fiscal Federalism theorists often implicitly make.

---

[10] A prerequisite condition for this question to be acknowledged one day by academics and politicians is the one of a successful EU on growth, employment and social cohesion grounds with a significant budget.

We see for instance why problems viewed under dimension 2 cannot be applied in a straightforward way under dimension 3. This, in turn, helps us to identify key conditions for applying the Fiscal Federalism perspective to the EU (dimension 3). Dimension 5 has already been summarised above and is also extensively investigated in Chapter 6.

Table 1.2: Fiscal Federalism and the EU: Five Dimensions

THEORY   REALITY

| **FF PERSPECTIVES** | **Actual FF SETTINGS in:** |

FISCAL FEDERALISM THEORIES

3
4
The EU
2
5
MEMBER STATES
1

Source: author

In the meantime, on the basis of the previous case studies, Chapter 5 proposes a set of variables likely to be decisive in any fiscal setting. Our empirical study is twofold. First, we describe the main features of the 25 European countries fiscal settings. We briefly review these variables for most European countries. We do not limit our analysis to considering 'usual' fiscal variables (*e.g.* the share of local government spending in total public spending), but we also pick a wider set of political and socio-economic variables, which, as we will show, may have a huge responsibility in shaping real-world fiscal settings. By doing so, we seek to exploit national experiences in order to increase our understanding of both theory and facts. This empirical study focuses on dimensions 1 and 2 in order to enrich dimensions 4 and 5. The underlying idea is to adopt an original viewpoint which would avoid traditional flaws of Fiscal Federalism. It also leads to interesting descriptive findings about fiscal settings *idéaux-types* and about the way the traditional Fiscal Federalism theory could be improved. The last chapter summarises our theoretical and empirical works. Above all, it reaches the following conclusion: the traditional theory of Fiscal Federalism can neither be applied *telle quelle* to the European Union nor to the European countries. Any change into existing fiscal settings requires a deep knowledge of political dynamics and of the institutional or historical context. This conclusion is then applied to shed new light on the EU budget, its means, its ambitions and its ends.

1.2.4. Fiscal Federalism and the European Union: First Conclusions

Chapter 1 has shown the following points. Fiscal Federalism is by no way a theory. It is a perspective, which welcomes different views (from neo-classical to a wide range of heterodox theories) but whose main feature is to study economic relationships in multi-level polities, such as the EU. Nevertheless, a broad consensus arises on an optimal assignment of functions, which should be taken as a flexible guideline. According to the traditional view, stabilisation and redistribution should be centralised, whereas allocation should be divided among the different levels of government, with a presumption in favour of decentralisation.

This perspective has a natural comparative advantage in mirroring some of the most debated economic issues in the EU. However, it was noted, this still leaves some place for sharp criticisms of the literature. The contested relevance of the Fiscal Federalism perspective should not make us throw the baby with the bath water.

We thus presented a new framework, which, in our opinion, could guide Fiscal Federalism theorists specialised in EU studies. This framework, summarised and discussed in Chapter 6, rests on the following reform recipe: an 'empirics-based' study, which takes into account the specific political, historical and institutional features of both the EU and its countries, with an emphasis on policy-making in specific areas rather than with extensive reference to a heroic decomposition of functions.

CHAPTER 2

Fiscal Federalism and
the European Cohesion Policy

Clément VANEECLOO

Chapter 1 discussed the overall potential relevance of the Fiscal Federalist perspective for the European Union. However, this was done in rather general terms. As we argued, there is a need to transpose our analysis in terms of precise policy issues. This chapter thus fulfils this task by focusing on the European Cohesion Policy,[1] which basically aims at reducing economic disparities across the European space and more specifically between European regions.

Compared to the loose framework presented in the previous section, this chapter directly tackles dimensions 3 and 4. Cohesion Policy is often presented as redistribution at the European scale. As we will show, the normative guideline of Fiscal Federalism says a lot about the distribution function. In this sense, theory provides useful insights for the understanding of the reality of this policy. However, the reverse is also true. Putting cohesion policy under scrutiny also provides rich lessons for the traditional Fiscal Federalism theoretical perspective. Notably, it leads to a critic of the latter's major (and often implicit) assumptions.

We first introduce this rather complex and ever-evolving policy, highlighting shortly its main features. Then, we show that, under certain assumptions, a Fiscal Federalism perspective can deepen our understanding of its justifications and functioning. However, we explain why these lessons should be considered with high caution. Indeed, the traditional theory of Fiscal Federalism is a 'suit', which does not fit Cohesion Policy very well. This preliminary conclusion regarding the lack of relevance of the Fiscal Federalist framework leads to the reversal of our analysis. We show that the understanding of the Cohesion policy is helpful for the normative theory of Fiscal Federalism and for the

---

[1] Here, we focus more in depth on Cohesion Policy in the EU(15). The recent arrangements for the ten new countries are still limited and are tackled in Chapter 4, together with the important question of the financing of enlargement.

updating of its hypotheses. By doing so, we propose some ways to improve its applicability to the EU.

2.1. Cohesion Policy: a Short Description

2.1.1. Objectives, Means and Specificity

The objectives and functioning of the Cohesion Policy are broadly sketched in the Treaty on the European Community. Articles 158 to 162, added in the aftermath of the Single Act, thus define its objectives, the repartition of competencies, its articulation with other European or nation-wide policies, its instruments and the modalities of decision-making or implementation. Moreover, it is complemented by numerous regulations (*e.g.* regulations (CE) No.1260/1999 or (CE) No.1783/1999) to render it operational by detailing the rules of the different Funds (see below). Already sketched in its Preamble,[2] objectives of the Cohesion Policy are detailed in Articles 158 (ex-130A) and 160 (ex-160C):

> In order to promote its overall harmonious development, the Community shall develop and pursue its actions leading to the strengthening of its economic and social cohesion.

> In particular, the Community shall aim at reducing disparities between the levels of development of the various regions and the backwardness of the least favoured regions or islands, including rural areas. (Art. 158 of the Treaty of Rome)

> [The ERDF] is intended to help to redress the main regional imbalances in the Community through participation in the development and structural adjustment of regions whose development is lagging behind and in the conversion of declining industrial regions. (Art. 160 of the Treaty of Rome)

The objective can be summarised as follows: ensuring economic and social cohesion of the EU by financially helping poorer regions to allow them to catch-up richer ones (convergence is measured in terms of GDP per inhabitant). From the way it is actually designed, one can also induce that it is a social policy as well, aimed at reducing inter-individual inequalities, or at ensuring equality of conditions. The Cohesion Policy thus currently focuses on southern Europe (Spain, Greece, Portugal, South of Italy), Ireland (formerly) and the poorest areas in rich

---

2 "RESOLVED to ensure the economic and social progress of their countries by common action to eliminate the barriers which divide Europe [...] AFFIRMING as the essential objective of their efforts the constant improvements of the living and working conditions of their peoples [...] ANXIOUS to strengthen the unity of their economies and to ensure their harmonious development by reducing the differences existing between the various regions and the backwardness of the less favoured regions".

countries (*Nord-Pas-de-Calais* in France, *Wallonie* in Belgium, New *Länder* in Germany, etc.).

Currently, Cohesion Policy is the second expenditure of the European budget. However, it is set to become the first one from 2009 onwards, and perhaps even before that date. The creation of the European Regional Development Fund (ERDF) in 1975 is often presented as the real kick-off of this policy. In reality, the coherent regrouping of all cohesion spending in a single policy only arose in the mid-1980s. Its importance has continually risen ever since, notably in 1988 and 1993, when Cohesion Policy doubled in nominal terms. The decision to leave it constant in real terms, at the 1999 Berlin Summit, symbolised a structural confirmation of its ever-growing status as it resisted the high pressure from some Member-States calling for its re-nationalisation. Other observers have been disappointed by this deal, seen as not being ambitious enough compared to the 2004 enlargement prospects. Cohesion Policy now amounts to more than 213 billion euros over the 2000-2006 period. This is more than 30 billion euros yearly, but only 0.4 per cent of the EU GDP. However, such a low rate in terms of GDP reflects the weakness of the European budget more than that of the policy. As agreed in the financial perspectives, it accounts for around one third of the European budget. This is set to grow gradually when accounting for the smooth rise of the spending devoted to the financing of the eastern enlargement. For instance, in 2006, cohesion policy including accession aid will already represent around 40 per cent of the yearly European budget. Note also that the statistical effect will concentrate the bulk of cohesion policy towards eastern countries from 2007 onwards. Poorer regions from the EU(15) area will automatically lose some funding, without being richer: the arrival of ten very poor countries will artificially increase their relative wealth (as the average level of GDP per inhabitant will fall). For the sake of simplicity, we will mainly focus on Cohesion Policy until 2006, as the precise design for the next period is not known yet (*cf. infra*).

Moreover, the importance of this policy (both in terms of budget and of media attention) will rise even more in the next budgeting period (2007-2013) due to the following factors: i) the planned stagnation in real terms of the Common Agricultural Policy (CAP), ii) the need to finance an enlargement which automatically leads the EU to unprecedented levels of cross-country inequalities, and iii) the recent proposals from the Commission in 2004 and the Parliament in 2005. However, recurrent calls for a 'fair return' by countries like the United Kingdom, Sweden or the Netherlands, or the automatic loss of funds by southern countries corollary to the eastern shift of the regional poverty problem (the above-mentioned statistical effect) made it impossible to predict the outcome of inter-governmental negotiations on financial perspectives, which took place in 2005. The European Summit, held in June 2005, led to a failure of negotiations, because of a mix of politico-economic reasons. Media attention was focused on the British refusal to drop its rebate. The UK, in turn, accused France of being over-anxious to keep 'its' CAP untouched. European countries eventually found an agreement before the deadline. Indeed, in December 2005, Financial Perspectives, were adopted by the Council. At the time of completion of this manuscript, they still required an inter-institutional agreement to be passed and, especially, the approval of the Parliament. However, the main lines and the political dynamics, as presented in Chapter 6, should be kept unchanged. When Financial Perspectives (2007-2013) are defined, the Council will decide on the general Cohesion Policy regulation.

Apart from its financial weight, Cohesion Policy is also distinctive in the sense that it is the most 'earth-grounded' policy of the EU. It is not just about financial transfers fixing ceilings, price or refund levels as is the case with the CAP. It is neither limited to financing of European-wide projects such as in the research policy. As we show further, the Commission plays a key role at all stages (including a significant role at the implementation stage) cooperating with a wide-range of national and regional actors to realise every year thousands of projects in all sectors (from culture to transport but examples are extremely numerous), led by agents of a different nature (public-private, societies-companies, etc.). This singularity explains why this policy attracts so many academics across all the social sciences fields: Sociology, Law, Economics, Geography, Political Sciences, with however, little multi-disciplinary work. Debates about its relevance seem particularly buoyant inside the fields of economics and political sciences.[3]

2.1.2. *Organisation: a Plurality of Rules, Policy Stages, Actors and Funds*

The organisation of the Cohesion Policy is a bit complicated for the novice. Table 2.1 below summarises some of its key components, but a full literary presentation is necessary. Cohesion Policy has to respect European *rules*, national laws and sometimes regional norms; it is run by different *actors* (at different levels of government or administration), which play a more or less extended role depending on the policy-making

---

[3] For example, the theoretical and empirical struggles are ferocious between and among different economic schools such as the New Economic Geography and/or the New Growth Theory. The same holds in Political Sciences, for instance, between partisans of the Multi-Level Governance (*e.g.* Marks and Hooghe, 2003) or State-centric (Moravscik, 1998) models.

stage (conception or implementation) and on the considered country; it can be run on a regional, national or trans-national basis; it is divided into numerous *Funds* aimed at different objectives, sectors and with various eligibility criteria. Besides, it is also highly interrelated with other national or European policies (*e.g.* the Competition Policy, the CAP, national policies of regional development).

Rules to which actors have to obey are European as provided by treaties or European regulations and respond to diverse concerns. This means that these rules are inescapable inside the policy-process. All of the actors, from the Head of European states to the ultimate manager of one of the thousands of financed projects, are constrained by them. These rules are the famous principles of the Cohesion Policy. The first principle is programming: the Policy is a sum of programs or plans, detailed for each region, and for each objective. Partnership simply means a wide range of actors should be involved (mostly the EC, MS and regional authorities) in strategic planning. Co-financing is made to avoid a substitution between European funds and pre-existing national funds (additionality principle). This principle also more than doubles the importance of this policy in real terms (as each European euro spent needs to be co-financed by at least one euro coming from another source, institutional or not). For the first time at the end of 2003, the so-called N+2 rule was also applied. This rule implies the loss of unspent funds if a particular region does not manage to subsidise enough projects effectively. It was introduced together with the performance reserve (according to the well-known carrot and stick principle). Other rules related to ex-post publicity, control or evaluation also apply to all European regions benefiting from these funds. As explained below, these European rules are complemented by national ones.

Actors are diverse and play different roles at different stages. To make it short, the Commission is mainly involved in preparing financial perspectives and regulations, in coordinating the different Funds, and in negotiating Community Support Frameworks (CSFs) with individual Member States or regions. Note that the CSFs are the main planning document for the six-year period (and revised half-way). As it is the ultimate financing body, it also intervenes more or less directly in project acceptance, control and evaluation. For instance, all the projects amounting to more than 50 million euros require an explicit agreement from the Commission, together with the compliance to extra rules. Moreover, it is fully responsible for the so-called Community initiatives (4 per cent of Cohesion spending). The role of the Commission is roughly the same regardless of the region or country, which is not the case for nations and regions. The main Directorate General (DG) is the DG Regio (DG XVI). However, the DG for Employment, Social Affairs and Equal Opportunities manages the European Social Fund (ESF) and the agriculture and fishery DGs also play a limited role. In the conception stage, Member States are the key players in the negotiation of financial perspectives, which complies with an intergovernmental bargaining and log-rolling logic. They also intervene in the conception and negotiation of Community Support Frameworks and according to the principle of subsidiarity are responsible for the implementation of the latter on the territory (including possible corruption and mismanagement). Consequently, they can decide on any appropriate rules and pass all laws (as long as they are compatible with the above-mentioned European principles) with regards to implementation. The diversity of these rules across countries is too wide to be even shortly summarised here. In general, regions are, to different degrees, also implicated in the writing of Community Support Frameworks. In the implementation stage, the agency responsible for the selection, monitoring and control of projects can either be national or regional, and administrative or political, depending on the country. However, it is always located within the regional territory. The Member State decides on the responsibilities of each level of government inside the country. As a result, the power of regions in the implementation of Cohesion Policy tends to be in line with the power they are usually granted in the national institutional design. For example, Belgian or German regions have more responsibilities than Greek or Irish ones. In France, regional power in the implementation of European regional policies gradually increases, but the Central State still retains most of it through the action of *Préfectures de Régions* and under the coordination of the DATAR (*Délégation à l'Aménagement du Territoire et à l'Action Régionale*). To complicate the whole process even further, regions in a similar country may even have different powers at the implementation stage of the policy. For example, in France, this is the case for the *Départements d'Outre-Mer* (DOMs) or for Alsace, which are awarded special additional powers. Eventually, Cohesion Policy also depends on regional norms and habits regarding practices or networks, which may affect the efficiency of the implementation in a given region.

The agency in charge also depends on the types of Funds and the eligibility condition. The Cohesion Fund is devoted to countries whose GDP per habitant is below 90 per cent of the EU average. It aims at financing transport and environment expenditures. Concerned countries are Greece, Spain and Portugal. However, the bulk of the Cohesion Policy are the Structural Funds: the ERDF, the European Agricultural Guidance and Guarantee Fund (EAGGF), the European Social Fund (ESF) and the Financial Instrument for Fisheries Guidance (FIFG). These four Funds are supposed to fulfil one or more of the three objectives. Eligibility at Objective 1 excludes eligibility at Objective 2 (though two parts of the same region may be eligible at either one of the two).

Table 2.1: Cohesion Policy, Facts and Figures

		2000-2006 period*			2007-2013 period**	
Objectives	*Instruments Used*	*Share of total Cohesion Policy **	*Eligibility criterion*	*Scope % of EU population -covered*	*Objectives*	*Instruments*
Objective 1	ERDF ESF EAGGF	64.1%	<75% of EU(15) average + under-populated areas Regional	25.7%	Convergence	ERDF ESF +Cohesion Fund
Objective 2	ERDF ESF	10.6%	Industrial decline, low employment conditions Regional	18.1%	Regional competitive-ness	ERDF
Objective 3	ESF	11.3%	Need for social employment-oriented measures National	74.3%	and employment (EES)	ESF
European Initiatives Interreg URBAN EQUAL	ERDF ERDF ESF	4%	Various Trans-national, regional, border cooperation	Potentially 100%	European cooperation	ERDF
LEADER+	EAGGF-guidance		'Problem' Cities	Urban areas		
			Gender equality	Mainly women		
Rural dev. Fishery (exc.Obj. 1)	EAGGF-guar. IFOP	1%			–	–
COHESION FUND	Cohesion Fund: Transport + environment	8.4%	<90% than EU(15) average national	Greece, Spain, Portugal, Ireland (west)	*Cf. supra*	*Cf. supra*
9 objectives	**6 instruments**	**100% 212 bil. euros**	**All European territory**	**100%**	**3 objectives**	**3 instruments**

*Objectives 1 and 2 respectively include regions eligible in a transitory manner (opting-out).
** based on the February and July 2004 proposals of the Commission.

Source: author, from various (EC) sources

Objective 1 is aimed at the poorest regions (below 75 per cent of the European average), Objective 2 at restructuring former industrial regions, and Objective 3 at territories (individual) needing training and skills upgrading. Objectives 1 and 2 are regional, Objective 3 is national. Once again, for the sake of simplification and not to mention transitory objectives and community initiatives, details of these policies are summarised in table 2.1. Although most details concern the current programming period (2000-2006), the table also displays the Commission's proposal for the next period (2007-2013). This proposal aims once more at 'rationalising' the policy, by reducing its number of objectives and instruments, by extending the prerogatives of the Member States and/or their regions, and by simplifying procedures. Last but not least, it should be noted that, although all European countries get some parts of the 'Cohesion pie', this policy is highly redistributive as it is mainly aimed at the poorest regions and countries (*cf.* section 2.3).

2.2. How Can Fiscal Federalism Inform Us about the Cohesion Policy?

2.2.1. A prerequisite: Cohesion as Part of the Redistribution Function?

All theories should correspond, at least very roughly, to facts. The first question that should arise when trying to understand a policy issue in terms of the traditional guidelines sketched in Chapter 1 is, thus, to determine to which Musgravian function it corresponds to. The Cohesion Policy has definitely nothing to do with stabilisation, as it is not by nature linked to conjuncture or cyclical smoothing of growth and employment (with the notable and odd exception of the recently created solidarity fund, which deals with natural catastrophes). Moreover, it is not allocation, as neither the EU nor the national or regional agencies in charge of the funds provide anything directly. Structural funds are not aimed at financing public goods, in the traditional sense of the term, as it is essentially run on a project financing basis. These funds finance all kinds of projects, both public and private projects in a desire to promote long-term competitiveness of beneficiary regions. This will be cleared upon in the next section, which deals more in-depth with the status and rationale of such a policy.

By process of elimination, Fiscal Federalism can thus inform us about the Cohesion Policy in two different manners. The first one is to consider it as a redistribution scheme, as does for instance the Sapir Report (2003). The second one is to see it as a complicated and vertical intergovernmental system of grants. The assumption that the Cohesion Policy corresponds to redistribution is often made in the literature, and that is the way we will consider it here. Table 2.2, at the end of this section, tries to make a distinction between redistribution and grants; it shows how difficult it is to disentangle these two elements in practice. Moreover, if one takes the broadest possible definition of Cohesion, this may also encompass redistribution and social systems. Section 2.2.3 tackles this last issue more in depth.

2.2.2. Redistribution: Lessons from Fiscal Federalism for Cohesion

If we make the assumption that Cohesion *is* redistribution, the traditional theory of Fiscal Federalism provides us with clear justifications of the Cohesion Policy. Indeed, as noted in Chapter 1, distribution should be centralised for reasons of systemic efficiency. This need for centralisation is already well justified elsewhere. For instance, Musgrave (1969, 1976), Oates (1968, 1972, 1999), Oates and Brown (1985), or Wildasin (1990, 1995), who, in particular, views the problem in terms of externalities, all insist on the need for leaving redistribution to the central government. Indeed, in theory, the alternative (decentralisation), together with agent mobility, would otherwise completely forbid any kind of redistribution to take place. Indeed, in a decentralised redistribution setting, sub-central levels of government are allowed to decide on the average amount of redistribution from rich to poor, fixing their own progressive income tax rates and allowances for raising revenues or consumption of the poorest. A decentralised system, where a given jurisdiction sets up an aggressive redistribution scheme, would lead to the outflow of rich households and companies – escaping the high fiscal burden – and an inflow of poor ones (presumably looking for higher fiscal benefits). Less generous jurisdictions would experience the reverse effect: an outflow of labour. Redistribution schemes would become impossible and the system explosive. As Musgrave (1976, p. 623) points out, this regional differentiation *de facto* influences agents' choices of location and leads to locational inefficiencies. Musgrave even adds that, in the US, such a differentiation of the system has contributed a lot to the migration flow of welfare recipients from relatively poor rural regions to richer urban areas. In short, redistributive fiscal settings (income and capital tax, but also personal and social benefits, including unemployment, housing, schooling, health when they are aimed at the poorest) should be the same on a territory where capital and labour mobility are high. Otherwise a kind of adverse selection phenomenon operates. The only 'solution' to this problem is to use segregation policies to constrain mobility, which would not be compatible with the European integration rationale and spirit. Note that if labour mobility is relatively low (*e.g.* Europe), decentralised redistribution in an heterogeneous space would theoretically act as a trigger for a rise in mobility. Admittedly, this however takes time. Moreover, it should be noted that if preferences are homogeneous, the only justification for a decentralised system is related to the administration cost of the system. And there might be economies of scale accordingly, which means centralisation of redistribution would be less costly.

Empirical evidence in mature countries seems to corroborate this theoretical intuition. For example, Feldstein and Wrobel (1998) show that massive redistributive policies of American States have failed to reduce skilled-unskilled wage inequalities, mainly because of wage mobility. This leads to a 'no-redistribution outcome' and *deadweight losses* because of interdependence of States (sub-central jurisdictions). Saavedra (1998) (cited by Oates, 1999) also shows that social spending among States is correlated (for a general survey, see Brueckner, 1998). Chapter 4 also highlights such mobility pressures in the case of the German unification.

Conversely, it is worth noting the few contributions advocating the decentralisation of the distribution function. The perspective here is a competitive one. It is adapted from Tieboutian analysis of the allocation function or from the Oatesian decentralisation theorem (Guihéry, 1999). It is for example the case of Pauly (1973) and Gramlich (1987b). These authors argue that a decentralised management of inter-personal redistribution leads to efficiency gains arising from smaller redistribution communities. Local redistribution, they argue, is then Pareto-efficient, as it allows to make beneficiaries and contributors closer to one another. Under a double assumption of interdependent utility functions and at given information costs, proximity enhances altruistic behaviours. Better access to information (supposed once again) leads taxation closer to its optimum. Finally, a last argument in favour of the decentralisation of redistribution is related to *laboratory Federalism*. The underlying idea (discussed and to a large extent contested by Oates, 1999) is that decentralised redistribution systems allow for diversity of practices and its corollary: a selection process of the best ones.

The consequences of such a fiscal federalist perspective analysis for the EU are straightforward (we still make the assumption that cohesion policy is redistribution). First, a EU with high labour and capital mobility (which is, indeed, both a means and a core end of the EU) would make decentralised redistribution systems explosive, unless one creates a complicated and politically, economically and socially costly system of segregation, impossible in traditional States and Federations. Second, this theory also tells us that, even without mobility, a decentralised system of redistribution would trigger mobility: a 'vicious' circle is perceptible here. Mobility makes decentralised redistribution useless or inefficient; even if there is no mobility at the beginning, such a decentralised system would make people more mobile (the time-span issue is important), thus leading to the necessity to centralise redistribution. Wildasin (1990) already predicted the rise of such demands for centralisation. Note that the exact same line of reasoning can be applied to Social Europe (see section 2.3.2). Lastly, the implicit argument for the decentralisation of redistribution is heterogeneity of preferences, which is assumed more than explained in the European case. The closer these preferences or the faster they converge, the lower the need for a decentralised system. However, to our knowledge, preference heterogeneity in the EU still forms more of an assumption than an objective evaluation. Very few, if any, economic studies try to understand what determines preferences in reality. The overall conclusion of this analysis in terms of Fiscal Federalism is that redistribution should become more and more Central (European) in the long-term (for most economists, mobility is perfect in the long-term), either in the form of greater harmonisation or of a full centralisation of the redistribution system. In other words, Fiscal Federalism tends to advocate towards the centralisation of the redistribution function in the long-term. Applied to the EU, and assuming Cohesion is redistribution, Cohesion Policy's European-wide scope is justified on economic grounds. It is likely to grow in the future as the results of the transfer of national (sub-central) systems to the European (central) level.

2.2.3. Lessons of Grant Economics for the Cohesion Policy

Nevertheless, it is important not to ignore the current reality of the EU. Households and labour mobility are still low, preferences are still said to be heterogeneous and sovereign national States are still very reluctant to loose the reins of distribution policies. In a sense, this can be viewed as a natural or historical tendency for self-discrimination. Moreover, as shown in section 2.3, Cohesion Policy imperfectly fits the redistribution suit tailored by the fiscal federalist framework. To state it simply, if cohesion is not really redistribution, are there any further justifications of the Cohesion Policy? If we substitute an assumption for another, the answer is positive. Indeed, if we make the assumption that the Cohesion Policy is a complex system of grants, whose main feature is inter-territorial redistribution, the theory of Fiscal Federalism still has much to teach us. This time, there is a lower need to make heroic assumptions about mobility or preferences.

Grants[4] are a privileged form of coordination in most multijurisdictional States. In most fiscal settings, grants are used to organise horizontal and vertical coordination:

> Vertical coordination seeks to allocate powers efficiently between the central level and local authorities in order to allow the equalization among communities of charges and advantages arising from public activities, without forbidding the possibility of a supply of collective public services adapted to the characteristics of the community. Horizontal coordination allows to structure relationships between territorial collectivities of similar level in order to equalize costs and advantages arising from spillovers [...] by far, financial transfers constitute the most common mode to coordinate decisions at different levels of administration (Derycke and Gilbert, 1988, p. 47).

Such a dichotomy is however far from holding in all cases. For instance, the German system of *perequation* mainly answers to concerns about territorial equity. Moreover, other means may be used to achieve the role assumed by grants such as i) tax-sharing, ii) fiscal spending *per se* as in the case of our first assumption about redistribution, iii) all other regulatory means and laws, principally in the hands of the central government (rarely studied). Tax-sharing is comparable to a grant (an unconditional/automatic/global grant from the central government to sub-central units), with a notable difference in the sense that it is stable and decided *ex-ante* (*i.e.* institutional). In a word, the study of grants allows to reach insights about most forms of fiscal coordination. More important, it allows to reach interesting conclusions about the Cohesion Policy.

For instance, the study of the effect of the various kinds of grants can be deduced in a partial equilibrium framework transposed from the consumer theory to grant and subsidies analysis (*cf.* Musgrave and Musgrave, 1984; Derycke and Gilbert, 1988; Costello, 1993; Gramlich, 1987a). Without entering into the details of such type of analysis, the message is the following: different types of grants have different effects on the consumption of the public good one wants to subsidise or on the fiscal capacity of a given region. For instance, when the grant has distribution or equalisation purposes, the grant should not be categorical; or when the grant aims at internalising externalities, the grant should be open-ended and categorical (Gramlich, 1987a). The purpose of Cohesion Policy is unclear here. Is it short-term distribution or long-

---

4   The underlying definition here is related to transfers, where grants are synonymous to a 'one-way transfer' as "a one-way economic relationship whereby party A conveys an exchangeable to party B without receiving in return an exchangeable of equal market value" (Boulding and Pfaff, 1972). Musgrave precises that "transfers thus defined involve redistribution so that a theory of transfers becomes a theory of redistribution" (Musgrave R.A. and P.B., 1984).

term action on competitiveness? The same holds for the suitable form of grant, which corresponds to it. For instance, it is not clear whether European grants are categorical or not: even though they bargain with the Commission, beneficiary regions more or less choose the sector or public good on which they want to spend the grants they receive. However, Fiscal Federalism still helps to explain some of the policy choices made. The additionality principle for instance is meant to avoid that States decrease public spending on matters subsidised by the Cohesion Policy. This principle seems to work in practice. On the other hand, this additionality requirement is lower for poorer regions. This means that creators of the actual grant system (Delors Commission) were aware of equalisation issues and differentiated fiscal capacities.

The study of grants also provides wide justifications for 'intergovern-mental redistribution'. Three different rationales may, then, legitimate grants between territories (as opposed to transfers between individuals). Financial transfers can be justified on efficiency, equity or political grounds as shown in table 2.2. As column 2 shows, many justifications for grants respond to mixed motives (*e.g.* double imperative of equity and efficiency for traditional redistribution). It should be noted that, both in practice and in theory, it is not always easy to see whether a grant is in fact inter-territorial redistribution (ITR) (see column 3).[5]

The literature traditionally agrees on three justifications for grants: i) the internalisation of externalities and spillovers, ii) fiscal equaliza-tion, and iii) the overall improvement of the fiscal system. Although Cohesion Policy can be justified on all or each of these grounds, these justifications seem more relevant in the context of mature nations than it is for the EU. As the last column points out, many other justifications can in fact perfectly suit the European reality. Most of these justify-cations are barely acknowledged, neither by Fiscal Federalism nor by the European Commission. Some of them actually play a significant role in explaining the size and working of the Cohesion Policy, but are not officially mentioned. However, the next section shows how important these factors are in reality.

---

[5] Numerous authors, hence, simply justify grants on inter-territorial distribution impera-tives, which seems idiosyncratic. Grants are also very often presented as being a way of achieving an optimal fiscal organisation, *i.e.* to offset the differences between the guideline and actual decomposition of functions. This, however, overlooks the fact that fiscal systems are institutionally and historically determined (Costello, 1993) and that any fiscal change may dangerously undermine the balance of a given fiscal system.

Table 2.2: Typology of Grant Justifications and Cohesion Policy[a]

GRANT JUSTIFICATION	Nature of the justification	Is it ITR?	CAN Cohesion Policy be justified for this reason?/ IS IT in practice?
Correcting inter-jurisdictional spillovers and externalities	EFFICIENCY	NO	YES/YES
Improving fiscal system, economies of scale, cheaper tax collection	EFFICIENCY	NO	YES/NO
Stabilisation in case of asymmetrical shock	EFFICIENCY Stabilisation	?	NO/NO
Inter-individual redistribution	EQUITY System efficiency	YES	YES/NO
Territorial or spatial equity, Equalisation of fiscal capacities	EQUITY EFFICIENCY POLITICAL	YES	YES/YES
Dispersing population, keeping places 'alive' (immobility)	EQUITY POLITICAL	YES	YES/YES
Internalisation of inter-temporal externalities	POLITICAL EQUITY	YES	YES/NO
Imposing central preferences to lower levels	POLITICAL	NO	YES/not officially
Improving integration dynamics, log-rolling tool	POLITICAL EFFICIENCY	?	YES/not officially

a. See Desjardins and Guihéry (2001), Oates (1999), Spahn (1993), Derycke and Gilbert (1988), Costello (1993), for similar typologies.

Source: author

To conclude regarding the lessons of Fiscal Federalism for the Cohesion Policy, this section has shown why the traditional theory of Fiscal Federalism advocates the centralisation of the redistribution function. This is because of a 'vicious' circle between mobility and differentiated redistribution policies. With more realistic assumptions about the EU, Fiscal Federalism, *via* its analysis of grants, also helps to legitimate Cohesion Policy. The effect of different types of grants varies. Consequently, one type of grant should be chosen according to the purpose it wants to serve. The additionality principle of the Cohesion Policy is thus justified as a means to avoid the flypaper effect. This simply suggests that the form of grant/inter-territorial distribution matters. However, the overwhelming focus on the fiscal forms and the ignorance of other political economy modalities accompanying these financial transfers is problematic, this analysis in terms of Fiscal Federalism should be taken with caution. Next section explains why the Fiscal Federalism perspective, as such, is not so relevant for the Cohesion Policy.

2.3. The Unfitting Suit: What Should the Tailor Do?

2.3.1. Why Is Fiscal Federalism only Partially Relevant for Cohesion Policy?

We have just seen that the traditional theory of Fiscal Federalism can potentially teach us many things about the justification and implementation of Cohesion Policy. To do so, however, we had to make a number of strong assumptions about this policy. Indeed, section 2.2 'reconstructed' the conclusions of the fiscal federalist framework 'as if' the latter had said something about Cohesion Policy. Actually, little analysis directly focuses on this policy in the traditional Fiscal Federalist framework. Most of the economic literature sees Cohesion in terms of convergence among heterogeneous territories (neo-classical or new growth theories and empirical works on the efficiency of cohesion policy), or in terms of the effect of economic integration regarding patterns of specialisation (traditional theories of international trade or New Economic Geography). New growth theories identify causes of endogenous development. Territories with better technology grow faster, hence triggering perennial inter-regional inequalities. Based on this rationale, cohesion policy is legitimised by its ability to reduce the latter dynamic. It should focus on increasing research and development, innovation, human capital and infrastructures in backward regions. New Economic Geography seems to show that integration, in the form of a reduction in transport costs, triggers agglomeration/desertification dynamics. These dynamics are due to migration or input-output linkages, at least in the short-term. This literature thus highlights a trade-off between efficiency (growth of the integrated space) and equity (harmonisation of living standards). Although it is not unanimous about the relevance of this policy, the New Economic Geography theory insists on the need to implement sound transport policies, combined to policies aimed at diffusing technology as widely as possible.

The neglect of Cohesion Policy by the fiscal federalism literature is a pity because, as already shown, it is maybe the most 'deeply European' policy in the strict sense of the term. One may regret that such a policy, which gives rise to many interactions between different levels of government, is not better investigated. These interactions are even perhaps richer than in a mature State, as they are both horizontal at the conception stage (negotiations between Member States) and vertical at the implementation stage (with three, sometimes four, levels of jurisdiction involved). In brief, Cohesion Policy is one of the most important and complex elements of the European fiscal setting.

We may however admit that the assumptions we made on the very nature of this policy do not hold in reality. Although the 'suit' we constructed may be the best one in the fiscal federalist perspective shop, it is as if the tailored suit did not fit this policy. In other words, the reality of Cohesion Policy does not have any existent theoretical counterparts in the fiscal federalist perspective. The assumptions one had to make happens in actuality to be a bit ill-at-ease with the actual policy described in section 2.1. First, for Musgrave (1959) and his followers, distribution is i) interpersonal, and ii) an equity issue. Regarding point i), Cohesion Policy is not interpersonal but inter-territorial. Inter-territorial distribution is viewed as a second-best option. However, the reason why Cohesion Policy's rationale is inter-territorial and not interpersonal once again has to do with political economy (see section 2.3.2). Disregarding this also means disregarding the (possibly *sui generis*) nature of the process of European integration. Concerning point ii), we have already pointed out the fact that distribution in fiscal settings has as much to do with systemic efficiency or political stability, than it has to do with equity. Next to the acknowledged and widely admitted permeability of functions, this may well have more important consequences. Possibly, the Musgravian decomposition may in fact not be suitable to understand States or polities where authority is very dispersed and fiscal interactions are numerous and complicated. Moreover, we have already explained that Cohesion Policy was made on a project basis, relating to education, vocational training, research, business spirit, environment, or transport. These kinds of projects may correspond to the allocation function with few inter-jurisdictional spillovers at play. But, as argued at the beginning of section 2.2, Cohesion Policy is not allocation neither. In this case, is this policy still justified? The answer is unclear in the traditional framework. Finally, the assumption that cohesion is redistribution, which may be true in a national context, does not hold in the European one. As shown by table 2.3, in reality, this policy is only partially redistributive, which contrasts with the 'letter' of the Treaty. This argument is reviewed in section 2.3.2, calling for a change in Fiscal Federalism traditional political assumptions. All countries get something and the actual level of redistribution is blurred. Even though the amount received by southern countries is high in per capita term, very populated countries like Germany, France, Italy or the UK get a big amount. Very rich northern countries also get some cohesion support for under-populated areas, a '*priviledge*' negotiated in 1995 as a compensation for their net contributor status. Moreover, when one takes the entire budget, one sees that the overall redistributive effect of the European budget is rather low, which often misleads theorists. Except Germany, and, to a lesser extent, the Netherlands, no country contributes that much. Indeed, as we deal with territories and not individuals, Cohesion spending cannot be assessed independently from the overall European budget. Cohesion is redistributive, in the sense that it gives relatively more money to poorer regions. But Cohesion is simply not redistribution in the Musgravian sense of the term. In short, European cohesion does not correspond to any of the traditional functions. It is a bit of all three.

Table 2.3: Budget and Cohesion, Who Gets What?

	Total Cohesion receipts 2000-2006 euro/hab [a]	Net contribution in % of EU budget [b]
Belgium	201	0.8
Denmark	162	-0.4
Germany	363	14.4
Greece	2342	-6.0
Spain	1419	-9.2
France	266	-0.2
Ireland	1072	-3.4
Italy	518	1.3
Luxembourg	214	0.0
Netherlands	209	3.2
Austria	224	0.2
Portugal	2305	-4.2
Finland	405	-0.1
Sweden	247	0.9
UK	282	2.8
EU 15	566	0.0

a. Cohesion receipts, amount received over the six year period, own calculations, includes Objective 1, 2, 3, Cohesion Funds and PIC.
b. Net contribution is calculated here as the total funds raised by a country for the European level over the EU budget minus the total funds given by the EU level to the budget in percentage of the European budget. A positive sign means a country gives more than it receives and conversely.

Source: author, own calculations from EC data

We also saw that European features (of low mobility and self-discrimination) did not make the centralisation of redistribution likely in a near future. Still, according to Fiscal Federalism, and making the alternative assumption that cohesion policy is a complex system of grants, the latter policy is still justified. But, once again, the three reasons traditionally advanced to justify grants: spillovers, fiscal equalisation, improvement of the fiscal system, are not very relevant in the European case. A political economy explanation is far more powerful. Cohesion in traditional States (where links between nationhood, cohesion and redistribution are straightforward) simply does not mean the same as cohesion in the European Union context. Ignoring it would once again lead to a misunderstanding of the European integration process.

A related issue deals with the form and extent of these grants. Fiscal federalists most often take these factors as exogenous coming from political choices, thus failing in explaining them. However, accounting for political factors behind these choices is a *sine qua non* to understand why a given fiscal setting exists and how it really works. Said conversely, disregarding these political factors just forbids to understand a given fiscal setting. The comparison Chapter 4 makes between Germany and the EU shows how much these political factors matter. This is not to mention the reductive vision of intergovernmental transfers, seen mostly as financial grants, but often not directly financial in practice (*e.g.* fiscal advantages concealed to Ireland by the other European states, the greatly innovative fiscal setting of Germany). All in all, it seems that a traditional fiscal federalist perspective hardly matches the Cohesion Policy case so far. Taking into account lessons deriving from the European practice may however help to improve its applicability.

2.3.2. Lessons from the Cohesion Policy for the Fiscal Federalist Perspective: Accounting for Political Factors

There are mainly three lessons Fiscal Federalism can draw from the practical functioning of Cohesion Policy. First, Cohesion Policy shows that distribution does not need to be of the form traditionally anticipated. The shift to a new kind of grant justifications, as stated by the objectives of this policy, is also acknowledged. Second, the organisation of this policy shows that the Fiscal Federalism assumption of a neat decomposition of a given political structure is not met in the practice of the EU. It is also suggested that the study of Cohesion Policy can potentially provide important lessons in terms of experimental Federalism. Third, we emphasise political factors, which have to be taken into account to understand this policy.

Tables 2.2 and 2.3 have shown that the Cohesion Policy is redistributive in nature, as it transfers funds from rich countries to poor ones. However, distribution in the European case significantly differs from the distribution function at the core of Fiscal Federalism. Whereas the former is inter-territorial, and aims at increasing capital stocks, human capital, infrastructure and environment, the latter is interpersonal and aims mainly at increasing poorest household revenues. The difference is huge. Indeed, inter-territorial redistribution is only a second-best in the Fiscal Federalism literature. Still, the strategy chosen by the Commission makes sense. It aims at giving the long-term means to the poorest and 'restructurating' regions to self-sustain their development in the long-term. Hence, most cohesion grants spent should, in theory, improve the long-term competitiveness of the recipient regions. This rationale comes from new growth theories. It is also rather close to the Listian 'infant industry' protectionist argument. The rationale behind the Cohesion Policy is to aim at enhancing territorial capabilities. The underlying logic is that of 'equality of chances or opportunities' more than 'equality of conditions'. Additionally, it is a significant break from national redistribution policies, still aimed at short-term revenue equalisation. The same holds for health and education, which are often seen as being highly redistributive allocative forms of expenditure.

Still, applying the pro-European reasoning of section 2.2 about redistribution to national redistribution and social systems is interesting. This small change in one of the assumptions of Fiscal Federalism – namely the decomposition of functions – explains why pressures on national systems may increase. Indeed, mobility and preferences were shown to be at the centre of the need for decentralisation/centralisation of redistribution policy. It is easy to see that this logic applies to Europe. The rising pressures on national social and redistribution systems[6] (referring to reality and not to Musgravian function of allocation and redistribution) will probably have to find a European answer, either in the form of heightened harmonisation or of a bigger European budget. This need will be higher as European mobility increases. National abilities to resist these centralisation pressures are also likely to decrease with increasing mobility. Moreover, this resistance is likely to decrease as (or if) preferences converge (or end-up converging).

With time, Cohesion Policy is likely to expand so as to encompass more and more social and distributive concerns. The ESF is likely to grow progressively. Consequently, these useful comments on Cohesion Policy and social Europe show that the analysis of Fiscal Federalism should emancipate from the heroic decomposition of function to focus on policy issues, in which the interest of the FF perspective still holds.

The second lesson for the traditional fiscal federalist perspective has to do with the way Cohesion Policy is organised in practice. Cohesion Policy complies with the principles of partnership and subsidiarity, which do not correspond to the centralisation *versus* decentralisation Fiscal Federalism spectrum. Subsidiarity applied to Cohesion Policy implies complementarity of the different actors, as shown by section 2.1.2. Partnership implies cooperation at most stages of this policy. The Cohesion Policy shows that as long as one actor remains ultimately responsible for the implementation of Cohesion, cooperation

---

[6] Here we refer to reality and not to allocation and distribution Musgravian functions. It should be noted that the notion of European cohesion is ill-defined. However, transposing this notion from a National context (where social and redistribution systems are the main tools of national cohesion), it is highly probable that the concept of European cohesion will also widen in the close future to encompass Social Europe.

may help to enhance effectiveness of a policy more than full centralisation/decentralisation would. In practice actually, this responsibility is shared by the Commission, national states, but also regional levels of government. The potential superiority of such an organisation can be theoretically explained. Indeed, the main arguments for decentralisation are heightened responsibility, accountability and information (related to preferences and cost conditions). Partnership allows to reap these benefits while, if well-implemented, it becomes possible to aggregate information from all levels. Moreover, as responsibility is (asymmetrically) shared, each level is under the scrutiny of the other levels of government. Corruption and waste are thus likely to decrease thanks to partnership.

Eventually, it shows that Cohesion Policy is a perfect field for experimental Federalism. Experimentation is not total because some rules are common everywhere in Europe and decentralised governmental units do not have full control of finances (little power for regions, shared power for Member States). Still the supply-side efficiency argument partly holds. As each Member States, and sometimes each region, is free to implement Cohesion Policy as it wishes, the way plans are shaped and respected, and the way projects are selected, monitored and controlled greatly varies across European regions. Although it has not been done yet by the Commission, it would be easy from there to select the best practices for regional development. Once again, and as opposed to Fiscal Federalism theory, full decentralisation may not be necessary and partnership may well be a sufficient condition.

More generally, the design of the Cohesion Policy is not always well understood by economic theory. Indeed, some empirical studies tend to accuse wrongly (*cf.* EC, 2004; Sapir Report, 2003) the Commission for the lack of inter-regional convergence. But this argument tends to omit many control variables, such as the impact of other national and European policies on convergence. Most importantly, it is based on the implicit assertion that, as the policy is European, the Commission should be considered to be the main responsible for its alleged failure. In reality, the conception phase is highly dependent on the Council: the Member States, *i.e.* on sub-central levels of jurisdiction. The implementation stage also depends on Member States' actions. To summarise, if the efficiency of the policy depends on the quality of coordination provided by the Commission, it also largely depends on the actions of sub-central (national and regional) levels of government.

All this emphasises the fundamental difference between the kind of political structure implicitly assumed by Fiscal Federalism and the EU. The EU is both innovative, as it creates new forms of governance, and under construction. Its governance is confronted to huge practical and theoretical challenges. The current political structure has both elements of supranationalism and of inter-governmentalism. This structure is both the outcome and a determinant of the dynamic process of European integration. Politico-institutional factors, thus, matter and are crucial for the shaping of the evolutionary European fiscal setting. Although it may share common features with the political structure assumed by Fiscal Federalism – a representative federal democracy – the EU does not correspond to it. Consequently, assuming that the EU problematic of supra-centralisation corresponds to the decentralisation one is not correct (*cf.* table 1.1).

The last point, perhaps the most important one, deals with high politics. It also illustrates the previous statement. The political nature of the EU, which is far from being a Federation, explains most of the discrepancies between the Fiscal Federalist guideline and the European fiscal setting. Our point of view is that the European fiscal setting should not be adapted to the traditional guideline. In contrast, the Fiscal Federalist perspective should incorporate these political factors in their analysis, as they influence the desirability and feasibility of any reform of the current fiscal setting. If Fiscal Federalism fails to do so, it will have to abandon its universalistic (applying to all types of countries or authority-dispersed entities) ambitions.

The example of the Cohesion Policy illustrates this point perfectly. The logic of this Policy is intergovernmental at the conception stage. It is negotiated in the realm of a more comprehensive fiscal package: the Financial Perspectives, which are analysed in depth in Chapter 6. In practice this policy is used as a log-rolling tool. This political behaviour is not really acknowledged in the Fiscal Federalism literature. The only exception is Spahn (1993), who explains that grants for a given policy issue can be used as a way to bribe lower levels of government initially reluctant to accept a precise measure about another policy issue. The justification comes from the fact that this allows to overcome under-standable resistance from losing players in zero-sum games. The loss may not occur at the end: players only need to think they will lose something or manage to make other players believe that they will. As suggested by Allen (2000) or Vaneecloo (2005), this is exactly the way Cohesion Policy works. It is used by MS and the Commission to reach agreement on other policy issues. Examples are numerous. For instance, the creation of the Cohesion Funds, in 1993, dramatically raised the amounts received by southern countries. This was done to overcome their resistance (especially Spain) to the Maastricht Treaty. The same strategy was conduced in 1988, as the increase of Structural Funds can mainly be explained by the desire to overcome the fears, or perceived threat, from southern countries about the single market. The invention of the under-populated area criterion also corresponds to the entry of very rich and potentially non-eligible countries (Sweden, Finland and Austria), which initially feared to be contributing too much to the European budget (table 2.3 shows it is not the case). Such an 'instrumentalisation' of this policy is not officially admitted (*cf.* table 2.2) and nothing tells us that it will carry on in the near future. However, in the last 25 years, it seems clear that the overall budgetary design of the Cohesion Policy has recurrently helped in reaching agreements on other important issues. This allows to ease the entire integration process or to make it faster. Assuming integration is a welfare-enhancing process in economic terms, the 'cohesion grants' thus help to achieve faster and deeper integration, which makes all countries better-off. The flaw of the traditional perspective, which does not take this intergovernmental behaviour into account, is obvious here. The European fiscal setting depends on the overall budget, *i.e.* the budget MS are willing to transfer to the European level. As the European budget is negotiated in package, as the Cohesion Policy is an important part of this package, and as it is in practice instrumentalised to reach broader agreements, any reform proposal about the European fiscal setting, which would not take this political log-rolling behaviour into account, would be doomed to fail. Chapter 6 goes back to this issue of interdependence between Cohesion Policy, the budget and the political process of decision-making.

2.4. Conclusion: Politics, Solidarity, Regional Development and the EU

To conclude, this chapter clearly showed the interactions between Fiscal Federalism and a major element of the European fiscal setting: the Cohesion Policy.

Lessons from theory are numerous. The relevance of using debates over the distribution function in the European context was discussed. It was showed that, as long as one stays cautious with regards to the way the Fiscal Federalism perspective is used, it is possible to reach interesting conclusions about the likely future of distributive and social Europe. This argument tends to suggest that, for reasons of system efficiency and equity, the EU should/is likely to/will take more responsibilities in social matters and redistribution in the future.

However, it was argued also, that the traditional perspective is a suit which does not fit Cohesion Policy very well. Or to put it more accurately, Cohesion Policy seems 'ill-at-ease' in this theoretical framework, *i.e.* in this 'perspective'. The last section consequently reversed our first point of view to address the question of the lessons from Cohesion Policy for the theoretical paradigm. A thorough study of this policy led to the following conclusions. Distribution in a fiscal setting can be inter-jurisdictional and still represents a first-best. Moreover, it was claimed, the EU is very innovative. The application of the partnership and subsidiarity (a mix of centralisation and decentralisation) principles can potentially lead to higher welfare gains than either of both alternatives. The traditional perspective of Fiscal Federalism could incorporate this singular setting as a way to achieve higher public sector effectiveness. Last but not least, Cohesion Policy also exemplifies the fact that political factors are to be taken into account if one wants to assess the effectiveness of any policy and the results or impact of any fiscal setting. For instance, the argument which tends to contest the role of the Commission in this policy, and the policy itself, is based on a deep misunderstanding of the reality of this policy. Indeed, both at the conception and implementation stages, Member States and their regions assume most decisions. They are as much responsible for the failure or success of this European Policy as the Commission is.

The last point, perhaps the most important, deals with high politics. The political nature of the EU – which *is not* a mature Federation, but a *sui generis political entity* – explains most of the discrepancies between the Fiscal Federalism guideline and the European Fiscal setting. Should the latter be blindly adapted to normative Fiscal Federalism? Probably not. In contrast, Fiscal Federalism should take the political nature of the EU into account, hence admitting that traditional assumptions do not hold in the European case and that its traditional political assumptions only correspond to mature Federations. The Fiscal Federalism theo-retical perspective should relinquish its universalistic ambitions (*i.e.* applying to all types of countries or authority-dispersed polities) to undertake more systematic positive analysis. Answering the question of what the EU really is should be seen as a pre-requisite for asserting what it should be.

CHAPTER 3

Fiscal Federalism
and the Stability and Growth Pact

Augusta BADRIOTTI

This chapter analyses the relevance of the fiscal federalist perspective for the European Union through a precise policy issue: fiscal policy and macroeconomic management in the European Union. This corresponds to the stabilisation tools of the European fiscal setting. The mechanism adopted in the European Union with the Stability and Growth Pact (SGP) has been effective during its first years of application, but has encountered enormous problems when its Member States (MS) started being confronted with economic difficulties. Fiscal Federalism theory can help us in defining a better environment, where fiscal relations are well defined and foster national growth. This chapter describes the current fiscal setting aimed at stabilising the Economic and Monetary Union (EMU), the SGP, and describes how national states have solved the crucial problem of economic stability within their borders. It also shows how the EU could improve this contested and limited stabilisation scheme. Finally, it defends the view that the traditional model of Fiscal Federalism is not applicable as it stands but needs some corrections to take into consideration political, national, cultural and historical characteristics of Member States.

Therefore, in analysing the particular European fiscal setting, focusing on the stabilisation function, Fiscal Federalism will be the driving force in evaluating the results found. Section 3.1 highlights what the theory of Fiscal Federalism says about stabilisation and what it means for the European Union (dimension 4 of our problematic). Section 3.2 will draw some lessons from the reality of national fiscal settings (dimension 1), and section 3.3 will put together the two previous lessons and try to build a new framework for the European Union. Section 3.4 concludes on Fiscal Federalism, stabilisation and the European Union (dimension 2).

3.1. Macroeconomic Stabilisation in the EU

3.1.1. Fiscal Federalism and Fiscal Policy in the EU

Fiscal Federalism traditionally focuses on the assignment of fiscal powers (namely taxing power) between a national or central government and lower tiers of government present in a country. Already from this rather limited definition of Fiscal Federalism, we see that this does not apply perfectly to fiscal relations in the European Union. In fact, the singularity of the European Union – with at least three different levels, sub-national,[1] national and supranational or central (EU) – comes from the existence of an intermediate level, which still retains most of the sovereignty (except for monetary policy) and from the fact that a consistent design of multilevel governance still needs to be found.

In the context of fiscal policy at EU level, national governments are left sovereign. The agreement on the Stability and Growth Pact (SGP) exemplifies the result of the actual economic governance in the Union. However, the SGP has several limitations. Mainly, it does not take into account national and very often peculiar institutional configurations of each Member State (MS). Precisely, it does not consider the decentralisation process that is present in most countries and that is changing and complicating the traditional fiscal relations among the new sub-national governments. Hence, the compliance with the Pact does not involve inferior levels of government, and issues relating to the accountability in terms of breaching of the rules established by the SGP may arise. The following chapter points out that this instrument (SGP) is not successful (from a Fiscal Federalism point of view) to reach stabilisation in the EU, because MS retain the ability to undertake national stabilisation policies, and because there is no binding guarantees that this agreement will be observed (for enforcement and accountability issues). The theory suggests that a new institutional set-up could be more suitable either through the creation of an independent body that controls European fiscal policy or through a wider EU federal budget where a system of grants and precise financial assignments allow every level of government to accomplish its tasks.

Fiscal Federalism can help us in describing and understanding this decentralisation wave and explaining why stabilisation should be centralised. We are going to show that the traditional Fiscal Federalism perspective concludes that the central level is the only one with the power to efficiently manage the stabilisation function (see Chapter 1 for a discussion of the traditional definition of Musgravian functions).

---

[1] Most European countries have more than two sub-national levels (*cf.* Chapter 5).

Hence, fiscal policy should be transferred at EU level. The next section describes the supranational (or central) level policy framework, the SGP, as it stands today.

3.1.2. European Fiscal Rules: the Stability and Growth Pact [2]

The Economic and Monetary Union (EMU) relies on fiscal rules designed to ensure that national policies maintain a stable fiscal position allowing margins for budgetary flexibility in case of bad economic conjuncture. Hence, fiscal stability is the precondition for financial and monetary stability and budget flexibility is needed to achieve stabilisation policy. The SGP was introduced with the prime goal to guarantee the stability of the unique currency and to support the economy-enhancing coordination of fiscal policies among the different Member States. The European Council of Dublin in December 1996 decided to propose a new version of the Maastricht Treaty to deal with the new context of the EMU.[3] The new Treaty signed in Amsterdam in 1997 strengthened the previous fiscal rules aiming at establishing fiscal discipline as the main topic for promoting the European economy. The SGP derives from two European Regulations (CE) No.1466/97 and (CE) No.1467/97 and from a resolution of the European Council of the 17th of June 1997. According to the SGP, Member States agreed on following a balanced budget in the medium term and to adopt corrective measures to attain the goals enunciated in the stability programme.

The SGP establishes that budget deficits cannot be larger than 3 per cent of GDP unless under exceptional circumstances (severe depressions), and that the deficit has to remain close to 3 per cent. Deficit can last only for a limited period of time. If these requirements are not met, the deficit is considered excessive and it opens the way to a procedure to force the adoption of corrective measures. The Stability and Growth Pact gives a detailed reference to what exceptional and limited period means. A recession is considered exceptional when real GDP decreases by 2 per cent with respect to the previous year. In case a recession happens unexpectedly, the value of reference of the GDP variation is 0.75. The Pact gives no specification of the concept 'closeness to 3 per cent': this shortcoming has led to a vivid discussion about the SGP recently (see section 3.3.3).

---

[2]   In this section the SGP is described in its original formulation. It does not take into consideration recent reforms. This, because to fully understand and evaluate how the discussion emerged, it is necessary to see all the aspects of the Pact, not only its recent changes. March 2005 reform will be discussed in section 3.3.3.

[3]   Already the Maastricht Treaty, Art. 104C and the attached Protocol on "Procedures over excessive debts" introduced for the first time the 'famous' parameters for debt and deficit ceiling but only in 1997 a formal protocol was added.

The SGP requires that each MS fixes a budgetary target in cyclically adjusted terms and let automatic stabilisers operate symmetrically. The lower this budget balance with respect to the 3 per cent threshold, the wider the margins for counter-cyclical policy without having the risk of an excessive debt. The choice of the medium-term target for the neutral phase of the cycle is dictated by three factors: the depth of expected recessions, the elasticity of the budget with respect to the cycle and the size of the discretionary measures that may be taken to enhance the impact of built-in stabilisers. Countries with debt ratios above 60 per cent of the GDP should also diminish it towards the threshold at a satisfactory speed. If the ratio increases, the excessive deficit procedure begins and states are supposed to pay a fine.

Each Member State of the EU must submit on a yearly basis its budgetary targets in multi-year documents of stability and convergence programmes. These documents are analysed by the European Commission that assesses their consistency with the EMU fiscal rules while the European Council, subsequently, makes recommendations to governments on the need to adopt corrective measures. The failure to respond to such early warnings brings sanctions. More accurately, it is supposed to lead to sanctions, as no EMU Member State has been fined yet. The country must pay a non interest-bearing deposit equal to 0.2 per cent of GDP plus one tenth of the difference between the 3 per cent ceiling and the actual deficit, up to a maximum of 0.5. In case the deficit continues in successive years, only the variable component of the sanction has to be paid. Whenever the deficit persists, the deposit is converted into a fine after two years. This has never happened in reality although some countries like Portugal, Germany, Italy and France breached the 3 per cent threshold for more than two years.

The Treaty envisages a multilateral surveillance with a procedure of early warnings sent by the Council to the Member State that faces difficulties in respecting the threshold and using the measures necessary to correct the budget deficit. This mutual surveillance requires that each year, member countries propose a multiyear programme of stability or a programme of convergence. It is the Council that evaluates these programmes to prevent excessive deficits taking place and to promote surveillance and coordination of the economic policy in the EU. Hence, the Council has to judge if the SGP proposed by countries helps in enhancing fiscal cooperation among states and if the economic policies of one member are coherent with the overall macroeconomic policy determined by the EU.

The approach taken by the EMU with regards to macroeconomic stabilisation, is summarised as follows:

- rules are defined on the basis of pre-determined numerical parameters,
- ex-post compliance with parameters is required each year,
- margins of flexibility are envisaged only in correction with
  exceptional cyclical events or events beyond governments'
  control,
- no special decision is made for investment expenditure,
- monitoring procedures are envisaged: yearly submission of targets, assessment of the results and peer pressure by the European
  Council,
- institution of the independent European Central Bank.

3.1.3. Why Fiscal Rules in the EMU?

It is important to understand the economic rationale behind the
current stabilisation setting: *i.e.* why fiscal rules have been chosen to
guarantee macroeconomic stability and what macroeconomic theories
and Fiscal Federalism tell us about it.

The introduction of fiscal rules arose from the need to guarantee the
stability of the common currency namely price stability, in order to put
some ties to the fiscal policy of the single Member States. Generally,
economic theory recognises that in international economics, cooperation
of fiscal policies could influence prices and real interests in a positive
manner (Rogoff, 1985).[4] More problematic is the application of fiscal
rules to a monetary union (Brunetta and Tria, 2003), mainly when the
latter is not an optimal currency area. For a good survey on fiscal rules
and the EU see among others Eichengreen (1997), Ackrill (1998) and
De Grauwe (2003).

In brief, the necessity to impose some fiscal restrictions on the possibility of single states to accrue debt derives from the hypothesis that an
imprudent fiscal behaviour of one member can bring negative externalities to the other members. The possibility for this to occur depends on
the behaviour of the central bank authority and national fiscal authorities, and gives rise to free-riding problems. This will only happen in the
case that the EMU participants can guarantee financial support against
problems of a state's debt insolvency or in the case of the central bank
bailing out.[5] Moreover, there exists no explicit guarantee that states will
help insolvent members, but nothing excludes this option should the
opportunity arise. Another argument is the impact of the debt on prices

---

[4]   The analysis on this topic is beyond the scope of this chapter.

[5]   The Treaty does not allow for this second possibility, prohibiting every kind of financial support to states from the European Central Bank (ECB neutrality).

through demand expansion effects. This leads to an increase in the real interest rate in all countries, but not all economists agree with this possibility.[6]

The main valid reasons why macroeconomic theories support the introduction of rules are that they are the most suitable instrument to assure the sustainability of the debt in the long run (without touching existing institutional settings, making this option, hence, fast and cost-less). Brunetta and Tria (2003) show that this decision depends on four parameters:[7]

- current debt stock over GDP,
- primer expected surplus in percentage of GDP,
- real long run interest rate,
- real long run growth rate.

The SGP considers only a particular version of the first one: gross debt over GDP, even if corrected over the cycle. The rule implying a deficit equal or inferior to zero means that, in the long run, the debt/GDP ratio will decline, at a pace dictated by the nominal GDP growth rate. The 3 per cent threshold for the current deficit has no impli-cation for the insolvency issue but aims to limit the discretion of national fiscal policy in the short run.

Now, no macroeconomic theory backs a zero debt argument. On the contrary, a small public debt serves to bypass the liquidity constraint households face. It can also lead to a bigger intergenerational equity, allowing present generations to enjoy higher welfare under the (implicit) hypothesis that future generations will be richer than the present one. Public debt allows an inter-temporal and intergenerational redistribution in that, capital goods benefits are usually spread over time and between generations. There are several proposals to face this limitation of the SGP, among which the introduction of a golden rule on public investment, to be discussed later on (Perotti, 2003).

A second point concerns the fact that fiscal rules, such as the SGP, interfere with national fiscal policies, directed to stabilise the cycle. Indeed, national authorities have two ways to react to recession: let automatic stabilisers work and create a cyclical deficit, or correct the deficit with a discretionary measure, hence applying a discretionary fiscal policy. The problem arises while asking if the rule of 3 per cent is sufficient to let discretionary fiscal policy work in case of necessity.

---

[6] To develop this subject further, consider the monetarists' criticism to fiscal policy and neoclassic economics.

[7] These parameters will be useful in evaluating in the followings the recent reform of the SGP.

That is also the sole instrument national countries have to influence the cycle, once losing monetary policy control. If the threshold of 3 per cent is not sufficient to let automatic stabilisers work, the flexibility of the SGP is likewise insufficient, and will lead to pro-cyclical policy in order for Member States to respect the threshold during recession. Even empirical analysis has problems in identifying whether the SGP has been an obstacle to counter-cyclical fiscal policy (Galì and Perotti, 2003 and Wyplosz, 2002).

In fact (macro)economic theories are both against and in favour of the effectiveness of counter-cyclical fiscal policy. Some empirical studies (Giavazzi, Jappelli and Pagano, 2000) confirm that extensive fiscal policies produce Keynesian effects on the economy: an expansion of the aggregate demand in case of a reduction of taxes or of an increase of spending and a reduction of the demand in case of restrictive fiscal activity. Other studies (Sutherland, 1995) show, on the contrary, that non-Keynesian effects arise, *i.e.* a restrictive fiscal policy could have an expansive effect. This is generally true in economies with a high and increasing structural deficit and witnessing bad reputation of budget authorities.

More generally, a counter-cyclical fiscal policy is usually not as efficient in regularising the cycle because the institutional framework in which these policies are implemented implies delays in this policy implementation, which prevents good timing (fine tuning) and causes useless if not harmful economic reactions.

Therefore, we can conclude that economic theory is not unique in evaluating stabilisation, but usually considers the SGP as a unsuitable instrument to guarantee stabilisation, mainly because the targets are ill-chosen and partial.

On the other hand, Fiscal Federalism (Oates, 1977) generally claims that stabilisation should be centralised: this derives from the Musgravian decomposition of state functions already mentioned. A first argument supporting this theory is that it is the central government that usually has the control of the monetary policy and of the money supply. When sub-national regions are small and economically open, they would, therefore, tend to have a very high marginal propensity to import instability. Any attempt at an active fiscal policy from one part would, thus, be rendered ineffective. This applies less well to the EU, but it is true that, mainly since the creation of the Common Market, all EU countries are completely open to the others. Also debt-financed expenditures by sub-national authorities would result in 'external debt', whereby the particular region in question would have repayment obligations to people in other regions within the single currency area, resulting in net real income outflows. When debt-financed expenditures occur at the central level, most debt-holders are located within the borders of the currency area, thus avoiding this problem. Finally, Oates argues that because of the degree of economic openness and closeness of regions within a single currency area, the regional economies will tend to move together, with any shock in one region rapidly transmitting itself to the other regions, for example *via* changes in inter-regional trade within the currency area.

To sum up, Fiscal Federalism suggests that tasks with large spillover effects across localities or large economies of scale should be centralised, while decentralisation prevails when heterogeneity of preferences and information issues are relevant.[8] Bini-Smaghi and Tabellini (2003) noticed that when governments are not assumed to be benevolent and are not focused exclusively on the conflict of interest among jurisdictions, but instead have political concerns or face other incentive constraints, the traditional theory fails.

In this paragraph it clearly transpires that actual fiscal framework in the EU does not correspond to what theories (either macroeconomics theories or Fiscal Federalism theory) establish, being rather like a kind of 'miscellaneous' entity from different theories. If from one perspective, this miscellaneous entity tries to avoid the internal 'mistakes' of each theories, from another perspective, such a framework could cause severe crisis and vivid discussion like the one which took place in 2004. It is therefore necessary to reform the SGP deeply and to establish a clear-cut macroeconomic governance in the EU.

3.1.4. *European Economic Policy:*
between Coordination and Federalism

Going back to the set up of the EU, we see that economic policies try to coordinate fiscal and monetary measures with the aim to control inflation, to reduce unemployment avoiding budgetary deficits and to stabilise the economy over a growing path.[9] But this economic gov-

---

[8] Some recent works on the EU and economic openness could undermine the application of Fiscal Federalism to the EU, because not all MS have reached so far the same level of openness among them within the EU. To gain advantages from a monetary union and from extension to a federal structure of the EU, the integrated area should form an optimal currency area, but this is not the case for the all 25 EU Member States (De Grauwe, 2003).

[9] This is what is specified under the Lisbon strategy but actual framework seems more focused to stabilise prices rather than foster growth. Generally, the economic goals of the EU are defined in this document. This is also the foundation of the socio-economic model of the EU. This strategy is although not taken into consideration by the ECB where price stability predominates every other concerns, hence dissatisfying Lisbon where all goals should have equal weight.

ernance set-up is atypical in that on the one side, monetary policy is centralised (as Fiscal Federalism theory says) and on the other, fiscal policy remains a prerogative of the Member States (contradicting Fiscal Federalism). Monetary policy is focused on the maintenance of price stability, the latter on balanced budgets.

In order to achieve these two targets, it would be necessary to create a policy mix of the two policies, hence, to associate to the centrally controlled monetary policy a centralised stabilisation or the administration of a real federal budget. However, Europe is still far from this stage. Generally speaking, the Maastricht Treaty gives too much importance to the constraint coordination (*i.e.* fiscal rules) and not enough emphasis to the federal set-up to support the economy. The Lisbon strategy gives guidelines for the policies for the first ten years of the 21st century: it envisages an economic growth based on knowledge, innovation and a society based on cohesion, and where the socio-economic development is taken more into consideration than ever before. However, no references are done to the construction of a more significant European budget or to the means to achieve it.

The euro and the growing interdependence of all European economies led to the coordination of the fiscal policies through the means of the SGP where balanced budget is the target and where only the automatic stabilisers can work. Hence, the Economic and Monetary Union is a hybrid fiscal setting combining together supranational and intergovernmental elements. It is the result of communitarian policies, as well as a central monetary policy and a series of policies still under the liability of MS.

The EMU manages these questions using a simple method: coordination. MS consider economic policies as a common business and coordinate themselves through the Council of ministers of the EU. These policies are different but should be consistent. In a central state, relations between economic policies are ruled by the national level, in federal or confederal states, the issue is rather complicated by the degree of liability attributed to sub-central levels of government for economic purposes. In such a context, the definition of fiscal powers, competencies among central state and lower tiers defines a given form of Fiscal Federalism. In the European case, the move towards the economic and monetary union makes economic national arrangements more complex than ever and should ask for a better defined assignment of functions.

We dare ask whether the choice of the EU is an appropriate one, whether coordination of the stabilisation is delivering the expected results. Our conclusion is that it is not, or at least not in the present framework. The answer to this question leads to supporting the need for a more federal structure in the economic governance of the EU, possibly through the adoption of a real European budget under a federal form and the establishment of a fiscal institution able to manage the fiscal policy needed by the EMU to sustain price stability, economic growth, welfare and employment as the theory of Fiscal Federalism suggests.[10]

One extra reason to support the idea that the actual setting is not good, is that in a monetary union, national economies are more interdependent and the presence of European public goods (see environment and transport networks, for instance) calls for the necessity to arrange economic policy in the euro zone. Economic interdependence comes from the augmented degree of commercial and financial trade, from the spillover effects of macroeconomic policies of neighbouring countries, and from the need to react together to international external shocks like oil shocks, wars or terrorist menaces.

The European construction intensifies these interactions and calls for good economic articulation of economic policies. The solution found, as in coordination, from a theoretical point of view, studies cooperation among different actors with different interests to pursue. Coordination is the result of the interaction of players when unilateral decisions will bring sub-optimality for the actors themselves. It is the study of the strategic behaviour of economic agents acting interactively.[11] Cooperation comes out while agents decide to find an agreement to reach the optimal solution: every other solution will lead to weaker results in terms of efficiency. Nevertheless, coordination is fragile, every player has to play honestly and the temptation to cheat is always strong. Two dangerous behaviours must be avoided in coordination agreements: i) free-riding, when one tries to make profit from the coordination effort without being himself completely engaged and ii) moral hazard, when an agent decides not to reveal all the information needed for the coordination and gains from this asymmetry in information. Often moral pressure from the partners is not enough to guarantee the good work of the coordination and some rules and procedures must be used to warranty a mutual multilateral surveillance. This choice between rules and discretion leads to different kinds of coordination. Coordination leads to reaching the optimum when there is such a mechanism that permits to reveal the true preferences of all players.

---

[10] This reasoning should be taken with caution. It does not mean that the EU should adopt a precise model of Federalism, but that it could itself become a new model of federation. In fact, as we will see in Chapter 5, Fiscal Federalism strictly speaking is rarely applied but beyond certain institutional similarities, every state has found its own way to organise fiscal interactions among its tiers of government.

[11] Game theory is the formal discipline that studies the interaction of economic agents and their strategic behaviours.

In the case of the EMU, the coordination is of intergovernmental form, both horizontal and vertical. In particular, the vertical form applies to the subsidiarity principle, principle establishing that a competence that is not efficiently implemented to one governmental level should be transferred to a lower one.

Macroeconomic coordination in Europe needs a policy mix of monetary and fiscal policies in order to sustain growth, employment and control inflation. The ECB, an independent European body, works by itself while fiscal policy is in the hands of the MS. This particular situation gives rise to new challenges: how to coordinate effectively national fiscal policies without centralising them? The EMU tried to respond by creating a European coordination model made up of different methods and involving different fields. Three coordination methods are now present in the EU. The first one is 'indicative', in which the EU gives guidelines to MS to satisfy certain common goals. It is a weak *ex-ante* coordination method that finds application within the Broad Guideline of Economic Policies, on the Guideline for Employment and the coordination between capital markets and goods markets. A second type is 'coercive' and takes the form of imposition of rules. The most famous is the SGP and some other rules of prévention such as the "no bailing out" rule (European Community Treaty Art. 103) among states and the prohibition to finance, through the creation of money, the deficit of a state (European Community Treaty Art. 101). The third type of coordination involves 'dialogues' and emerged as a response to the democratic deficit that the EU suffers. The most important form of dialogue is the institution of the Eurogroup, an informal round table discussing subjects concerning the single currency. Established by the European Council of Luxemburg in 1997, it deals with the meeting of the Ecofin Ministers of the euro area to discuss subjects of common concern for the euro. It is an informal body that has no decision-making power. The other one is the so-called Cologne process, where a macroeconomic dialogue on monetary, fiscal policies, economic growth and employment is held twice a year. Mainly these two last forms of dialogue testify to the inadequateness and limitations of the actual coordination taking place in the EU that can nevertheless be considered as the starting point to present a new European Fiscal Federalism model.

Another problematic aspect concerns the consistency of budgetary procedures and institutions at national level with the constraint imposed by the new EU framework.

National fiscal policies have to insure a certain level of coordination and achievement of certain 'broad economic guidelines'. A tighter coordination in fiscal policy could achieve more effective discretional aggregate demand management in reaction to wide aggregate shocks.

Active and discretionary fiscal policies for stabilisation are often pro-cyclical because fiscal policies operate at lags and it is very difficult to choose the appropriate fiscal measure over the business cycle. Further-more, Persson and Tabellini (2003) strengthen the dependence of MS governments in the so called 'electoral policy cycle' according to which national policies could be strongly influenced by political decisions taken to please the median voter in order to be re-elected. This possibility could lead to a conflict between EU agreements and MS political agenda, further weakening the credibility of the Pact.[12]

The voting of the 25th of November 2003, in which the Council under majority voting decided to suspend the sanction procedure for France and Germany, adds further credibility issues to the architecture of the SGP. In fact, in that context, the Pact showed not to be binding, at least not for all MS. Germany, mainly, has always been seen as one of the strongest (economically and hence politically) MS. The problems it is facing now made other MS reflect on the possibility to find them-selves in the same situation and consequently they preferred to vote against the sanction procedure. This is very dangerous because it under-mines the credibility of the SGP from its basis (rules commonly established should be respected by all MS and there should be no voting possibility to suspend them). If an agreement is not enforced, it is not binding, if it is not binding, there is no coordination anymore. To be really binding, an agreement (the SGP) needs a precisely defined system, which allows for flexibility in extreme cases but not every time MS want to change something.

Stabilisation in the EU is already centralised, in the sense that mone-tary policy is centralised, and to develop a harmonic environment, fiscal policies are supposed to be coordinated. For Fiscal Federalism, centrali-sation through coordination is, theoretically, equivalent to centralisation through a common budget. However, this is not equivalent in practice because of the enforcement/sovereignty issue of MS.

In this section we have seen how macroeconomic stabilisation works in the EU, what the economic theory and Fiscal Federalism say about stabilisation: an ill-defined framework emerges. Fiscal Federalism calls for centralisation and enforceability while the EU is neither a central (in the traditional sense) nor a sovereign state. The analyses of stabilisation under dimension 4 of our problematic shows that SGP is a failure. We have seen that macroeconomic theories criticise the target chosen terming them as ill-defined. Fiscal Federalism theory predicts a com-

---

[12] Some agrees that recent reform of the Pact could be the result of such a process as many 'big' EU countries (facing deep budgetary problems) have renovated their government: Germany on September 2005 and Italy in April 2006.

plete centralisation of stabilisation, but in the EU, only monetary policy is centralised while fiscal policy remains national although constrained. This constraint is not credible, enforceability is not possible because MS maintain their sovereignty in fiscal matters. And also, EU coordination mechanisms (being the SGP, only one mechanism together with the Eurogroup and the Broad Economic Guidelines) suffer from the lack of a well defined system. The EU being a peculiar political structure (more than a 'union', less than a mature federal state), Fiscal Federalism theory *telle quelle* cannot be applied. The European policymakers are well aware of this and are trying to develop a new model of European Federalism based on tighter cooperation but the difficulties are still enormous.

Leaving aside for a while Fiscal Federalism, we now try to see which lessons a broader approach taking into consideration national fiscal settings can deliver for the improvement of the EU setting and of the Fiscal Federalism perspective.

The question of whether it is possible to improve the present fiscal policy framework naturally arises. Next section tries to answer taking certain national experiences as a guiding reference (dimension 1).

3.2. How Can National Frameworks Bring Insight for Stabilisation Policy?

3.2.1. Decentralisation of Decision Making and Fiscal Discipline

Stabilisation policy is an old issue: the problem of fiscal coordination between different levels of government has become critical in the EU, but deals from the very start with single MS. In this section the scale of study shifts from a supranational point of view to a national one, taking into consideration the experiences of national countries on stabilisation issues.

In each member country, regardless of the degree of fiscal decentralisation, the national government has sole responsibility for formulating the SGP. In many countries, sub-national governments enjoy enough fiscal autonomy to determine as a consequence of their actions whether EU rules are respected or not, but they are usually not accountable for the final outcome. There is, evidently, a potential free-rider problem. Since then, in many cases, there is a need to develop some domestic stability pacts, a legal or procedural framework for ensuring that the fiscal behaviour of local entities is consistent with the EU commitments.

The common pool problem is clearly exacerbated by a larger vertical fiscal gap: sub-national governments have every incentive to overspend when a large share of financing is raised by the national government. A solution could be to reduce the gap giving to local entities enough local tax revenues to finance their expenditure. However, this would not solve the free-rider problem because sub-national authorities may rationally decide not to raise the revenue required since they have the option of being bailed out by the central government. A way of reducing the spending and deficit bias arising from the coordination problem in the budget process is to either delegate authority or a commitment from the whole government to a set of spending limits on expenditure allocations negotiated at the beginning of the budgeting process. Making local authorities responsible for both taxing and spending decisions reduces any vertical fiscal gap as much as possible.

Once that the common pool problem is solved, fiscal discipline cannot be taken for granted. Even in presence of local financial autonomy, a local entity will still be able to gain access to the common pool of national tax resources when the budget constraint is soft: in an environment where the central government would eventually provide some financial assistance, this means setting a system of controls and incentives to harden the budget constraint for lower tier governments. The literature on budget procedures shows that a fragmented process is likely to be conducive to higher levels of expenditures and deficit. Hence, fiscal decentralisation makes budgeting in the public sector a more fragmented process. Thus, less fiscal discipline is to be expected, and fiscal rules are needed (Pisauro, 2001). We can easily extend the same reasoning to the EU level.

Several factors make the securing of fiscal discipline difficult in a decentralised setting. Sub-national governments do not take into account all effects at the national level in their decision-making. Strategic behaviours could also develop (free-riding). Often the central government has provided discretionary financial support to local tiers running into financial difficulties or has bailed them out. Expectations of a rescue from the central government create a moral hazard problem and make it likely that sub-national governments implement fiscal polices that are unsustainable. Overlapping responsibilities and the lack of a clear match between decision-making and financial responsibilities could weaken accountability and create an upward bias in the public spending. Central authorities, on the contrary, could raise minimum standards or transfer spending responsibilities without taking full account of mandates that could raise taxes or run deficit.

To avoid the risks of a loose fiscal policy, there exists a wide array of instruments, roughly divisible into three categories:

– central government exercises tight control on sub-national authorities by imposing strict administrative controls;

- central government maintains extensive fiscal autonomy at sub-national level relying on market forces to secure fiscal discipline;
- fiscal coordination either through fiscal rules imposed by the centre or by creating cooperative institutions.

In the cooperative approach, fiscal objectives are established through a negotiation process involving central and sub-national authorities. This approach is found in most federal countries as well as in unitary states like Denmark. All this reasoning can be applied to the EU considering the latter as the central level of government and where the EU and its MS negotiate fiscal objectives from time to time without a fixed scheme such as the current SGP.

3.2.2. Strategies and Mechanisms to Ensure Fiscal Discipline

The need for fiscal consolidation has become more and more pressing, especially under the present economic downturn. Countries have relied on a wide range of strategies. Sometimes fiscal rules have been imposed on sub-national governments, or fiscal co-ordination has been reinforced through cooperative arrangements. Other times financial and administrative sanctions have been also introduced. Other countries have relied on market mechanisms to secure fiscal discipline.

The literature on budgeting institutions identifies two broad solutions: delegation of authorities (hierarchical approach) and the commitment to a set of fiscal rules. It also suggests three main strategies to ensure macroeconomic management in a decentralised setting: fiscal rules, macroeconomic consistency and market discipline.

A variety of fiscal rules for sub-national governments exists. Fiscal rules targeting the overall budget deficit are present in Austria, in Belgium, in Finland, in Sweden and in Spain. The operating deficit target is present in France. A deficit target is simple and easily understood by the wider public but could fail to prevent debt accumulation due to off-budget items. In some other countries (Hungary, Poland and Portugal) they take the form of a ceiling on sub-national debt establishing limits on debt services, debt-to-revenues ratio or debt-to-GDP ratio. These targets are better suited to address long term sustainability and intergenerational equity.

Nevertheless, a debt ceiling can be circumvented: through sales of assets, outsourcing of debt to local public enterprises outside the government sector or by selling and leasing back fixed capital. In practice, multiple fiscal regulations are usually applied to sub national governments, with fiscal rules combined with restrictions on taxing rights or borrowing constraints.

Optimal fiscal rules should meet several criteria. Fiscal rules should be adequate relative to the final goal: if fiscal consolidation is the goal, overall debt should be the target or at least an indicator strongly correlated with debt accumulation. They should be consistent with other policy objectives. Fiscal target should be well-defined and the framework should be transparent. In particular, the division of responsibilities across governments should be clearly stated and the availability and quality of data should be assured. Increased transparency helps to make the rules less easy to circumvent. Rules should be simple to understand gathering stronger popular support. Fiscal rules should be flexible and able to handle unexpected events or cyclical downturns.

Some degree of flexibility is present in the fiscal framework in most countries. Some EU Member States have also introduced more ambitious fiscal targets than the 3 per cent deficit ceiling and close to balance budget over the cycle included in the SGP. This pressure comes from the need to face problems such as ageing populations.

A number of enforcement mechanisms are in place across countries to strengthen sub-national incentives to comply with fiscal regulations. Sanctions have also been introduced to enhance the credibility of fiscal rules decided at the sub-national level. In Austria and the Slovak Republic, sub-national tiers failing to reach the fiscal targets could be fined, while in Italy and Spain, a region causing the country to breach the SGP rules would have to pay the associated penalty. In Denmark, grants to the counties were cut in 2003 in response to a violation of the agreed tax freeze. Similarly in Portugal, state transfers are to be reduced if spending ceilings are exceeded or if financial information is not provided in time. A number of countries have introduced different types of administrative sanctions or procedures. In Belgium, central authorities may limit sub-national borrowing. Other countries have introduced auditing or co-operative bodies to deal with sub-national authorities that fail to comply with fiscal targets. In Finland and Spain, defaulting authorities are obliged to present a plan for correcting any fiscal deficit, while Italy and France have introduced cooperative bodies to deal with sub-national governments, which fail to comply with the regulations.

Efforts to coordinate fiscal policy across government levels have encountered fairly widespread problems: in Sweden and Finland, only approximately two thirds and three quarters of the municipalities, respectively, achieved balance in 2001. Fiscal rules have in some cases been circumvented by creative accounting techniques like in Italy, where paying a kind of arrears to suppliers has partly circumvented local deficit targets. Furthermore, despite the flexibility embodied within existing fiscal frameworks, coping with cyclical developments has not always been satisfactory.

Market discipline could play a more prominent role in enhancing fiscal discipline. In Canada and the United States, for example, credit ratings in bond markets seem to act as a disciplining factor at all levels of government (Poterba and Ruben, 1999). For financial markets to exert effective discipline on sub-national government borrowing, several conditions need to be satisfied:

- sub-national authorities should not have privileged access to borrowing in any form. One implication of this is that public loans should be obtained in the private market;
- adequate information on the borrower's existing liabilities and repayment capacity had to be readily available, so that potential lenders can correctly discriminate between borrowers;
- no bailout of sub-national authorities facing problems has to be anticipated;
- the borrower has to respond to market signals.

An alternative way would be to create a market for tradable deficit permits or taxing rights (Casella, 1999). This would recognise that fiscal policy slippage creates negative externalities, by putting aggregate financial stability or efficiency goals at risk, while minimising the compliance costs of achieving a global target. It should be noted that a system of transferable deficit rights is in place in Austria and it is based on agreed fiscal targets for each individual Land; for municipalities as a group in each Land, a mechanism is in place allowing the transfer of an overshoot to another participant.

As aforementioned, the issue of intergovernmental fiscal relations is essential in the EU. It is an inherent contrast between the imposition on each member country of targets on public deficit and debt and the relative high and increasing degree of fiscal decentralisation that characterises public finances in several countries. To ensure that the fiscal behaviour of sub-national entities is consistent with the European commitments, many EU members have introduced some kind of legal or procedural framework, rather like an internal stability pact or domestic pact. The following two tables summarise some features of fiscal policy in the EU at national level.

Table 3.1: The Use of Fiscal Rules and Sanctions in Selected Countries

Type of fiscal rule	Type of sanctions in case of non-compliance		
	No sanctions	*Administrative sanctions*	*Financial sanctions*
Deficit target[a]	Finland, Sweden	Belgium, Spain	Austria, *EU*
Operating deficit target[b]	Italy, Portugal		Slovak Republic
Debt ceiling[c]	Hungary	Poland	Portugal, *EU*
Expenditure ceiling	Germany	Belgium	

a. Usually takes the form of a balanced budget requirement.
b. May also take the form of a 'golden rule'.
c. Limits on debt service, debt-to-revenue ratio or debt-to-GDP ratio.

Source: author's elaboration from OECD 2003

Table 3.1 shows that MS apply different rules to their lower government tiers, and the way to enforce them varies: in some cases (Finland for example) municipalities are only obliged to make a plan of how to cover any deficit in the balance sheet (peer pressure), in other cases (Belgium), the regional level monitors the municipalities budgets and has the power to enforce expenditure cuts and tax increases if necessary (administrative sanctions). Few cases (Austria) contemplate the possibility of a financial fine to governments that fail to reach the target (financial sanctions).

Table 3.2: Strategies for Ensuring Fiscal Discipline

Administrative control[a]	Centrally imposed rules	Formalised co-operation	No institutional co-ordination
France, Greece, Ireland, Luxembourg, United Kingdom	Finland, Hungary, Italy[b], Poland, Portugal, Slovak Republic, Sweden *EU*	Austria, Belgium, Denmark, Germany, Netherlands, Spain	Czech Republic

a. In practice, such controls result in limited fiscal autonomy at the subnational level.
b. A domestic stability pact has been imposed by the central government, but the enforcement of the pact is left to a co-operative institution.

Source: author's elaboration from OECD 2003

Table 3.2 summarises the strategies applied by MS for ensuring fiscal discipline. This table emphasises the main coordination strategy in place in different countries. However, the relationship between different government tiers is complex and the distribution of countries in this table is therefore not clear-cut.

The emerging picture is that there is a wide differentiation on how national countries ensure fiscal discipline.

We have seen how fiscal settings can be effective in improving the management of the multilevel economic governance. The next section tries to resume which lessons the EU can learn from that.

3.2.3. Lessons for the EU in Macroeconomic Management from National Countries

In this section, we will draw some lessons from national experiences for stabilisation. Shifting now to a positive perspective, is the reality of fiscal settings as the model predicts? The answer is no and it is evident when one analyses real fiscal relationships inside sovereign countries as done in section 3.2.2. Even unitary states, not traditionally defined as federal, present some sort of fiscal settings in which the theory does not find application. Often, to develop a consistent fiscal framework, national countries use different means of coordination (leaving to sub-national tiers some fiscal autonomy depending on the traditional strength of regional and local bodies). Fiscal rules, market discipline, delegation of (some fiscal) authority, binding pacts, a bigger common budget, transparency in the fiscal policy process: all these are different means of fiscal coordination that fiscal settings present in multilevel governments.

Transparent Fiscal Policy Framework:
First Step to Improve European Fiscal Setting

There exists a series of conditions for a federal system to have coherent and sound fiscal relations among different tiers of government and fiscal discipline. The International Monetary Fund (IMF, 1999) prepared a Manual on fiscal transparency in which it is stated that "powers and accountability need to be based on stable principles and agreed formulae and that should be clearly stated".[13] Financial resources assigned in various forms (own revenues, shared revenues, grants to sub-national entities) should be sufficient to match the expenditure assignments. Own revenues should be such as to guarantee sub-national governments some degree of manoeuvrability of their budget. On the expenditure side, over-detailed mandates should be avoided not to restrain local ability to efficiently manage expense.

Recent procedural changes in the budget process in the UK (Code for Fiscal Stability) and in New Zealand (Fiscal Responsibility Act) emphasise the role played by transparency in national accounting. A working example is the Australian government with its 'Charter of Budgetary

---

[13] IMF (1999), par. 26.

Honesty' in which the government is obliged to specify temporary tax and expenditure changes and the 'process of their reversal'. The major aim of such a Fiscal Stabilisation Policy Act would be to increase the costs of reputation for governments in case of deviation from *ex-ante* principles.

These national experiences can be extended to the EU (Calmfors, 2003), introducing a Fiscal Stabilisation Policy Act establishing well-defined objectives to existing long-run balance goals for fiscal policy. Fiscal Stabilisation Policy Act should also give guidelines about the use of automatic stabilisers and discretionary actions. To move in the direction of a more appropriate distribution of responsibilities neither the Council nor the Commission have adequate instruments. The Council's main task is policy and surveillance functions but has not the required degree of transparency and equity to conduct the coordination of the fiscal policy. In the same way, the Commission has no authoritative power of surveillance because its warnings and recommendations have to be approved by the Council.

The SGP needs to enhance the political ownership of EU policy coordination in order to strengthen its effectiveness. Member States' ownership of budgetary policy coordination could need an adjustment of the European coordination process and national budgetary process (a significant step was done in 1995 with the introduction of the SEC 95 for the accounting measures) and the creation or strengthening of national institutions that control over the budgetary responsibility.

Transparency and clarity in the assignment of competencies have increasingly been demanded by Member States and citizens. Clarity and transparency are essential in management efficiency and public accountability. Transparency is crucial if fiscal rules, cooperative agreements or financial markets are effectively to discipline subsidiary fiscal behaviour. Budget reports should be comprehensive, encompassing the information needed for the relevant trade-offs between different policies to be assessed. It is important to have an accounting system that delivers a picture as accurate and timely as possible, at both budgeting and reporting stages, of the impact of the government's activities on its overall financial position. In a number of countries, sub-national public finance data is often available with a significant time lag such as in Germany, Italy, Poland, Portugal and Spain. In most countries, sub-national public finance data is on a cash basis. Traditional cash accounting can lead to a misleading picture of commitments undertaken, since payments can be accelerated or deferred. In contrast, accrual accounting recognises the final implications of transactions when they occur, irrespective of when cash is paid or received. It is important to have a common basis for accounting systems in order for EU-level assessment of national budgetary performances to be easier and faster.

Delegation of Decisions: Second Step to Improve European Fiscal Setting

Another step to solve the problem of credibility and transparency of the fiscal policy could be either to establish an independent advisory Fiscal Policy Council, with the task of providing regular input into the budget process, or to delegate the actual decisions on fiscal policy measures to stabilise the economy to a Fiscal Policy Committee in the same way as monetary policy has been delegated to the European Central Bank (ECB) (see among others the contributions of Ascari, 2003; Blinder, 1997; Calmfors, 2003; Pisauro, 2001; and Wyplosz, 2002).

This attitude towards fiscal relations involves delegation of authority and decisions. It involves administrative controls on borrowing and expenditures at the level of local revenues. With a high vertical fiscal imbalance, the UK is a practical example of this, where the central government has the power to cap local taxes and to strictly control administration borrowing. The idea of administrative control is itself part of the notion of fiscal settings: the transparency of budget institutions and a good public expenditure management system can make a difference in supervising the financial behaviour of multilevel governments. According to this approach, the agenda setting of fiscal powers should be assigned to a leadership that won't suffer from the opportunity cost of public revenues, *i.e.* in the European context, a supranational governmental body or an independent fiscal policy board. Such an approach is followed in Australia and Germany. They are united by the delegation of the coordinating role to a fiscal council composed either by the finance ministers across all levels of government or by independent experts.

Another way to delegate authority, mentioned earlier, strengthens the importance of fiscal rules and is namely based on the American experience (Von Hagen, 1991 and Inmam, 1996). In some cases, rules are written in the state constitution like in the UK or in Germany, in others in ordinary laws. Wide consensus is found around the power of fiscal rules to enforce budget discipline to maintain a lower deficit and allow better reactive power to negative shocks (which is of central importance in the EMU). Presently, fiscal rules imply the loss of flexibility in fiscal policy, which makes it more difficult to pursue counter cyclical or tax smoothing objectives (this is one of the recent critics directed at the actual fiscal policy design in the EU).

We have seen that multilevel fiscal settings across levels of government allow a better framework than Fiscal Federalism, overcoming traditional flaws of Fiscal Federalism, giving a more flexible framework to analyse the real setting of fiscal policy interactions among governments. A number of useful real-world examples on how to 'improve Fiscal Federalism' in Europe (*i.e.* the European fiscal setting) can be found.

This section clearly demonstrates that in actual fiscal settings, centralisation is not always chosen in stabilisation policy. Therefore, theory and practice contradict themselves and a further question arises: is stabilisation centralised at national level the same as stabilisation centralised at the EU level? A political economy approach may help to solve this issue. The following section discusses the main limits of the present European setting, and the lessons it gives for the improvement of the institutional setting of the economic governance in the EU.

3.3. Improving European Stabilisation

3.3.1. Limits of the SGP

Up to now we have seen what theories and practice say about stabilisation: from one perspective Fiscal Federalism theory calls for centralisation of fiscal policy, from another, real set-ups show it is possible to keep it decentralised as long as enforceability power and strategies for ensuring fiscal discipline are well defined. We now try to draw a new set-up for the EU taking into consideration these previous lessons: the summary of the main limits of the SGP is a good starting point.

The SGP has been working since 1999: during the first three years it was well observed, only in 2002 Portugal with Ireland were the first States to be object of a procedure of excessive budget deficits by the Council. During the same year, France and Germany exceeded the 3 per cent of the GDP ceiling and the Commission forecasts the same scenario until 2006/07. An early warning was addressed to both but on 25th of November 2003, the Council, under majority voting, decided to suspend the procedure. This political decision once more displays the weakness and limitations of the SGP. Rules are usually designed to be binding but in the present context, the SGP demonstrated it was not. Since then, many criticisms followed and voices soared to ask for its reform.

Already since the early application of the Pact, several criticisms came out but during these last years of economic downturn they multiplied.

Two limits are usually identified. The first one is that it is an overly strict mechanism, which does not take into consideration the specific situation of the single MS. The second one is more about its coercive nature and the possibility to introduce a more federal set up.

The first critique says that the SGP reduces the flexibility of national fiscal policies against asymmetric shocks. The rigid threshold of 3 per cent has to be observed. Only very few exceptions are considered whereas a MS needs full manoeuvrability of all instruments of fiscal policy to face asymmetric shocks or long stagnations properly. The mechanism of the SGP is asymmetric and pro-cyclical: it does not force MS to reduce expenses and increase revenues in periods of expansion. As a consequence, many MS adopt a pro-cyclical policy during expansion periods becoming, hence, impossible to build-up a surplus for a downturn period where deficits tend to increase under the pressure of the stabilisation of the budget. Alternatively, the SGP discourages public investments, the high level of which is essential for guaranteeing a certain quality of public services. Imposing equilibrium in public accounting implies the hampering of the financing of public investments through borrowings. The threshold is indifferently applied to all MS without taking into consideration the level of the deficit, its nature and the nature of the public expenditures or the level of inflation. Furthermore, a null deficit is a very contestable economic goal. Economic theory discussion about the optimal level of public deficit is far from being unanimous about this null level as mentioned in section 3.1.2.

The second critique previously mentioned considers the coordination in place with the SGP as coercive and not innovative (Dévoluy, 2004). The objects are ill-defined and sometimes contradictory and the economic coordination is of a negative type. The financial object to prevent the insolvability of MS is insufficiently clarified and neglects an important monetary variable: inflation rates. The SGP says nothing with regards to this. Every MS can adopt its own economic policy without eventually taking into consideration the effects this policy could have on the other MS; this coordination does not internalise the impact every national policy has among the other partners. A deeper coordination is needed to positively coordinate governments, the Commission and the ECB, but is impossible in the present framework. This is hindered by the independence of the central bank that makes the determination of the policy mix necessary to completely coordinate European economy, harder although not impossible. Furthermore, the SGP reflects the economic predominant environment and when the environment changes, discussions regarding its renewal start.

3.3.2. *Recent Discussion and Proposals for the Reform of the SGP*

The discussion concerning the weakness of the SGP also developed throughout all of the academic and institutional world. These proposals can be summarised under the two approaches described in previous sections: better fiscal rule architecture and institutional reform.

The first group of suggestions concerns the enhanced definition of the targets for every MS, strengthening the fiscal rule approach and establishing a level of deficit for every country taking into account the level of the deficit, the inflation rate and the structural reforms undertaken. Disregarding the deficit level, expenditures for public investments such as costs of investments are imputable in one budget year, while their effect is usually spread over several years. Therefore, expenditure in infrastructures, in R&D and education should not be placed at the same level as current expenditures. A good example is the so-called golden rule used in Great Britain that authorises the financing of public investment through borrowings to finance the depreciation of the capital. This rule, however, gave rise to numerous difficulties namely with regards to the definition of public investment that is different from one MS to another. Pisani-Ferry (2002) proposes to leave to MS of the euro zone the choice between the procedure of excessive debt and a "Pact of sustainability of the deficit".[14] The MS able to keep the ratio of their debt under 50 per cent of the GDP and presenting transparent and exhaustive public accounts could be exempt from early warnings for excessive deficit.

The second group of proposals puts forward institutional reform concerns: coordination improvement cannot bypass through an improvement of the institutional device aiming at creating surveillance institutions independent from national governments or to introduce into practice a real European model of Fiscal Federalism.

The proposal of a Committee for Fiscal Policies derives mostly from a proposal by Calmfors and Wyplosz. According to them, the determination of fiscal policy could be split into two parts: the nature of expenditure, the fiscal structure and the fixation of the balance of the budget and the public debt. The first one needs a democratic control having to reflect the preferences of the citizens, but the second one could be assigned to a Committee independent from national governments whose long term target is to guarantee the sustainability of the

---

[14] This proposal gains favour with the enlargement because the Ecofin will become larger and difficulties in finding agreements are likely to become stronger.

public debts and in the short run to define a level of deficit able to support the economy.

A radical approach recently proposed by Ascari (2003) and Calmfors (2003) is the establishment of an independent advisory Fiscal Policy Council (FPC) with the task of providing regular stabilisation reports, serving as a basis for fiscal policy decisions as it actually happens with the Bank of England and the Bank of Sweden. The idea is to influence the fiscal policy agenda by increasing the reputational cost for the government for attaching a low weight to considerations about stabilisation and long-run fiscal sustainability. To give more political weight to the FPC means to give more power to its recommendations through the discussion in specific parliamentary sessions or even the obligation of governments to respond formally to the Council's proposals. As mentioned earlier, some examples of this kind of delegation of decision to auditing committees are already present in Denmark with the Economic Council, in Germany with the *Sachverständigenrat* and in Belgium with the *Conseil Supérieur des Finances*. These Councils differ in any case in their composition, alternatively made-up of the representatives of governments, of central banks or academic economists.

Of course, these possibilities could raise, if not accurately controlled, political credibility issues, but the relative success of the ECB demonstrates that this could be a good proposal.

There are several arguments, which demonstrate that macroeconomic stabilisation is to a large extent a question of technical findings to achieve the objectives of minimising fluctuations. Of course, issues such as the size of expenditure, the structure of taxes and the path of government debt involve value judgements on how to conciliate income distribution with social efficiency. Hence, only stabilisation decisions should be delegated while the other fiscal policy decisions would belong to parliamentary decision-making. Coricelli and Ercolani (2002) suggest how this will change the role of the Commission, which should only verify the coherence of the expenditure plans already evaluated by the auditors. This authority or Committee would work as the ECB. This will guarantee the stability of the parameters in the medium-long run but at the same time the possibility to use fiscal instruments for counter-cyclical purposes, without loss of credibility, guaranteed by the reputation of the independent institution. As for the ECB, where it is independent in the choice of the instruments to reach certain goals established before, these institutions could follow the lines and goals established by the parliament and be put under control by some control mechanisms.

A traditional model of reference for this institutional set-up is the one presented by Wyplosz (2002). The Committee decides on the annual budget balance and the parliament maintains the right to decide which tax and expenditure policies are pursued to reach the target annual budget set, allowing the parliament the most important policy of income redistribution and social efficiency. The Committee will determine the variation around the path of government debt over the cycle and it will not acquire full control over the stabilisation effect of fiscal policy.

Limits and criticisms to the SGP received voice even inside the EU institutions. In particular, the reflection of the Commission on the SGP started on November 2002 with the Communication on 'Strengthening the coordination of budgetary policies' and progressed further on with the constitution of a study group, a 'High Level Group of Independent Experts' to analyse the consequences of the implementation of the Lisbon agenda and to evaluate the impact of the Enlargement. This group chaired by André Sapir proposed the so-called Sapir Report or 'An agenda for a growing Europe' (2003). We will briefly report some results and comments on the economic governance framework suggested in this report.

Six main problems are identified with respect to the SGP: weaknesses in the political ownership of the SGP by the MS; difficulties in establishing clear and verifiable budget objectives which take account of underlying economic conditions; failure of some members to run sound budgetary policies in good time; deficient enforcement procedures of the SGP; failure of the SGP to develop into an effective coordination framework for dealing with country-specific circumstances in a consistent manner; and communication difficulties on the merits and workings of the SGP.

They put forward a series of proposals:

1. Combining effective surveillance and political ownership of Member States, by creating a budgetary surveillance network comprising of the Commission and independent national fiscal auditing boards (FABs) with no policy role but only assessment power.

2. Improving economic governance and coordination, by allowing the Commission to play a stronger role in the implementation of the treaty rules, by strengthening the coherence between national budgetary processes and aggregating national stability programmes into a euro-area stability programme and by entrusting a euro-area Ecofin Council.

3. Providing incentives to good behaviour in good times, by allowing the introduction of voluntary *rainy-day funds* that are consumed in slowdowns and replenished in upturns.

4. Fostering symmetry along the business cycle, by redefining the exceptional conditions under which the 3 per cent deficit threshold can be breached as a recession, rather than a GDP contraction of 2 per cent.

5. Permitting a higher degree of country differentiation in the implementation of the SGP, by giving more weight to debt-to-GDP ratios in the budgetary surveillance process, and by accepting higher structural budget deficits for low-debt countries.

The proposal of the Group requires certain institutional changes, with the creation of independent national FABs and of a euro-area Ecofin Council, and the possibility to set up rainy-day funds. Hence, tighter coordination could be achieved among the euro-area MS, the states mostly affected by the weak coordination mechanism in place. According to the report, the lack of 'authority' is the main weakness of the SGP: a network comprising of the European Commission and independent national fiscal boards, according to the Group will be the best solution to face actual flaws of the SGP. This refers back to the enforceability issue: an institutionally stronger system of auditors could give more credibility to the maintenance of the stability target. The Sapir Report tries to consider all previous proposals and putting them under a common framework in order to create a sound system. Although the discussion about the reform of the SGP is always on the agenda, until now no profound changes were achieved. The opportunity, offered by the Intergovernmental Conference for the European Constitution and the ratified EU Constitution, was lost in that no agreement was reached about these discussions. The constitution ratifies the previous situation and in a certain way renders changes more difficult because they imply the voting of all EU(25) MS. Even the recent reform in March 2005 discussed hereafter remains under the logic of an internal adjustment and does not solve intrinsic contradictions and limitations of the SGP and Economic governance. The institutional improvement solution will now become more and more difficult.

Brief Chronology of the SGP (non)Implementation

As aforementioned, criticisms towards the SGP rose immediately after its application, but it is only during the last three/four years that it has been seriously under pressure because of the difficulties encountered by (big) MS to comply with it. In 2002 already two countries received the so-called early warning procedure: Ireland and Portugal. The following year, it was the turn of Germany and France but the European Council decided to stop the procedures. Since then, other countries began to face budget threshold problems: Portugal, France, Germany and Italy. As the last three together represent three quarters of the EMU

GDP and are among the founding, MS they used their political influences to ask the Commission to 'soften' the SGP.

The first early warning sent by the Commission concerned Ireland in 2001. The Council on 12th of February 2001 judged Ireland's Stability Programme 2001-03 inappropriate with a budgetary surplus of about 4.7 per cent of the GDP. The Council therefore decided to issue a recommendation to Ireland under Article 99(4) of the EC Treaty.

Soon after Ireland, an early warning was sent to Portugal too as the deficit outcome for 2001 was estimated at 2.2 per cent of the GDP. This procedure was meant to prevent the occurrence of an excessive deficit. The Council decided not to follow the Commission's proposal in response to firm commitments by the Portuguese Government. The new Government in 2002 revised upwards to 4.1 per cent of GDP the budgetary deficit for 2001, making Portugal the first Member State to exceed the threshold value. In October 2002 the Commission, initiated the excessive deficit procedure in accordance with the Treaty (Article 104(3)). The Ecofin Council endorsed this proposal in November 2002. Portugal was asked to take all necessary measures to put an end to the excessive deficit before the end of 2002 and to reduce the public deficit to less than 3 per cent in 2003. The Government committed for new Stability Programmes for the 2003-2006 period, improving the coordination on budgetary policy and fiscal discipline and the quality of national statistics.

The public deficit in Portugal fell back in 2002 and 2003 to below 3 per cent of the GDP. The Commission recommended that the Council terminate the excessive deficit procedure against Portugal. On 22nd of June 2005 the Commission assessed the updated Stability Programme, observing that Portugal's deficit was again above 3 per cent of the GDP. On a recommendation from the Commission, the Council initiated a new excessive deficit procedure against Portugal in September 2005.

The third country to receive an early warning was Germany. The budget deficit stood at 2.7 per cent of the GDP in 2001, exceeding by a large margin the target set in the October 2000 update of the Stability Programme (1.5 per cent of the GDP). Accordingly, the Commission proposed the early-warning procedure. At its meeting on 12th of February 2002 the Council decided not to follow the Commission's recommendation as the German Government had strongly committed itself to ensuring not to breach the reference value and gave a firm commitment to reach a close-to-balance budget position by 2004. 2002 Germany's budget deficit reached 3.8 per cent of the GDP and the total debt exceeded the 60 per cent boundary value, rising to 60.9 per cent of the GDP. On 19th of November 2002 the Commission called for an excessive deficit procedure. The Council followed this recommendation at its meeting on 21st of January 2003.

Shortly after, France began to suffer from an excessive increase in its budget deficit in 2002 (2.7 per cent of the GDP according to Commission calculations instead of the 1.4 per cent announced in the 2001 Stability Programme). The Commission opened an early warning procedure in November 2002 and the Council addressed recommendations to the French Government on 21st of January 2003.

France and Germany couldn't fulfil the Commission's requirements for excessive deficit. Hence, the Commission activated the next stage in the excessive deficit procedure in November 2003 with a view to encouraging both countries to correct their deficits at least by 2005. However, on 25th of November 2003, the Council under majority voting decided to suspend the sanction procedure for France and Germany.

On 5th of July 2004, the Council noted the existence of an excessive deficit in Hungary. It recommended to the Hungarian authorities to take action in the medium term to decrease the country's deficit to below 3 per cent by 2008.

In 2004, Italy joined the club too. The Commission recommended a warning to Italy because of the risk that its budget deficit would exceed the 3 per cent threshold in 2004. The Ecofin held on 5th July 2004 decided not to issue an early warning because of the additional budgetary commitments made by the Government. In June 2005, the Commission adopted a report on Italian public finances, recommending that an excessive deficit procedure should be initiated against Italy. The Council officially launched the procedure on 28th of July 2005.

In the same year Greece and the Netherlands received an excessive deficit procedure. The Council decided to initiate the excessive deficit procedure at the Ecofin meeting on 5th of July 2004. The Greek Government was asked to put an end to its excessive deficit situation at the latest by 2005. In April 2005 the Commission assessed the Greek Stability Programme, concluding that, despite the efforts of the Greek Government, the outlook for 2005 and beyond was uncertain. In June 2004 the Commission initiated the excessive deficit procedure against the Netherlands. With the reduction in the Dutch deficit from 3.2 per cent in 2003 to less than 2.3 per cent in 2004, the Commission recommended on 18th of May 2005 to suspend the procedure as the Netherlands was firmly back on the path of healthy fiscal consolidation.

2004 has been a crucial year: internal economic difficulties became stronger and the pressure to reform the SGP was spread throughout Europe.

Finally, during the Spring Ecofin meeting on 20th of March 2005, EU economic ministers agreed on 'softening' the Pact. As we will see, the direction of the reform is only partial because it does not respond to criticism based on economic reasoning but it is more the result of opportunistic national (big) governments' behaviour towards a softening of the excessive budget procedure, the time span to reduce it and the fine.

At the European Council meeting on 22nd and 23rd of March 2005, the finance ministers reached a political agreement on improving the implementation of the Stability and Growth Pact. The Commission subsequently drew up proposals concerning Regulation (EC) No.1466/1997 and Regulation No.1467/1997. The proposals were adopted and Regulations No.1055/2005 and 1056/2005 of 27th of June 2005 amend the original Regulations (Regulation No.1466/1997 and Regulation No.1467/1997).

This brief chronology shows the most relevant steps of the (non)implementation of the SGP. 13 countries over 25 (non euro zone countries are asked to submit a Convergence Program) received at least one early warning during the last four years. If one could say that already such a high percentage of non "virtuous" countries is a sign of the failure of the (architecture) of the SGP, the death hit has been given by the political behaviour of the Council that refused to transform the early warnings for Germany and France into a fine as foreseen by the SGP. For this reason the Ecofin held on 25th of November 2003 can be considered as the grave of the SGP, two years before its recent loosening with March 2005 reform.

Table 3.3: Excessive Deficit Procedures: Chronology

Country	Date of the Commission report (Article 104-3)	Last update
Year 2006		
Germany	19 November 2002	1 March 2006
Italy	7 June 2005	22 February 2006
United Kingdom	21 September 2005	24 January 2006
Year 2005		
Hungary	12 May 2004	11 November 2005
United Kingdom	21 September 2005	21 September 2005
Portugal	22 June 2005	12 September 2005
Netherlands	28 April 2004	18 May 2005
Greece	19 May 2004	6 April 2005
Year 2004		
Greece	19 May 2004	22 December 2004
Hungary	12 May 2004	22 December 2004
Czech Republic	12 May 2004	22 December 2004
Cyprus	12 May 2004	22 December 2004
Malta	12 May 2004	22 December 2004
Poland	12 May 2004	22 December 2004
Slovakia	12 May 2004	22 December 2004
The Netherlands	28 April 2004	22 December 2004
France	2 April 2003	14 December 2004
Germany	19 November 2002	14 December 2004
Greece	19 May 2004	5 July 2004
Czech Republic	12 May 2004	5 July 2004
Cyprus	12 May 2004	5 July 2004
Hungary	12 May 2004	5 July 2004
Malta	12 May 2004	5 July 2004
Poland	12 May 2004	5 July 2004
Slovakia	12 May 2004	5 July 2004
The Netherlands	28 April 2004	2 June 2004
United Kingdom	28 April 2004	
Year 2003		
France	2 April 2003	25 November 2003
Year 2002		
Germany	19 November 2002	25 November 2003
Portugal	24 September 2002	28 April 2004

Source: EC Website, March 2006

The new Pact states that:

1. medium term objectives for budget position have to take into account the heterogeneity of economic and budgetary position, and development of fiscal risk towards the sustainability of public finances;

2. more attention should be placed on the debt and its sustainability, reaffirming the need to reduce government debt to below the 60 per cent of GDP at a satisfactory pace;

3. deadlines for taking effective actions and measures will be extended. In case of 'special circumstances', the initial deadline for correcting an excessive deficit could be set one year later (the second year after its identification, *i.e.* three years after its occurrence);

4. structural reforms that enhance growth will be taken into account when defining the adjustment path to the medium term objective in countries near the 3 per cent threshold. For pension reform, the deadline is five years.

This new Pact, under German, French and Italian pressure, also foresees special circumstances, aimed at excluding some expenses from the calculation of the deficit. According to the Council, these expenses should be related to the implementation of policies in the context of the Lisbon Strategy, policies to foster Research and Development or innovation (as Italy and the UK asked for). Germany and Poland obtained that the cost for EU enlargement would also be taken into account.

Furthermore the Council introduces a new paradigm for EU MS and for EMU II MS: a cyclical adjustment cut of the public debt equal to 0.5 of GDP, a value increasable when total output exceeds potential output and decreasable in bad circumstances. A new definition of a deep economic crisis is given: a deep economic crisis 'occurs' when the annual GDP growth rate is negative or when actual output is low compared to potential output, during a long-lasting period.

From an economic point of view the only relevant innovation is a partial application of the 'golden rule' according to which deficit should be evaluated taking into consideration the quality and the nature of expenses and the overall sustainability of public finances. Nevertheless, beyond this statement of purpose, no exact formulation for the introduction of the golden rule was given.

Hence, the overall architecture of the SGP has not been changed. It is only more flexible and discretional and relies more than ever on the good will of each MS. The absence of objective rules undermines the nature of the Pact in that the reform is more the result of pressures from certain countries, creating dangerous disparities between the 25 MS. Differences also relate to the way the reform has been presented to national citizen. Benelux countries affirmed with strength that they will continue all efforts to comply to the parameters, and no special circumstances will be considered to evaluate their deficit, while France, Italy and Germany consider the reform as being a victory against the 'oppressive' rules that hindered their national growth.

Table 3.4: Executive Summary of the Fiscal Policy in the EU

	Macroeconomic management	**Stabilisation**	**Fiscal discipline**
EU current setting	*Monetary policy* and *fiscal policy* are not managed at the same level	*Monetary policy*: centralised (ECB) *Fiscal policy*: constraint but at national level only	*Fiscal rules*: SGP *Financial sanction* (theoretically binding but with enforceability issue) *Coordination*: Eurogroup, Broad economic guidelines and SGP
Fiscal Federalism	Unique level manages monetary and fiscal policy	Centralised	*Coordination* and *common budget* are the same
Proposals			
Institutional reform (Calmfors, 2003, Coricelli and Ercolani, 2002, Wyplosz, 2002)	Independent 'central' authorities for monetary and (part of) fiscal policy	*Monetary policy*: centralised (ECB) *Fiscal policy*: partially centralised, independent advisory Fiscal Policy Council	Coordination of MS through the 'Broad Economic Guidelines'
Better fiscal rules architecture (Pisani-Ferry, 2000)	*Monetary policy* and *fiscal policy* are not managed at the same level	Monetary policy centralised Fiscal policy nationally constrained	Euro-area Ecofin
Sapir Report (2003)	Budgetary surveillance network by the Commission and Fiscal Auditing Boards	*Monetary policy*: centralised (ECB) *Fiscal policy*: constraint but at national level	*Fiscal rules*: improved SGP, euro-area Ecofin *Coordination*: European economic governance Financial incentives: voluntary rainy-day funds
20th of March 2005 SGP Reform	No big changes as the issue 'who controls the controllers' remains; No effective policy mix because of political compliance of MS	*Fiscal policy*: constraint at national level but more flexible and discretional	*Fiscal rules*: SGP with a 'soft' golden rule and taking in consideration heterogeneity of MS *Financial sanction* (theoretically binding but with stronger enforceability issue as the deadlines have been softened) *Coordination*: no changes

Source: author

Although this reform constitutes a significant step towards the improvement of the SGP, it has not solved the intrinsic contradictions and problems of the old SGP. Even more it weakens European economic governance. The chance to change institutional framework was lost once again (after the EU constitution).[15] And once more the problem of enforceability and surveillance of the SGP has not been solved. The surveillance remains a prerogative of the Council who is made up by MS, most of them facing actual deficit problems. The crucial issue – *who controls the controllers* – remains as no improvement in the governance, either through the delegation to an independent authority or through the creation of a bigger budget, was implemented.

The proposals presented here are numerous and table 3.4 summarises them, but are these new set-ups applicable? Do they take into consideration all economic, social institutional and political features? What challenges arise? Chapter 6 will partly try to address these issues.

3.4. Concluding on the Relevance of Fiscal Federalism for EU Economic Governance

One object of our work was to revise studies and proposals about the reform of the SGP under a Fiscal Federalism perspective. We have seen what happens in reality and what the theory predicts. We can conclude that we are far from having a coherent and uniform response able to support economic growth and cohesion from one side and to adequately represent a model to be exportable for the integration of the new MS. A new institutional set-up is needed where national governments are free, to a certain extent, to manage their fiscal policies in order to better represent their citizens, acting within the competencies given by a stronger supra-structure, the EU.

Intermediate agencies could serve as discussion round tables in which these two contrasting forces try to find an agreement through a delicate balance between coordination, fiscal rules and enforcement power. A reference example could be the Australian Loan Council (ALC), in which Federal and State borrowings are co-ordinated. Most states have adopted some sort of balanced-budget rule and State borrowing is not guaranteed by the central government. The states are required to explain overruns in the borrowing allocations set by the Loan Council.

To work efficiently and effectively, this mechanism needs a well defined and bigger budget. The EU is still far away from it.

We have seen the theory of Fiscal Federalism and its meaning for stabilisation (section 3.1): a first glance solution will be centralisation but this contrasts with some national settings. Indeed even in federal states and not only in unitary states the tension between centralisation

---

[15] Although not all is lost because of French and Dutch 'no' could lead to a re-discussion and hopefully to an improvement for what concerns its economic part.

and decentralisation is always present like a dialectic force driving multilevel fiscal relations (section 3.2). The debates and the reform proposals are numerous; nevertheless until now no explicit step in the change of the economic governance has been taken (section 3.3).[16]

In previous chapters, we dealt with the lessons the EU could learn from the Fiscal Federalism theoretical perspective and from the practice of national fiscal settings. A description of what traditional theory (in the line of Musgrave, Tiebout and Oates) helped us in understanding its main flaws and the need to change it, and in our opinion also to improve it. Recent contributions in this strand of literature give good hints on the way to reflect about the EU, the EMU, Enlargement, Cohesion Policy and macroeconomic stabilisation.

Our main object was to decompose traditional ways of reasoning about Fiscal Federalism and its applicability to the EU: we identified five original dimensions in which our problematic was split into. A circular path was envisaged in the analysis of the macroeconomic stabilisation. Starting from what the theory says about stabilisation and what it means for the European Union (dimension 4 of the problematic), we have seen that the present context offers many challenges. To solve these, valid experiences are provided by Member States themselves, which in their own internal fiscal settings came up with various solutions (dimension 1).

This chapter showed that stabilisation is often centralised but many approaches are possible, hence the 'absolute' centralisation of this policy as predicted by the traditional Fiscal Federalism theory cannot be taken as a rigid paradigm. The cycle shut down enclosing new variables with the traditional ones: political, national, cultural and historical characteristics.

The current set-up implies responding to macroeconomic shocks with the use of fiscal policy instruments at the European level, thereby leading to stronger demands for a bigger EU budget and possibly for EU deficit-spending. Chapter 6 will also summarise these lessons.

An extensive European Fiscal framework internalises the external effects or externalities of national policies. These externalities could have either positive or negative effects on the activity level of the other partners. The SGP is born to avoid the negative externality given by a loose fiscal policy to the partners but it does not take into account the positive externalities.

---

[16] Although the Recent SGP reform is important, it looks more like an attempt from bigger states to gain internal political support than a real improvement that could enhance structural economic changes and boost growth.

There is disagreement over which areas of policy making should be transferred to supranational European institutions, there is also disagreement on how much power should be given up to European political bodies in those areas. The traditional approach to Fiscal Federalism, dating back to Oates and Musgrave ignores second-best arguments related to incentive constraints on the policy formation process. According to Persson *et al.* (1996) decentralisation of authority may correct existing distortions in the economy or in the decision-making mechanism. Furthermore, Fiscal Federalism abstracts from political decision-making inside governments when individuals have different preferences. Centralisation or decentralisation of decision-making may affect the coalition formation process and the balance of power between various interest groups. To keep into consideration these aspects, it will be useful to adopt a broader political economy approach that addresses the second best effects of centralisation, as well as its effects on coalition formation.

Fiscal organisation and economic governance are inseparable. In order for the European budget to fulfil its tasks without provoking endless discussions, it is necessary for these tasks to be well defined and that its administration held by a real European economic governance.

The EU being a complex structure of multilevel governments it is natural that, in order to design a new framework that goes beyond the previously mentioned flaws, we keep into consideration such experiences. National experiences allow to re-evaluate the actual 'coordination level' in the EU, suggesting that two options are possible:

    i) the delegation of the 'European' fiscal management to an independent body;

    ii) the creation of a bigger budget.

The creation of an independent body can serve in the short run as a counter-alter to the fear of excessive centralisation of powers at the EU levels. This authority will deal only with fiscal policy aimed to stabilise the EMU and to also confront the challenges that the newcomers will face adopting the euro. The actual system (the Ecofin) cannot address in a proper way the delicate question of the single currency stabilisation while the majority of the system is made up of MS not (yet) inside the EMU. An independent body (either a FAB, or FPC, see section 3.3) guarantees that (a part of) national fiscal policy will be focused on the stabilisation of the economic area in which the single currency circulates.

Of course, the 'European Project' does not stop here (however uncertain the future of the Constitution is) but slowly proceeds in its aim to create an integrated Europe, economically, culturally and politically.

Fiscal Federalism will not be applicable as it stands but needs some corrections to take into consideration political, national, cultural and historical characteristics of MS.

Decentralisation of authority may correct existing distortions in the economy or in the decision-making mechanism (as Fiscal Federalism predicts) but going forward, it must take into account political internal government decision-making when individuals have different preferences (as it is the case in the EU where representatives from different nations happen to meet). Centralisation or decentralisation of decision-making may affect the coalition-formation process and the political outcome. To take into consideration these aspects, the theory of Fiscal Federalism should broaden its perspective by including political economy arguments, a wider approach that studies the second best effects of centralisation, as well as its effects on coalition formation.

In any case, even the simple enforcement of balanced budget rules (as the SGP) by national governments requires additional enforcement powers (credibility of sanctions) at supranational level which in turn requires a higher legitimacy of supranational institutions (qualified majority voting), which in turn reinforces the need for political reforms (transformation of the Commission, of the European Council). Such a new framework would lead in the medium run to an enlarged budget, when the EMU will be established to all the EU MS and to a more ambitious and, possibly efficient, European Fiscal setting.

The budget will manage only expenditures that are relevant to the whole Union and that develop a European identity and solidarity. Specific national expenditure such as defence could be diverted to the European budget. This budget could operate in deficit, financed by the issuing of European bonds that will also widen the portfolio choice of private investors. Of course, the European Parliament should have the power to impose certain taxes and should control the mix of expenditures and revenues that forms the European budget.

Asking for a fiscal setting based on an abstract and theoretical fiscal federalist model is, at least for the moment, too ambitious but steps towards Fiscal Federalism can be undertaken. First, a more constructive multilateral surveillance system is needed for better targeting of the common objectives and its analysis, making it a result of a deep dialogue.

Second, an increase in the number of co-financed projects would also be welcome. Before increasing the weight of the European budget significantly, it will be a good step to introduce in national budgets projects of a European dimension. This concerns projects like the "European growth initiative" that promotes investments in fields such as transport networks, energy, telecommunications and R&D.

CHAPTER 4

Fiscal Federalism, German Unification and European Enlargement

Margherita FORNASINI

This chapter deals with the interactions between the theory of Fiscal Federalism and the reality of the biggest national fiscal setting in the EU. It aims in particular at highlighting lessons from the German national experience for the EU and for the Fiscal Federalism perspective (dimensions 1 and 2 of the problematic presented in Chapter 1). It is divided into three sections. Section 4.1 deals with lessons one can draw from German unification for Fiscal Federalism. It analyses the great territorial, demographic, financial and economic changes induced by unification. The federal government approach to unification was reactive to the political unrest following the fall of the Berlin Wall and char-acterised by a great inventiveness in the forms of aid provided. Aids not only comprised grants but also bonds, direct investments from West to East, the creation of THA, an agency to help firms in their convergence to the western standards, etc. This section thus aims at highlighting the fact that there is an interaction between the theoretical scheme of German Fiscal Federalism and the setting where this scheme is applied. Changes in the setting due to unification triggered a need to change the entire German fiscal setting/model. We also note the impossibility to leave aside political and social factors to understand how a particular fiscal setting works and evolves. Fiscal Federalism theory under-estimates their importance.

Section 4.2 compares the German Federalist system and the EU 'federal' structure, with particular attention on similarities and differ-ences between German unification and the 2004 EU enlargement. In the comparison with German unification, the latter EU enlargement approaches it in terms of significance and difficulty. Matters to be faced are numerous: transfers to the Central and Eastern European Countries (CEECs), the exchange rate, migration, trade development, unification of different 'identities of people' and so on. Many similarities and differences will be outlined and some lessons will be drawn. For the theory of Fiscal Federalism, once again it is important to consider political factors to understand a fiscal setting and to make the Fiscal Federalism perspective applicable to the EU. With regards to the EU, this section shows the need to keep in mind the real situation of the acceding countries and that convergence of the new EU Member States towards the EU(15) standards is likely to be a long process. Section 4.3 presents our conclusions.

4.1. The German Unification and Fiscal Federalism

This first section highlights lessons, which can be drawn from German unification for Fiscal Federalism (dimension 2 of our problematic). To achieve this goal, we start with a description of the East German economy at the moment of unification, going on analysing on the one hand, the consequences of unification, and on the other hand, the several ways used to help the former German Democratic Republic (hereafter GDR) to face it. To deal with this unprecedented phenomenon, the German government made choices also considering political and social factors (for example facing the problem of conversion rate or of unemployment). The German unification shows that, actually, it is not possible to leave aside such factors and that unification (like enlargement) is not simply an addition of territories to a previously existing state. Instead, Fiscal Federalism deals with the means of coordination between different levels of government and tries to determine which function is better carried out by which tier of government. Theory tends to disregard the particular political and social settings of countries, which in reality influence, as we will show, its application and feasibility.

4.1.1. The East German Economy

After the fall of the Berlin Wall in 1989, German unification in 1990 extended the western German legal, economic and social security system to the new states. At the same time, it extended the currency area of the DM in the five new *Länder* and East Berlin with a conversion rate of 1:1. Furthermore, eastern Germany joined the European Common Market and thus could have new trade markets.

However, in reality, Germany was facing an economic challenge of unprecedented scale. In fact, it is important to keep in mind that the economic situation of eastern Germany that came out from 45 years of socialist planning economy, was disastrous and absolutely unable to compete in the open market environment of the west.

During the socialist planning period, western economic competitors had very limited access to the market of Eastern Germany: in fact East German trade had mainly occurred with the other countries of the communist block. This trade was based on agreements among these nations, which assured outlet markets to East German products independently of their standards of quality. In 1989, over two thirds of East German exports went to eastern block countries: 40.3 per cent to the USSR and 32.3 per cent to other Member States. After the unification, a double problem occurred in the GDR: on the one hand, the dissolution of the eastern block and the political collapse of the USSR removed eastern European markets from the GDR's industry, because newly liberalised economies were not able/willing to pay western prices for the low quality of East Germany's products. On the other hand, simultaneously, East Germany was not able to attract western trade partners, and consequently to sell in western markets, for various reasons: firstly, in accordance with the equal right to work, the socialist governments in GDR had increasingly substituted labour for capital, creating a distortion in factor markets, because there was abundance of labour and scarcity of capital. This abundance of labour led GDR's industry to manufacture low-cost products with high labour intensity that however lacked in quality, a necessary feature to attract western trade partners.

Secondly, the obsolete GDR's industrial stock disallowed to face western competition. In fact, at the time of unification, the majority of GDR's firms needed fundamental restructuring and needed to assimilate management techniques in a new open market economy context. The solution could be, and later on was in many cases, privatisation, but until privatisation occurred, GDRs' firms were provided with capital to allow them to operate even in deficit in order to protect workers from unemployment. From a strict economic point of view, inefficient firms have to close down, not to waste resources. In contrast, in the reality we are describing, the government made different (and apparently pareto-suboptimal) choices for social reasons, *i.e.* saving jobs, which evidently can be, and at that time were, stronger than the economic ones.

In sum, at the time of unification, East Germany had an obsolete capital stock, a washed-out infrastructure and a big environmental problem.

4.1.2. Analysing Consequences of Unification

Unification surely had positive consequences for East Germany, for West Germany, for the whole of Germany and for Europe as a whole, which are briefly discussed hereafter. As for the first one, the western legal, economic and social system was extended to the new *Länder*, which also joined the European Common Market, having the possibility to develop trade in western Germany and Europe. As for West Germany, it increased its territory and population respectively by 44 per cent and by 26 per cent. As for the whole of Germany, this event ended the separation of 80 million Germans that had lasted for 45 years and restored the united country's unrestricted sovereignty (Prey, 1995). Above all, German unification was not only the mere incorporation of eastern *Länder* into the territory of the Federal Republic of Germany (hereafter FRG); on the contrary, it marked important events with great meanings for the whole of Europe and the world, like the end of the Cold War, which meant the beginning of a new 'way of life'. Moreover, with its first territorial enlargement towards Eastern Europe, it impulsed the European integration of eastern countries and helped to stabilise other former Comecon economies.

Nevertheless, unification had also some, and probably insufficiently foreseen or considered, negative consequences. Two of them were the worst post-unification problems: unemployment and excessive migration. As aforementioned, from the liberal economic point of view, East Germany was 'over-laboured' and, despite the financial efforts made to help firms protect their workers, unemployment was a huge concern in East Germany. According to official statistics, in 1992 – the worst year for the labour market – 1.7 million people, that is 14.8 per cent of the work force in GDR, were unemployed. Furthermore, during the same year, an average of 370,000 people worked short periods, 388,000 people took part in job-creation schemes, 426,000 people trained in vocational programmes and 811,000 retired early (Prey, 1995). In addition, in the following three years, the negative trend went on.

As a consequence, massive migration from East to West Germany began. At the very beginning, the most important incentive to leave the GDR was the uncertainty about the political future of eastern Germany; in fact, many citizens feared the possible return of the communist regime that could soon close the borders again. However, there is also another reason for massive migration in the early 1990s. In fact, despite the great financial transfers from West to East Germany, amounting to 50 per cent of East Germany's GDP per year, there was a real collapse of the GDR's economy after unification, with the consequent loss of a million jobs in the East. In 1990, the Akerlof Group made a study on migration incentives in GDR, with the result that the lack of work for a sufficiently long period and differentials in earnings were the main ones, for GDR's people, to move to the West.

According to Heiland's survey, between 1989 and 1990, almost 600,000 people (roughly 3.7 per cent of the eastern population) migrated from East to West Germany. Afterwards, from 1991 and 1995 East-West migration declined (in 1994 the emigration rate was 1.04 per cent), partly because of the improvement of living standards in the East but above all because West Germany was involved in the European economic slowdown in late 1992 and thus finding a job in the West had become even more difficult. Another wave of migration began in 1996 because of the bad employment situation in the east due to the big structural changes needed by the East German economy. Speaking still of East to West migration, according to official statistics it remains as high as 50,000 people per year.

The federal government had two basic targets to face unemployment: people and firms. We analyse the transitory fiscal setting set up by Germany to manage unification.

Helping People

As for the first target, a way to provide for the unemployed was through the extension of unemployment insurance to East Germany. But payment of unemployed benefits was very costly and, in the long run, would not solve the problem itself. Another way was the introduction of 'qualification vouchers': through financial incentives, unemployed workers would train on the job, they would receive qualification vouchers limited only to a certain monetary amount and to an application in the five new *Länder*. These federal government's decisions were taken on social grounds. Unemployment, in fact, always has dramatic social consequences, which can lead to demonstrations and disorders. In particular, this happened in 1990 in the GDR, because of the unprecedented size of the phenomenon.

Referring to the framework constructed in Chapter 1, the German unification experience provides a lesson for Fiscal Federalism theory: the German government used means such as social vouchers or unemployment insurance to protect jobs in the East. This shows, on the one hand, the social problems' big influence on the government's decisions and, on the other hand, the great innovative character of the German fiscal setting compared to Fiscal Federalism theory, which mainly provides the means for grants to make transfers.

Helping Firms: Restructuration and Privatisation

The second way to deal with unemployment was through help given to firms. As aforementioned, East German firms were not competitive. Thus, a restructuring process was necessary. During the socialist regime, the whole national industry was organised in *Kombinate* and only 316 *Kombinate* controlled the entire industry.

The *Treuhandanstalt* (THA), an agency created to help firms in their convergence towards western standards, divided these *Kombinate* in more than 13,000 independent units. It was able to sell some of them immediately after their dismantlement but, as for the majority of eastern firms, they could not attract investors because of their lack of competitiveness and of their polluting impact.

So, a fundamental restructuring process took place. Firstly, inefficient firms without possibilities of economic improvement had to close
down as soon as possible, not to waste capital further. For the remaining
firms, a possible alternative was a structural policy primarily aimed at
saving jobs, it was intended at providing the direct intervention of a
public organisation to support firms. However, this would somehow
have signified a continuation of socialist economic policy and such a
protection was not a long-term solution for unemployment and the non
competitiveness of firms. Moreover, the THA was not able to make
feasible decisions because it did not manage to tackle the huge diversity
in the East German productive system.

The second alternative was the market process which meant that
eastern firms could achieve an adjustment to western standards under
economic criteria; only firms able to withstand them would have
survived. In this way, inefficient firms would have been eliminated
without wasting financial aid.

Nevertheless, the federal government decided in favour of structural
policies, with employment as the main objective. They sometimes
sacrificed efficiency for social reasons or for keeping political stability,
using for example subsidies to existing firms even with the risk of also
protecting inefficient firms, under the justification of saving jobs.

After the restructuring of firms, where possible, privatisation was the
next step. A possibility in the implementation of privatisation was to sell
the firms in order to attract domestic and foreign investments. Western
buyers would have provided old eastern entities with new technology
and management experience, so that selling the firms would be the
quickest way to achieve adjustment. However, there were obstacles to
the implementation of privatisation, such as obsolescence, bad environmental conditions and increasing losses by eastern firms.

Despite the flaws of eastern firms, the THA worked to sell them,
with a social *leitmotiv* that was focused on job preservation. This once
again shows that governments cannot leave social factors aside when
taking decisions on economic policy. Social problems like unemployment shape political behaviours which are a major determinant of the
overall shape of any fiscal setting. The importance of these interrelated
social and political factors, testified through the analysis of a concrete
reality, shows the need for Fiscal Federalism theory to take them into
account.

4.1.3. The Different Forms of Aid to East Germany

The economic disaster of GDR implied the need for financial aid from the West. This is in particular due to the principles at the basis of German federalism. One of these is fiscal equalisation. German Basic Law assures adequate financial instruments to any layer of government, to give it the ability to perform its functions. This is achieved through fiscal equalisation, that is the redistribution of financial resources between federal units with stronger spending power to those with weaker spending power (Börzel, 2003). Another one is the principle of uniform living conditions in the whole country written in the Constitution. Consequently, all this had also to be extended to East Germany after unification. All efforts had to be made to conform living standards in the East to those in the West as soon as possible. To reach this objective, financial transfers were provided, which, at the very beginning, as mentioned earlier, were used to support eastern firms in order to protect workers from unemployment. Later, they were used to improve, or, in many cases, to upgrade an infrastructure system. During the first five years after unification, the federal government, together with the *Länder*, municipalities, the EU, the German Unity Fund and the Social Security Insurance, transferred a sum ranging from 68.71 billion euros in 1991, in constant rise to reach 108.13 billion euros in 1995, to the new *Länder* and East Berlin (Prey, 1995). According to Kenschnigg-Kohler's study (1999), transfers to East Germany rose from 40 to 46 per cent of the total gross transfers between 1991 and 1995, reaching 5 per cent of West Germany's GDP in 1995.

As highlighted, unification meant an enormous financial burden for the Federal Republic of Germany. To support it, the federal government alone was not able to provide the necessary funds, thus, the financing project involved all levels of government: Federation, *Länder* and municipalities.

Three main fiscal policy options to finance transfers to the former GDR were applied: cutting expenditures, raising taxes and issuing bonds.

Cutting government expenditure seemed to be an inexpensive way to prevent a raise in future budget deficit that, in 1989, was at its lowest level since 1973. However, in the mid-1980s, the government of FRG had already introduced a tax reform whose third stage of tax cuts had to be made in 1990, the year of the unification. So, the budget fell by one percent of West Germany's gross domestic product and further cuts in Government expenditure were very difficult.

Another way to finance unification was to raise taxes. Such a solution will be analysed later on (see section 4.2.5).

The third possibility was to issue government bonds. This issue created a flux of capital for the transfers to the East without a decrease in disposable income in the West, in order to make people better accept the financial burden of unification. But any expenditure based on public debt signifies borrowing at the cost of future generations unless investments turned out to pay for themselves (Prey, 1995). In the early 1990s, however, elections were imminent and the government did not want to transfer the costs of unification directly to the taxpayer, that is the voter. Thus it chose to finance it through funds and bonds, even if it had become clear early on that, for the conversion of a socialist economy, a temporary increase in budget deficit was not enough and the government had to introduce new taxes, as we will show in section 4.2.5.

Again, in choosing financial instruments to support GDR, the federal government diversified the forms of aid acting on political grounds, trying to put off the rise in taxes as much as possible so as not to provoke political instability.

Rate of Conversion

As we have seen, the German government showed great inventiveness in the choice of financial means to help the East, not limiting this choice at grants *per se* and did not always act under strictly financial grounds. This also occurred in particular with regards to the choice of the rate of conversion. They decided for a rate of 1:1, even if this would have increased wages and consequently the labour costs for eastern firms, leading to higher unemployment. From a strict economic point of view, a devaluation of the Ost Mark (OM) appeared to be a logical measure but the concern was to maintain the purchasing power parity between the Ost Mark and the DM in post-unification. This economic policy choice was mainly based on socio-political grounds. The federal government feared to lose the votes of 16 million Easterners and the political and social instability that a different choice would have provoked, since in fact demonstrations had not stopped in the GDR. Slogans like 'One for one', or 'We will never be one' (Prey, 1995) showed that Easterners would not have felt 'German' without such parity.

The German Unity Fund

According to the unification Treaty, the German *Finanzausgleich* had to be extended to the eastern *Länder* as soon as possible, to achieve the equalisation of living conditions.

Let's briefly analyse the German *Finanzausgleich*. The German Federalism is cooperative, that is, it is based on the consent of all public institutions taking part in the execution of a task. The interaction between Bund and *Länder* is present in the decision-making process, where states are represented throughout the Bundesrat, and in the share of responsibilities for expenditure and revenue legislation. They also share the main tax yields (income tax, corporate income tax and value added tax),[1] whose vertical distribution is set in the Constitution. There is also a horizontal equalisation of financial burden, *i.e.* between richer and poorer *Länder*. This is an instrument of solidarity to the poorer regions and to avoid conflicts. As described in Chapter 2, the EU has a similar instrument in the cohesion and structural funds that are used to help the development of poorer regions in Europe.

The other main feature of German Fiscal Federalism is the fiscal equalisation system, the redistribution of financial resources between federal units with stronger spending power to those with weaker spending power (Börzel, 2003). All this to achieve the aforementioned uniformity of living conditions.

Despite what the unification Treaty sets, the fiscal equalisation scheme did not include the new states until 1995. In the opposite case, there would have been a big revenue transfer from western to eastern *Länder*. This met with strong opposition from western *Länder* because their financial burden would have been too heavy.

Instead of their inclusion in the fiscal equalisation scheme, the new states received subsidies from the German Unity Fund, a bond issue to finance economic development in East Germany.

Initially, the German Unity Fund was co-financed by the federation and the western states and, at the beginning, was made up of 58.8 billion euros, 20 of which coming from the Federal government. In 1992, the fund was raised through a one-point increase in the VAT and through a further contribution from the Federation. Afterwards, the federal government was forced to introduce surcharges in taxes, in 1991-92 the income tax, the mineral oil tax and the insurance tax rose.

Additionally, two types of grants were paid to the eastern *Länder*. Type A grants, payable to both East and West German states, were designed to raise per capita revenues (after horizontal equalisation) to 90 per cent of the national average (Watts, Hobson, 2000); type B was directed primarily to the eastern *Länder*, to support them in the construction of modern infrastructures.

The distribution of the fund to the states was based on population size. The recipient states, as a second step, had to pass on 40 per cent of their grant to their local governments.

---

[1] For additional details, see Spahn and Föttinger (1997: 229) and Seitz (1998).

In 1995, the law on fiscal equalisation (*Finanzausgleichgesetz*) was extended to eastern *Länder*. The financial burden always fell on a small group of states (North Rhine Westphalia, Baden-Württemberg, Bayern and Hessen), constantly in favour of new *Länder*. This led to political tensions and to donor states' complaint to the Constitutional Court. In June 2001, they agreed on a reform of the fiscal equalisation system, which has come into force in 2005 and will last until 2019. Such new regulations are called 'Germany's Solidarity Pact II'.

Both the exclusion of the new *Länder* from the fiscal equalisation system until 1995 and its reform of 2001 show that the original scheme could not work after unification and its direct impact. They had to change it in conformity with the change of setting. There is an obvious interaction between a theoretical scheme and its practical application to a setting.

4.1.4. Improving German Federalism: Germany's Solidarity Pact II

With Germany's Solidarity Pact II, many elements of the German Fiscal setting have been reformed. For example, from 2005 onwards, a higher VAT volume is distributed in order to increase the help to weaker states.

As for horizontal fiscal equalisation, a change concerns the 'marginal transfer rate',[2] that is the money that can be skimmed off from financially strong *Länder* (contributing states) to weaker *Länder* (recipient states) and is based on a graduated tariff. This rate is provided in the fiscal equalisation scheme to ensure that every state attains at least 95 per cent of the average fiscal capacity (Seitz, 2000). Currently, in 2005, for contributors above 110 per cent of the equalisation point,[3] the transfer rate is 80 per cent of per capita fiscal capacity in excess of average fiscal capacity. For contributors between 101 per cent and 110 per cent of the equalisation point, the transfer rate is 66.6 per cent. For contributors between 100 per cent and 101 per cent of the equalisation point, the transfer rate is 15 per cent of per capita fiscal capacity in excess of average fiscal capacity. Since 2005 there has been a change to a steady and linear tariff, so that donor states have to expect a rate of 75 per cent at most. This tariff is applied only if a state reaches 120 per cent of the average financial strength of all states (Beierl, 2001).

---

[2] For details on calculation of fiscal capacity: Guihéry, "An economic assessment of German fiscal equalization schemes since 1970: what prospects for a unified Germany", Institute of Transport Economics, Université Lumière, Lyon, France.

[3] *Ibid.*

The amount of funds for vertical allocation has been reduced from 770 to 520 million euros annually starting from 2005.

Always starting from 2005, funds transferred to Bremen and Saarland (traditional recipients among West German *Länder*) because of their 1990s budgetary crisis have been discontinued.

The allocation of funds that East German states receive from the central government to improve their economic performance has been set at 10.5 billion euros in 2005 and will be gradually lowered over the following years to a low point of 2 billion euros in 2019 (Werner, 2003). Finally, the central government takes over all annual debt repayments of the 'German Unity Fund', so that the western *Länder* will be relieved of this burden.

Germany's Solidarity Pact II has been passed also because of complaints arising from three western states to the Constitutional Court. They did not want to carry on persistently being donor states in the financial equalisation system, which was always in favour of the same states (eastern *Länder*). This clearly shows that a theoretical scheme (as the German Federalism was) cannot be applied *per se*, but needs to be linked with the actual setting and, if necessary, renewed. However, more importantly, this shows the influence that political and social factors have had on the current breakdown in the German fiscal setting. In fact, people's discontent for the all too heavy financial burden in the aforementioned three *Länder*, due to the original fiscal equalisation system, influenced their appeal to the Constitutional Court, and the political weight of such states surely influenced the reform implementation.

The analysis of the German unification shows that disregarding political factors halts the understanding of a given fiscal setting: here a lesson can be drawn from the German experience for the Fiscal Federalism theory, which underestimates them.

4.1.5. *Assessing Results of Unification and Its Lessons for Fiscal Federalism Theory*

To achieve the uniformity of living conditions in the whole of Germany, many efforts have been made in the East, in particular in the fields of infrastructure and environmental modernisation, through interventions to reduce pollution, to build a modern telecommunications network and to improve the public administration system.

As for the eastern industrial sector, the situation is still contrasted. Competitiveness improved as shown by the rises in the export quota (*i.e.* the companies' proportion of foreign sales as part of their total turnover) (Bertsch, 2002) from 11.8 per cent in 1995 to 21.2 per cent in 2000. The improvement in this sector was also possible because of the increase in investments, whose amount, from 1995 to 1999, was double in the East that of the West. However, productivity in the new *Länder* is still lower than in the West. Some of the reasons for this are the relative inferiority in management culture, in organisation and the lack of big companies in the East that leads to a weaker position of eastern firms in the international markets. If it is true that, as aforementioned, the export quota in the East doubled from 1995 to 2000, it is also true that it is still largely lower than the West one, that was 37.5 per cent in 2000 as Bertsch (2002) points out.

In addition, a large gap between industrial sectors in the two parts of Germany still remains regarding innovation and R&D. The main reason is the low presence of big companies in the East and the vast majority of medium-sized firms, which, in many cases, are not able to face the high costs to finance Research and Development. An adopted successful solution is the creation of networks of firms in order to share such costs.

Furthermore, the dramatic problem of East Germany is, still in recent years, unemployment, which is twice as high as in the West (according to the Federal Foreign Office, in 2002, in West Germany the unemployment rate stood at 7.6 per cent and in East Germany at 17.7 per cent).

Concluding, since unification East Germany has already made some steps towards attaining the western economic level, but years will still be required to really equalise the standards of living in the two parts of the country.

As highlighted, the German unification determined a new fiscal setting in the country. The phenomenon was characterised by great inventiveness in the various forms of aid provided. They used several financial means, not only grants but also bonds, direct investments from West to East and raises in taxes in the West. Moreover, indirect forms of aid were provided too, for example through the THA, a body created to help firms in their convergence to western standards and economies and in creating or improving their management culture to guide them towards privatisation. We can remark that the process was very dynamic, with many changes in fiscal settings over time, like the exclusion of eastern states from the fiscal equalisation until 1995 and the reform of this latter in 2001, because it was no longer applicable in a setting that saw such a big imbalance in the financial burden distribution, due to unification.

But the main feature of the German setting after unification is the predominance of political and social factors in influencing economic policy decision, above all pressures to save jobs, which led to measures like social vouchers or unemployment insurance but also to much more. In fact, for example through the THA, the government decided, under social grounds, to let some eastern firms operate even in deficit, at least at the beginning, to preserve jobs. But more importantly, they decided on a rate of conversion of 1:1, with the aim of maintaining the purchasing power parity between the Ost Mark and the DM, as a consequence of massive demonstrations in the East.

Referring back to our problematic, the analysis of section 4.1 shows that a theoretical scheme of Fiscal Federalism interacts with the particular setting where it is observed. In this section, a first lesson for the theory of Fiscal Federalism can be drawn: this latter ignores political factors which the analysis of reality shows being of great importance; such factors have to be taken into account to make the Fiscal Federalism perspective applicable in reality.

4.2. Comparing German Unification and European Enlargement

The aim of this section is to highlight similarities and differences between the German federal system and the EU, focusing in particular on the comparison between German unification of 1990 and the EU enlargement of 1st of May 2004. The question that will lead our reasoning through this section is the following: are there any good and exportable lessons drawn from national experiences for the EU? We answer positively. To do so, we concentrate on lessons one can draw from the German experience.

4.2.1. The EU Structure and the German Federal Model

The EU may be described as a system of multi-level governance, where sovereignty rights are shared and divided between supranational, national and sub-national institutions (Börzel, 2003; Marks and Hooghe, 2001).

At present, the EU already has some features of a federal state, which is a state with two or more levels of government shaping the same political system and taking part independently in the decision-making process. In particular, federal units can really influence it through a Chamber that represents them. The EU already shows some of these features, for example the presence of at least two orders of government, acting directly towards their own citizens, the presence of 'shared government' in areas where the jurisdiction of the EU and the Member States overlap (Börzel, 2003) and the representation of smaller states.

So, with German unification, the eastern states joined a Federation, with the enlargement, the CEECs (Central and Eastern European Countries) joined a system of multi-level governance being not a mature federation but having some federal features. In particular, the 'shared competencies' and the representation of smaller states (federal units) are two features that bring the EU federal structure nearer to the German federal model, which is a model of cooperative federalism (Börzel, 2003).

The literature on federalism usually distinguishes between two ideal-type models, going back to different interpretations of Montesquieu's ideas about organizing political power as *séparation des pouvoirs* and *distribution des pouvoirs* (Börzel, 2003). *Séparation des pouvoirs* or dual federalism is represented mainly by the USA, each level of government has an autonomous sphere of responsibility and, for each sector, one tier of government has both legislative and executive power. Thus, here the separation of powers is clearly a vertical one. The federal units cooperate with the central government voluntarily through intergovernmental conferences and have fiscal autonomy and independent sources of revenue.

The second model, *distribution des pouvoirs* or cooperative federalism, mainly represented by Germany, is called 'cooperative' because it is based on the consent of all the public institutions, which take part to the execution of a task. It is characterised by the division of labour among different levels of government, each of them taking an active part in the decision-making process and being represented by a Chamber of the political system.

In general, as for taxation and rates, the central level makes the laws and the federal units are responsible for implementing them (Börzel, 2003). But the main feature of this model of Federalism is not only the sharing of legislative and executive competencies but also the sharing of tax yields, with a redistribution system from financial stronger federal units to financial weaker federal units.

At present, the EU presents some elements that are closer to cooperative federalism, in particular to German federalism, rather than to dual federalism. In fact the sub-central units (the *Länder* for Germany and Member States for the EU) are not 'mere administrative agents' of the central government but were created before the creation of the *Bund*/EU. Moreover, they still maintain an important role today, being represented in the Council of the EU, (like in Germany where the *Länder* are represented in the *Bundesrat*) with a voting power based on their population size and a veto power on financial issues. Another important similarity is obviously the share of competencies between the central and the state level (the EU and Member States – the Federation and *Länder*). As for the EU, the European Treaties allocate jurisdiction and resources especially to the two main orders of government, that is the EU and Member States; such Treaties are not unilaterally amendable by one order of government alone, but require the endorsement by the governments and a given proportion of the voters or of a majority in the legislatures of the Member States (Börzel, 2003). Speaking about Germany, as noticed above, *Bund* and *Länder* share responsibilities both for expenditure and revenue legislation. The Constitution specifies the assignment of revenues to the *Bund* and *Länder* and major revisions in federal financial arrangements can only be made by amending the Constitution, which requires a two-thirds majority in both the *Bundestag* and the *Bundesrat* (Rodden, 2000).

Another similarity is that, both in Germany and in the EU, political decisions require a strong consensus. In fact, in the first case the *Bundesrat* possesses an absolute veto on all federal legislation affecting the *Länder*. In practice, about sixty per cent of all bills fall into this category. In the second case precise percentages of consensus are required, for example when dealing with the endorsement of the European Treaties.

On the other hand, differences between German federalism and the EU can also be pointed out. Firstly, the lack of a real counterweight to the Council in the EU institutions, which is instead present in the German model, where the power of the *Bundesrat*, representing the *Länder*, is counterweighted by the *Bundestag*, that represents the Federation. Because of this deficiency, at the EU level there is a risk of stronger prevalence of territorial interests with regards to European interests. Moreover, in the EU there is no real system of party integration, which is instead present in Germany.

But the really important difference is due to the fact that German federation has a significant spending power, while the EU lacks a tax and spending capacity to guarantee redistribution and stabilisation (see Chapter 6).

4.2.2. Comparing Initial Conditions

West Germany had virtually no time to prepare for the unprecedented economic adventure of unification. Nevertheless, at that moment, its economic situation was very good. From 1986 to 1990, German exporters achieved the highest balance of trade surplus, 305.75 billion euros (Prey, 1995) and FRG investments on equipment increased more than in the previous twenty years. West Germany exhibited a deflation after five consecutive years of seeing decreases of inflation and budget deficits and, after 1985, unemployment had been decreasing at an increasing rate.

As for the EU(15), according to the European Commission Spring 2004 Economic Forecasts, economic growth of the euro area rose by 0.4 per cent in the third quarter of 2003 and by 0.3 per cent in the fourth quarter. After a period of stagnation, it showed a moderate rise in domestic demand and a surge in exports. Yet, compared to 2002, the euro area exports (intra and extra) of goods and services did not grow at all in 2003, but the carryover for 2004 is 1.1 pp. As for the euro, it appreciated by 10 per cent over the past year. Investments, after a period of contraction, in the fourth quarter of 2003 had a sharp upturn at 0.6 per cent. Furthermore, in the last quarter of 2003 industrial production increased by 0.5 per cent (compared to the previous year) in the euro area and by 0.1 per cent in the whole of the EU. After three consecutive quarters of sharp contraction, output in the agricultural sector expanded again in the fourth quarter of 2003.

One of the problems of EU governments is their spending, which continued to increase at an annualised rate of 2.4 per cent in the second half of last year. This happened for example because of the rescuing of highly indebted public or private companies and of the picking-up in public orders for infrastructure and defence.

We can now distinguish an important difference between German unification and the EU enlargement, which lies in the starting conditions of the country: on the one hand, FRG was, in 1990, in an economic situation not far from excellent, on the other hand, the EU(15) showed only a slow recovery a few months before enlargement. Another difference is also clear: the possibility of unifying Germany came suddenly, it was forced through political unrest, and the government was reactive in its approach to unification. This contrasts with the planned or proactive EU approach to the enlargement.

East Germany in 1990 was in a bad economic situation, offering low quality products and inadequate services and lacking experience with western-style marketing and management strategies (Prey, 1995). In fact, as quoted before, in accordance with the equal right to work, the socialist governments had increasingly substituted labour for capital, creating a distortion in factor markets, with an abundance of labour and scarcity of capital. This abundance of labour led the GDR's industry to manufacture low-cost products with high labour intensity that however lacked in quality, a necessary feature to attract western trade partners. Moreover, it suffered from macroeconomic phenomena such as massive over-employment, an antiquated capital stock, poor infrastructure and an obsolete technology (Prey, 1995).

As for the accession countries, the European Commission Spring 2004 Economic Forecasts remark that private consumption increased by about 4.5 per cent in 2003 and in particular in the Baltic States, Hungary and the Czech Republic. The purchasing power of households was supported by several factors: low inflation, that was at the level of the euro area in the accession countries as a whole (2.1 per cent), increased borrowing, as a result of the development of the banking system, and anticipated spending because of the expectation of price rises in 2004. In contrast, investment was weak (except in the Baltic States), because of the global situation and the stalling reform process in these countries. Exports did well, in spite of the lack of demand in the EU; this happened because they are benefiting from the foreign direct investments of the past (Slovakia in particular). Employment declined, particularly in Poland, in 2003, unemployment rate remained high at 14.3 per cent on average. Most governments balances in accession countries turned out better than expected. Only the Czech Republic deficit significantly rose. On average, the general government deficit in the CEECs is estimated to be 5.7 per cent of GDP in 2003, ranging from a surplus in Estonia to a deficit of 12.9 per cent of GDP in the Czech Republic. On the other hand, the accession countries suffer from limited resources, needing infrastructure and social programmes.

We can observe that both the new *Länder* and the accession countries emerged from socialist regimes characterised by a centrally planned economy but with an important difference: while in East Germany such a regime had just fallen at the time of unification, in the new Member States the transformation into a market economy has already, at least partly, taken place, or at least begun, before their access into the EU (Busch, Müller, 2004).

A further similarity can be outlined. As described above, the eastern *Länder* economic development in 1990 was lower than the western one. The same applies for the CEECs. In 2003, their levels of income on average barely reached the 40 per cent of the EU(15) average. Analysing GDP, we can distinguish a first subset of more advanced countries, with per capita GDP ranging from 60 to 90 per cent of the EU(15) average (Cyprus, Slovenia and the Czech Republic), a second subset of middle income-economies (Malta, Hungary and Slovakia), with per capita GDP ranging from 50 to 60 per cent of the EU(15) average, and a last subset of backward countries, whose GDPs are comprised in the range of 20 to 40 per cent (Poland, Estonia, Lithuania, Latvia, Bulgaria and Romania).

4.2.3. Advantages and Problems of German Unification and the EU Enlargement

Both German unification and the EU enlargement have led to a significant increase in territory and population. German unification has led, according to Prey (1995), to an increase of almost 44 per cent in territory and of more than 26 per cent in population, whereas the last European enlargement has added ten countries and increased population by approximately 107 million (roughly 30 per cent). With unification, the western German legal, economic and social system was extended to the new states. Furthermore, East Germany joined the European Common Market, it could therefore trade on new markets, finally allowing the West German social security system to spread out to the population in the East. In the EU enlargement case, the new Member States are now an integrant part of the European Common Market and trade will benefit this.

Yet, while the EU(15) was the main trading partner of the new Member States already before the 2004 enlargement, absorbing roughly 68 per cent of their total exports, East Germany's trade before 1990 had mainly occurred with the other communist block countries. It was based on agreements among these nations that assured outlet markets to eastern German products independently of their quality standards. In 1989, 72.6 per cent of East German exports went to the eastern block countries: 40.3 per cent to the USSR and 32.3 per cent to the other Member States (Prey, 1995).

As a result of the enlargement, the European trade market is made-up of 25 countries and the European Union is a bigger player in the World Trade Organisation and in other trade-related international bodies. Trade liberalisation can take place in the enlarged Europe with the break-up of residual tariffs and non-tariffs (essentially anti-dumping) protection and the application by new members of the same common external tariffs at the existing EU countries as well as the trade agreement with other areas (Behir, Fontagné and Zanghieri, 2003). A second meaning of enlargement is that economic integration brings about a convergence in product quality. There is one market for firms of all 25 countries and consumers will benefit from the quality of products available in CEECs, catching up rapidly with the EU(15) standards.

Here, an important difference between the two phenomena is outlined: as noted above, at the moment of unification, there was an enormous gap between East and West Germany in the quality of standards of products, this gap can be smaller for the acceding countries. There are at least two reasons for this: firstly, while the unification took place only one year after the fall of the Berlin Wall, giving no time to strengthen the East German economy, in the enlargement case, the new states had much more time to restructure, at least partly, their economies. Furthermore, always because of the difference in the moment of occurrence of the two phenomena, West Germany did not practically have the time to transfer money to the East before unification, while the EU(15) helped the new Member States also before 1st of May 2004, through specific programmes in order to prepare them better for enlargement. Such programmes are: Sapard programme (Special Accession Programmes for Agriculture and Development), ISPA (Infra-Structural Policies for

Pre-Accession) and Phare programme (Poland and Hungary Action for the Reconstruction of the Economies).

The first one was introduced to modernise agriculture and food industry in central and eastern European countries, to improve product quality and to promote respect for the environment. The second one wanted to help the CEECs to promote infrastructures projects in the areas of transport and environment, in order to make infrastructures compatible with those of the EU(15). Finally, the Phare programme supported investments for the modernisation and adaptation of the CEECs economies administrations to Community standards.

Between 2000 and 2003, a total of 3.12 billion euros per year was transferred as pre-accession assistance to the accession countries, half through the Phare programme, a third through ISPA and the remaining through Sapard.

Using these programmes, the EU(15) tried to reduce the gap with the CEECs' economies also before the enlargement, trying to avoid the repetition of the situation of FRG immediately after unification, that forced it, notably in order to keep political stability, to provide such extensive financial transfers.

4.2.4. Supporting New Comers: the Exchange Rate Issue

As for the exchange rate, a difference between the two situations can be outlined, in fact with unification the currency area of DM was immediately extended to the new *Länder* and East Berlin with a rate of conversion of 1:1, while the CEECs will not immediately adopt the euro.

As aforementioned (see paragraph 4.1.3), the extension of the DM currency area had great consequences on East Germany's economic performance. The objectives they wanted to carry out with monetary unification were: to provide East German people with a starting financial basis, to put in liquidity for daily exchanges and to support GDR firms. But the problem concerned the real value of the Ost Mark. Choosing a rate of conversion of 1:1 for payments and financial assets would provide East Germany with purchasing power and liquidity. On the other hand, with the conversion of wages at 1:1, they would lose their advantage over low labour costs, with a consequent higher cost for firms, leading to higher unemployment. This would lead to the increase of social security payments and to an increased budget deficit.

Despite all of these considerations, the FRG government decided on a conversion rate of 1:1, with the aim of maintaining the purchasing power parity, fearing the socio-political instability that a different decision would lead to.

As for the accession countries of the EU, learning from the German experience, they should take care of consequences at the moment of the euro adoption. The German experience shows that such a decision cannot be taken without consideration for political and social pressures. In the GDR, demonstrations had an undeniable influence on the conversion rate decision and probably some pressure will be present also at the moment of the euro adoption in the CEECs.

Another remark can be made. If in the German unification case, the financial burden on the West could also be linked to the shared identity of people (all being German), this is more difficult to say in the European case. Learning from German unification, the walk of the CEECs should firstly be towards an adjustment of political and economic criteria, to make their purchasing power more similar to the West before taking decisions with regards the euro conversion rate.

4.2.5. Supporting Newcomers: Solidarity Fiscal Settings

It is surely possible to stress benefits that East Germany received from unification: massive transfers from the West, in terms of German GDP, roughly 4 per cent throughout the 1990s (Busch, Müller, 2004); to finance pensions, health expenditures, unemployment benefits; to support businesses, tax subsides and to build or modernise the infra-structure system. The THA (*Treuhandanstalt*) was able to achieve the privatisation of more than 10,000 companies in a period of about five years and, in spite of mistakes, this attracted capital and management know-how from FRG and from abroad.

Particularly remarkable was the rebuilding of infrastructures, with the improvement of roads, railways and the telecommunications system, the preserving of castles and churches in the East and the 'renaissance' of Berlin as capital city of the unified Germany.

Yet, something went wrong with unification. For example, despite the big amounts of transfers, no help was provided at a psychological level, which led to a damage in the self-confidence of Easterners and, worse, encouraged dependency because, relying on the transfers, some people developed a habit of not even trying to help themselves (Walter, 2002).

Secondly, there was the problem of 'old property rights'. The FRG government decided to solve it through the restitution for the majority of private property claims. Expropriated people by the Nazi-regime and by the GDR government regained properties proving that ownership was available and unchanged. Yet, there were some problems in this method: for example, multiple-owners often had an interest in the same property, in which cases, compensation was used. Secondly, the system of restitution provoked a very long judicial process. This, on the one hand, damaged the self-esteem of Easterners who had taken care of properties for decades and were now 'deprived' (Walter, 2002) and, on the other hand, forced old owners to have to wait for a long time for restitution. Financial compensation would probably have avoided such problems.

Moreover, unification extended the social benefits system, whose costs were already prohibitive for FRG alone, to a further 16 million people in the East, making the situation impossible to be sustained in the long term. The bad general economic situation of the GDR must be kept in mind. For a while, the boom in the construction sector, because of the demand for infrastructures (rebuilding), saved the situation, even allowing for the possibility of growth in the first period after unification, although the real situation came out later.

But in Germany, at the very beginning, decision-makers under-estimated the real financial burden of unifying two countries with so many differences in economic, social and political fields. On the contrary, they considered the financial needs of GDR as transitory and considered unification as ultimately self-financing, with the initial increase in public spending financed largely by government borrowing (Von Hagen and Strauch, 1999). This may be partly due to the good economic situation of FRG at the end of the 1980s and to the increase in government revenues in the early period of unification.

Thus, despite the real situation, the unification Treaty stated that the living standards in the East had to reach those in the West as soon as possible. The policy of equalisation of living standards generated a need for financial transfers from the western *Länder*, through the federal government, to the eastern *Länder*.

Here a parallel with the EU situation can be highlighted: in both cases, motivation for financial transfers is based on the realisation of faster integration, whose benefits would be reaped by respectively the whole of Germany and the whole of the EU. Furthermore, in both cases we remark an increase in centralised tendencies. As for Germany, the federal government increased its role as a mediator between West and East Germany in the financial aid policy. As for the EU, the logic of market integration and a strong preference for preserving the welfare state favours an increasing centralisation of national policy competencies at the EU level.

As noticed above, at the beginning they did not consider that carrying out unification would need long-term financial transfers. At a certain moment, it became impossible to deny the additional financial needs of East Germany but the federal government had promised, for political reasons, to finance unification with no additional fiscal burden for its citizens. To solve this problem, in 1991, they introduced the 'solidarity surcharge' on personal income tax, assuring this was a temporary measure, but, after an interruption in 1992, they reintroduced it in 1995, at a rate of 7.5 per cent. Always in 1992, a one-point increase in the VAT rate was also decided. Later on, the federal government stated increases also in the mineral oil tax and in the insurance tax rates and, in particular, in income and corporate income tax laws. From 1991 and 1997, a long sequence of tax initiatives affecting almost any major tax categories occurred.

Another aspect of the matter is that there is no guarantee that financial transfers would let achieve the goal of a faster and widespread convergence. German unification exemplifies this case. As noticed above, this enlargement has been very expensive, with roughly 4 per cent of the German GDP transferred throughout the 1990s to the East (Busch, Müller, 2004) but, in spite of this, the gap between the two parts of the country is still wide.

Continuing comparing German unification and the EU enlargement, in the first case financial transfers to the East increased more and more. As for the EU, according to the Spring 2004 Economic Forecasts, including pre-accession aid, about 31 billion euros (about 7 per cent of the new countries GDP) is available in payment appropriations in the period 2004-2006 for these latter. As for the CEECs' contribution to the EU budget, it is expected to be of about 13.5 billion euros, leaving them as net beneficiaries overall. So, as in the unification case, the EU budget will give to the new states more than it will receive. But with an important difference: the EU has earmarked less than 10 per cent of its total budget until 2006 for the CEECs', an area of 75 million inhabitants, only one tenth of German transfers to the new *Länder* (Barnevik, 2002), which have only 16 million inhabitants. One explanation of the bigger size of transfers in Germany can also be found in the strong common identity of German people, which contrasts with the strong national and even sometimes nationalistic differences between new and old European countries.

Another reason against an excessive financial help is also the possible danger it can create. In fact, it may result in a disincentive for lower levels of government to avoid an excessive deficit and to pursue expansion of their revenues. Because they know there is the central government that helps them anyway, they could be not stimulated to take such responsibilities upon themselves.

Still about transfers, a German mistake which the EU has to try to avoid deals with the way of using transfers. For example in Germany, the privatisation of the state-owned retail chain was made selling wholly to some western companies, ensuring them the access to the eastern market but not *vice versa*. Always because of privatisation, the biggest percentage of the eastern productive capital was under western control. In a nutshell, they did not use transfers mainly to improve the existing capacity in the East but to increase capacity utilisation in the West. The EU should not make such a mistake. A remarkable attempt to avoid it is the use of the aforementioned programmes to improve the CEECs economic situation previous to the enlargement.

4.2.6. The Migration Issue

The German unification can be considered an informative experiment for integrating an economically less developed country into a modern western economy (Busch and Müller, 2004). As pointed out previously, unemployment was a huge concern in East Germany after unification. As a consequence, migration towards the West began. Despite the efforts to equalise the two parts of the country as soon as possible, disparities remained very deep, increasing the incentive to migrate, making migration turn into a negative phenomenon because it was excessive.

The phenomenon of migration can be analysed in the EU enlargement situation too. According to Sinn, the solution of harmonisation of social systems to reduce it would impose a excessive burden equal to 5-7 per cent of the western European GDP, which no one in the West would accept. He proposes the solution of limiting access to the benefits of the western social systems for the period of adjustment of the CEECs to western standards of living.

But the aim we want to achieve here is not to propose a solution or to judge that a solution is better than another. Our aim is rather to stress that migration is bound to be an important phenomenon the EU should not to disregard or underestimate. The following table tries to summarise the findings so far.

4.3. Conclusion

Chapter 4 draws lessons from the German experience for the EU and for the Fiscal Federalism theory (respectively dimensions 1 and 2 of the problematic pointed out in Chapter 1).

In section 4.1, a detailed analysis of the German unification has been outlined. A first aspect we can remark is that the unification triggered great changes in Germany, not only territorially or demographically, but especially in the financial and economic fields. Secondly, the federal government approach to unification was reactive to the political unrest following the fall of the Wall and was characterised by the very different forms of aid provided to the East. On the financial side, not only grants were used, but also bonds, direct investments from West to East and rises in taxes in the West. This latter measure, indeed, was put off as much as possible, because it had been promised, on political grounds, not to increase the fiscal burden of citizens. Indirect forms of aid were provided too, like the creation of the THA (*Treuhandanstalt*).

Table 4.1: Pros and Cons of German Unification

	PROS	CONS
1) Social system	Extension of the western German legal, economic and social security system to the new states. Extension of the currency area of the DM with a conversion rate of 1:1	Extension of the social benefits system, whose costs were already prohibitive for FRG alone, to further 16 million people in the East, making the situation impossible to sustain in the long term
2) Forms of aid	Massive transfers from the West (in terms of German GDP, roughly 4% during the 1990s.) to finance pensions, health expenditures, unemployment benefits, to support businesses, tax subsides and to build or modernise the infrastructure system	Despite all the efforts made, not only through financial means but also through the creation of THA, to help firms in particular for saving jobs, unemployment was a huge concern in GDR (with a top of 1.7 million unemployed people in GDR in 1992)
3) Movement of people	Free movement of people because of the fall of frontiers	Excessive migration from East to West Germany (between 1989 and 1990, almost 600,000 people, roughly 3.7% of eastern population)
4) Infrastructure system	Rebuilt of the infrastructure, with the improvement of roads, railways and the telecommunications system. Preserving of castles and churches in the East and the 'renaissance' of Berlin as capital city of the unified Germany	The economy collapse of the GDR to face. For a while, the boom in the construction sector, because of the need to rebuild infrastructure and the work to preserve monuments, saved the situation, making even possible a growth in the first period after unification, but later the real situation came out
5) Property rights	Decision to solve the problem of expropriated people by the Nazi-regime and by the communist government	'Old property rights' matter: choice to solve it through the system of restitution, which provoked a very long judicial process. Damage to Easterns who had taken care of properties for decades and now were 'deprived' and to old owners who had to wait for a long time for restitution

Source: author

Referring back to our problematic, the analysis of German unification shows the deep interaction between the theoretical scheme of 'German Fiscal Federalism' and the setting where this scheme is applied (dimension 2). The German setting changed over time because of unification and its consequences, which firstly led to the exclusion of the eastern *Länder* from the fiscal equalisation system until 1995 and secondly led to its reform in 2001. In fact, the unification determined a heavy financial burden, which, according to the original fiscal setting, always fell on the same states (Baden-Württemberg, Bayern and Hessen in particular). After their complaint to the Constitutional Court, it became clear that the original scheme was not applicable anymore in the German setting, in consequence of the excessive imbalance in the financial burden distribution it created.

The analysis of German unification shows the big influence of political and social factors not only on economic policy decisions (*e.g.* the '1 = 1' exchange rate) but also on the form of application of German Federalism. In fact, people's discontent for the overly strenuous financial burden in the aforementioned three *Länder*, due to the original fiscal equalisation system, was a factor that influenced their appeal to the Constitutional Court and the political weight of these *Länder* influenced the implementation of the *Finanzausgleich* reform of 2001.

The main lesson one can draw from the German unification experience for the theory of Fiscal Federalism is to take into account political factors, because disregarding them means that such a theory cannot be applied in practice (dimension 2 of the problematic).

The hostility of the above mentioned three *Länder* finds a symmetry in the actual difficulties next faced by the determination of Financial Perspectives at the EU where OMS fear to lose the advantages they enjoy so far. This is one reason which led to the non-ratification of French and Dutch Constitution Treaty.

Section 4.2 compares German unification to the 1st of May 2004 EU enlargement. The two phenomena approximate one another as for significance and difficulty. Matters to be faced are numerous: transfers to the CEECs, the process for the introduction of the euro, migration, trade development, unification of different 'identities of people' and so on.

The main lesson the German unification suggests is that the EU has to keep in mind the real situation of the accession countries. This includes being aware of the fact that political and social factors cannot be left aside when taking decisions of economic policy. The German experience also suggests that, sometimes, decisions of economic policy, which can be unpopular, are necessary, if one does not want the future situation to worsen.[4] Despite the undeniable positive consequences of unification, it is also true that, still after more than ten years, the national

---

[4] An example occurred again under our eyes with Chancellor Schroeder. Facing a severe slowdown of German economy, he was forced to introduce unfair reforms that costed its place during last federal elections.

German debt continues to grow to finance unification. To avoid the repetition of the German mistakes, assistance to new EU states have to be aimed at giving them a real chance of access to western markets and, above all, have to account for the fact that convergence of CEECs towards the EU(15) is likely to be a long process (dimension 1 of the problematic).

Like after unification, the present situation of Germany is very difficult, thus important decisions, and sometimes not easy to be accepted from a strictly social point of view, are needed. In fact, during the spring of 2005, North-Rhine elections took place in Westphalia, which resulted in an important victory (44.8 per cent) for the Christian Democrats (CDU) in a state where Social Democrats (the old Chancellor party) had always won. The loss in this *Land* led the Chancellor to announce early elections in autumn 2005, which eventually lead to the victory of the Christian Democrats. In particular, high unemployment rates have gradually been eating away voters confidence in SPD coalition, this is the core problem to be faced with respect to the sluggish German economy.

One solution proposed by the CDU coalition has been an increase in VAT from 16 per cent to 18 per cent in case of victory, that is a rise in taxes, like what happened some years after unification.

Another lesson one can draw from the German unification for the theory of Fiscal Federalism (dimension 2) is that for this latter the unification and the enlargement are theoretically equivalent, since it considers them as additions of new territories to previous entities. The analysis of section 4.2 shows that this is an incomplete way to see such phenomena. This is not the case as there are important differences between the two assimilation processes. One of the most interesting ones concerns the lack of a strong European identity as compared to the strong common identity of the two German sisters. Another difference deals with the financial effort made (in the case of unification) and planned (as for enlargement) in order to face the two events. The German one is higher than the European Union one. Notably, the higher financial effort made in Germany reflects the importance of historic and political factors. Whereas both events seem to have a similar 'historical' nature (but wider in the EU, and more intense in Germany), the greater 'financial generosity' comes from a correspondingly greater political will.

In conclusion, the German unification experience suggests that, to face all of the several aspects the EU enlargement involves, (*i.e.* transfers to the CEECs, the exchange rate, unification of different 'identities' of people, etc.) decision-makers have to take into account the entire complexity of the phenomenon (dimension 1).

Finally, it is also possible to underline some of the flaws of the European policy and budget. Comparing the EU and Germany from the political and budgetary point of view, we can draw lessons for the EU (dimension 1). Germany exemplifies a state with a real representation of federal units in a 'second' Chamber. This guarantees the share of competencies between higher and lower levels of government, given that about 60 per cent of the bills require the *Bundesrat* consensus to be passed. If on the one hand, it is true also that the EU has a Chamber of representation for the Member States (the Council), on the other hand its ambitions are completely constrained by the sub-level of government (unlike in real federal states) because unanimity is the voting rule. Qualified majority voting would be necessary in most fields, including fiscal matters. In consequence of this situation, the main problem is that the EU has no spending capacity, while the German federal government has a real spending capacity that it uses also for redistributive purposes, making transfers to the *Länder* and municipalities (for example grants paid to financially weak *Länder* to raise their fiscal capacity to 99.5 per cent of the states average and to reduce fiscal disparities). At the EU level, the Council could be transformed into a Chamber of the States with real powers of taking fiscal decisions; the European Parliament could be given the right to take part in decision-making on an equal footing with the Council. In fact, the European Parliament is the Chamber, which represents the will of citizens that directly elect its members, thus, it has to concur with decisions both in terms of spending and revenues. With a reform allowing for Council voting by majority and a Commission with real executive powers, the economic policy could still be managed mainly by the Member States but with an effective coordination at the European level. The unanimity voting rule on the one side and the small size of the budget on the other side are the obstacles to remove. The issues of the voting rule within the European Council and of the EU budget will be dealt with in more depth in Chapter 6.

Table 4.2: Comparison between German Unification and the EU Enlargement

	SIMILARITIES	DIFFERENCES
1) Typology of the 'accessed' states before and after unification/ enlargement	Acquisition of states stem from a socialist regime characterised by a central planned economy.	In East Germany the socialist regime had just fallen at the time of unification, in the NMS the transformation into a market economy has already, at least partly, taken place before their access into the EU.
	In both cases the new Member States have joined a federal structure.	This structure is a real Federation as for Germany and a system of multi-level governance with some federal features as for the EU.
2) Approach to unification/ enlargement and changes due to the phenomena	In both cases significant increase in territory and population: for Germany almost 44% in territory and more than 26% in population. For the EU: addition of ten countries and increase in population by approximately 107 million (roughly 30%).	Different approaches to the phenomena: the possibility of unifying Germany came quickly, it was forced through political unrest, and the government was reactive in its approach to unification. This contrasts to the planned or proactive EU approach to the enlargement.
3) Trade	Important advantages for the richest/'accessed' countries, for example new trade markets and, consequently, possible further trade development.	The EU(15) was the main trading partner of the NMS previous to the 2004 enlargement, absorbing roughly 68% of their total exports, while the East Germany's trade before 1990 had mainly occurred with the other communist block's countries.
	With unification and enlargement possibility of free movement of goods (across the whole Germany and in all the 25 countries of the Union) based on the market process.	Before unification, the GDR trade was based on agreements, which assured outlet markets for its products apart from their quality standard, which were very low. This gap in quality can be smaller for the CEECs because they had more time to restructure, at least partly, their economies before the enlargement.
4) Financial transfers	Financial transfers' motivation is based on the realisation of a faster and widespread integration, whose benefits would involve respectively the whole Germany and the whole EU.	There is no guarantee that financial transfers allow to achieve the goal of a faster integration. German unification exemplifies this case: in spite of the financial transfers, a gap between the two parts of the country is still present. The EU has the possibility not to repeat such a situation.
	FRG transferred big amounts to the East (roughly 4% of German GDP throughout the 1990s). The EU is transferring, between 2004 and 2006, 31 billion euros to the CEECs and receiving a lower contribution to the EU budget from them (13.5 billion euros). In both cases they transfer more than they receive.	The EU has earmarked less than 10% of its total budget until 2006 for CEECs, an area of 75 million inhabitants, only one tenth of German transfers to the new *Länder*, which have only 16 million inhabitants.

130

5) Currency	In both cases presence of a new currency: the DM for the new *Länder* and the euro for the CEECs.	With unification the currency area of DM was immediately extended to the new *Länder* and East Berlin with a rate of conversion of 1:1, while the CEECs will not adopt immediately the euro.
6) Centralist tendencies	Increase in centralist tendencies. As for Germany, the federal government increased its role as a mediator between West and East Germany in the financial aid policy. As for the EU, the logic of market integration and a strong preference for preserving the welfare state favours an increasing centralisation of national policy competencies at the EU level.	
7) Starting conditions		Difference in the starting conditions of the countries: FRG was, in 1990, in an economic situation not far from being excellent, the EU(15) showed only a slow recovery a few months before enlargement.

Source: author

CHAPTER 5

Learning from the Diversity
of National Political and Fiscal Experiences

Augusta BADRIOTTI, Margherita FORNASINI
and Clément VANEECLOO

Getting a clear picture of the diversity of the internal inter-governmental organisation(s) of EU Member States, both fiscal and political, is a difficult but rewarding task. The main obstacles to engaging in such a study are linked to methodological and data collection limitations inherent to any comparative study. However, this chapter shows that the exercise is 'worth the pain'. Before turning to the lessons one (EU policy-makers, scholars or citizens) may draw from national experiences, it seems useful to sum up some of our main findings so far.

Firstly, we showed that the agenda of the literature on Fiscal Federalism was at least legitimate and original, at most a *sine qua non* for anyone seeking to understand the current European debates. The EU is an ever-evolving polity. Relationships which are at the core of this process, both between levels of government and between jurisdictions at the same level, give rise to many conflicts, concerns or mutual benefits of a 'vital' nature. Consequently they are often, if not always, quoted in economic contributions to the European debate.

The real value-addition of the Fiscal Federalism perspective is to acknowledge explicitly the central importance of the vertical and horizontal restructuring of the public sector. The attempt to make it endogenous to the integration process should also be noted. However, it was argued, traditional Fiscal Federalism literature suffers from significant shortcomings. For instance, it tends to study fiscal settings in isolation to political variables. Moreover, despite numerous claims of applicability to all kinds of countries, both unitary and federal, it still suffers from a strong 'Anglo-Saxon type federation' bias.

Chapters 2 and 3 actually undertook a big 'reconstruction' process in order to allow useful lessons about the EU reality to be drawn from the dominant normative vision of Fiscal Federalism. They notably showed that political and organisational factors were pre-eminent in the design of the current European fiscal setting. Chapter 4 drew useful lessons from German Unification – a specific and one-off national experience – for the EU. For example, such things as historical cohesion, political will/imperatives were shown to be decisive in explaining the reforms of the German fiscal setting in the aftermath of unification.

All in all, previous chapters recurrently did three things: i) they criticised the reductionism of most normative contributions from the 'theory' of Fiscal Federalism, which constitutes a constant yardstick for many scholars in the field; ii) they emphasised the necessity to take into account the specificity of the European experience when one seeks to understand the actual EU fiscal setting. The leading role of political variables, traditionally eluded by Fiscal Federalism economists, were also underlined; iii) they suggested that the normative view also needed to encompass the latter, in order to keep its relevance and its 'potential status or label' as the general theory of intergovernmental relationships.

This empirical chapter is a natural continuation of the previous one, which was a clear example of the analytical usefulness of national examples. Here, the underlying idea is that, in order to understand the current process of an on-going and uncertain experience (that of the EU), it is necessary to grasp the lessons from more mature (but also man-made) national settings. A warning is however necessary: our analysis is comparative, positive and still superficial in some ways. Our perspective may disappoint statisticians or econometricians, but the lack of comparable data is partly responsible for such superficiality. Nevertheless, it still represents significant added-value. As much as possible, the underlying methodological choices or limitations of our analysis are explained at the beginning of the first section, or presented in the methodological appendix.

The following comparative study is interesting in many ways. First of all, it gives a wide picture of prevailing fiscal settings in the EU. Regrouping countries according to a set of precise political, fiscal and socio-economic criteria leads to the identification of various ideal-types. Intuitively, national fiscal settings matter for European integration at least for one reason. As individual Member States still retain their veto power on fiscal matters, national positions are likely to be determined by the internal fiscal organisation (their advantages and drawbacks, recent reforms, prevailing modes of coordination).

Once again, it is worth referring back to the dimensions of the relationship between theories and facts highlighted in Chapter 1. In the following chapter, we focus on dimensions 1, 2 and 5. We thus try to determine lessons from national experiences for the EU and for the Fiscal Federalism perspective. Additionally, we defend the idea that drawing lessons from the latter for national experiences is, above all, conditioned by an adequate incorporation of political and historical specificities.

Section 5.1 clarifies the scope and aims of our empirical framework, and insists on methodology and data collection issues. Section 5.2 identifies empirical 'regularities' and various European ideal-types. Section 5.3 interprets our results in a comparative way and draws some conclusions on the relevance of our setting for the Fiscal Federalism theory and fiscal settings. Section 5.4 concludes.

5.1. A Comparative and Constrained Empirical Framework

This section clarifies the aims of this empirical chapter. It also makes explicit the underlying arbitrary – but necessary – choices which had to be made. It presents some of the most salient methodological difficulties facing economists working in this field. It then goes on to introduce the various political, economic and socio-economic dimensions of national fiscal settings (experiences).

5.1.1. Aims, Choices and Methodological Concerns

Unfortunately, it is almost impossible to analyse in a comprehensive way the full range of issues implied by intergovernmental relationships in a given national fiscal setting. In a European-wide comparative study, this constraint has to be multiplied by 25, which, in turn, calls for the need to specify the scope and aims of our empirical investigation.

Our first aim is to get a picture as clear as possible of national fiscal settings. This includes the division of competencies, taxation, revenues, expenditures among the different levels of government. This also includes the main relationships between the latter, which are both numerous and complex. The previous chapters highlighted the potential role played by historical, political, and organisational factors in explaining national settings. As we argued, a fiscal federalist perspective ought to take the latter into account explicitly. Consequently, we include a set of political, institutional and socio-economic variables. For the time being, we consider some of these variables to be explanatory variables (of prevailing fiscal settings), others as control variables. However, as we shall see, neither such distinctions nor the direction of causalities is clear-cut.

However, this distinction has the merit to help identify various ideal-types. The criteria for classifying various national fiscal settings are *a priori* arbitrary, as no formal explanatory model was sketched beforehand. However, this is preceded by a one-to-one analysis of the various dimensions of the intergovernmental structural problem. The steps of this empirical method are well-identified and the relevance of various classifications is discussed.

This leads to our third aim. This consists in using such a loose and descriptive framework in order to identify '(ir)regularities' in the various fiscal settings of EU Member States. Indeed, what is true/holds for 25 EU countries is most likely to be true/hold for the EU as a whole. Most importantly, the construction of related indicators leads to the investigation of a set of correlations between the various dimensions: political, socio-economic and fiscal. As we will show, it provides evidence, which can improve the vision of traditional empirical debates, and backbones the main insights provided so far.

These national experiences, as such, allow to circumvent the scope of possibilities for the EU. Moreover, the pace and path of the integration process still depends on nation-states' authority and will, the latter being itself constrained by the features of national fiscal settings. Contrary to most of the highly prolific empirical literature, we made the arbitrary choice to undertake an exhaustive, comparative and to some extent 'superficial' analysis of European fiscal settings rather than a specific and in-depth one. This comes from the belief that comparative analysis constitutes a better source of information for the EU than any singular and well-documented case would ever be. Of course, our results do not pretend to constitute neither a set of hard evidence nor a series of clear and undisputable causal links. They should be seen as a set of presumptions, which may be of importance for the understanding of both national countries and the EU (*cf.* Chapter 6). Consequently, great rhetorical care will be placed on conclusions presented in section 5.4. The analysis of the fiscal settings of the 25 EU countries could be an endless task by itself. The same holds for their comparison. For example, comparing EU countries in pairs – a useful exercise as shown by Vaneecloo, Badriotti and Fornasini (2004) with regards to Italy and Belgium – would produce 300 contributions (*i.e.* 25x24/2). This just proves that any empirical analysis has to make difficult but necessary choices. We preferred to get a rough image of every EU countries (no one can be a specialist of all of them) rather than a precise picture of a few. Such cross-country wide-ranging evidence of EU countries is surprisingly scarce (see for example Darby *et al.*, 2003; OECD, 2002; COR, 2004) and mostly refers to the IMF Government Financial Statistics data basis. Consequently, this should be seen as a first step for future research in this promising field. Put differently, our methodology does not take into account all 'subtleties' of national systems and is constrained by the quality of available comparative data. Although such future research is likely to keep its descriptive status, it will be improved over time.

Two important methodological concerns should be kept in mind before investigating national fiscal settings. The first one relates to the difficulty of collecting relevant, satisfactory national data and uses them in a comparative framework. The lack of data is the first difficulty when trying to get an idea of the fiscal setting in a given country. This scarcity is more salient for new entrants and usually a bit less so for federal countries. This makes it difficult to get accurate data concerning sub-national levels of government. Worse, fiscal figures, labelled in the same way in different countries, often relate to different realities (either different kinds of expenditures, tax, or unfitting fiscal basis). Some countries label some specific spending as being sub-central just because the sub-central level is the last level of government through which the spending transits, even though choice/discretion on where, to whom, and how money should be spent belongs to the central level. Consequently, it is hard to find data coming from a homogeneous data set. This is particularly relevant for fiscal variables, where one gets very different figures according to the data definition. This often implies a certain amount of double-counting (for instance with regards to inter-governmental grants) or the oversight of important fiscal revenues or expenditures. Despite recent initiatives in cross-country data harmonisation such as the SEC 1995, lack of data, together with national accounting and historic fiscal specificities, lead to a scarcity of comparable data. Few data sets including all existing countries and on a wide number of variables are available (notable exceptions include the OECD, IMF and to a lesser extent the Eurostat data basis; but they are still limited). The data basis on which this chapter is drawn was hence constructed by using many sources, summarised in the Appendix.

The second methodological problem arises from the consideration of time. Indeed, our analysis applies to the current period, *i.e.* the beginning of the millennium. However, fiscal settings can only be understood in the context of the entirety of the (de)centralisation process. Existing data sets are in many cases too recent. Constructing new temporal data sets 'from scratch' is too time-consuming. Note that in most countries, the beginning of the decentralisation process often only really took-off in the 1970s, to accelerate again in the 1990s. But such a rough summary of the evolution over time of fiscal settings is obviously unsatisfactory. The same mixed records should be noticed regarding current reforms. For instance, although they have been 'voted' in many European countries (France, Italy, most CEECs, etc.), further reforms are still under way, being vertically negotiated by the various levels of government or encountering implementation problems. Their short-term outcomes are difficult to predict. The authors are, thus, conscious that a given fiscal setting (and reform) is only fully understood when one considers it as a part of a wider process, looking both back and looking ahead. Still, 'History' of the fiscal setting can also be partly captured by the present political and institutional variables.

5.1.2. Dimensions of Analysis

At various points, our work showed that a given fiscal setting is in fact something very broad and that it may owe as much to institutional, political and historical factors as it does to economic considerations (efficiency and equity criteria). To understand the actual degree of decentralisation or the inter-governmental structure in a given country, one needs to take many variables into account. For example, measuring a simple decentralisation index is not enough, but it is what is often done (World Bank, 2002; Wallis and Oates, 1988). Most comparative studies on decentralisation mainly focus on (a few) fiscal variables (*e.g.* tax autonomy, expenditures or spending assignments of regional/local government as a percentage of total public spending). The importance of the 'institutional' dimension is a good example. Faithful to the intuition (not a theory as such) in previous chapters, we argue that studying decentralisation in isolation, without acknowledging the institutional framework in which the latter operates, is likely to give a warped image of any fiscal setting. An example is that federal countries tend to give more prerogatives to regions than to localities, and that regions in federal countries tend to have more power than those in unitary states. However, this 'regularity' is becoming less and less relevant as some unitary States, such as France, Italy, the UK or Greece are also devolving an increasing amount of power to regional levels. Another example is the existence and nature of 'representatives and offices' of the Central state in regions. It is untrue to say that a country is not decentralised just because the 'central' State is responsible for most of the expenditure. In fact, the decisions of the representative of the Central state in 'power' in the region often depend on regional influence(s) from consumers, producers, voters or more generally citizens. He (she) often manages an efficient administrative network, gathering as much information about the preferences of his (her) jurisdiction's inhabitants as the regional body would in its place. In such a case, despite a strong 'formal' degree of centralisation, the State may be in fact very decentralised (*i.e.* 'de-concentrated') and very responsive/accountable to local or regional preferences and cost conditions (referring once again to the normative version of Fiscal Federalism).

The opposite holds if Central state policies heavily depend on the regional government's good will, such as in Belgium or Germany.[1] Conversely, a country where the region is responsible for most fields, on the ground, but where the Central government keeps the main regulatory power, a final say, or a revocation power, in most cases may not be as decentralised as it looks. Such examples are numerous and often concern such important competencies as education, health or social security. For instance, a foreign observer could think that education in France is a very decentralised competence. Formally, municipalities are responsible for *kindergarten* and primary schools, the *départements* are responsible for secondary schools (*collèges*), the *régions* are responsible for high schools (*lycées*) and the Central government is responsible for Universities. In fact, the reality is much more complicated. Indeed, the Central government still decides on the programmes, finances the main expenditure (teachers' salaries), and recruits the staff under national competitions. Sub-national authorities construct and maintain the buildings, provide grants to allow families to buy books, etc. Note that universities also historically benefit from a special autonomy status. This explains why so much attention/time should be devoted to data analysis/collection. This also explains why the normative view of Fiscal Federalism may be misleading: the initial theoretical configuration from which its logical deductions are derived is too simplistic. The hypotheses of clear decomposition of the Musgravian functions, clear and full accountability from all levels of government, higher level of information for lower levels, absence of distinction between policy-shaping and policy implementation (etc.) seem too removed from the reality(ies) the normative view is supposed to 'shed light on'.

Here, we build indicators that respectively include institutions and political variables, fiscal settings and control variables. Consequently, the analysis of European fiscal settings provided in the next sections draws on three interconnected dimensions. The first one is the politico-institutional dimension. As we show, one of the most striking features of European countries is the diversity they exhibit in terms of institutional and organisational forms. This heterogeneity makes any comparison difficult. However, acknowledging such a diversity also constitutes a *sine qua non* for anybody aiming at understanding in-depth a given fiscal setting. The most obvious example most probably comes from

---

[1] Belgium is a good example of the 'real complexities which do not appear in simple data' since regional levels (Regions and Communities) are responsible for the implementation of most Central tasks, and the discretionary interpretation of central regulations from various jurisdictions (*e.g.* for Regions Wallonia, Flanders and Brussels) is huge. On the other hand, the social security system, job benefits... are still managed under the Central rule.

Eastern Europe. How to understand CEECs current fiscal framework without taking into account the fact that they were subject to the rule of a heavy-centrally planned socialist structure? How to understand the comparative homogeneity of these countries without acknowledging the standardising logic of the USSR? Similarly, how to understand the relatively weak role played by localities in Federal States without highlighting the conversely high status given by their constitution to the regions? Examples are numerous; and, obviously, they cannot be captured in a single summary data. The table in the next section presents our selection of such institutional and organisational indicators. The selected variables to capture the political dimension are: type of country, existence of special status region, number of levels of government, administrative tradition, to which we add a number of institutional interaction variables, including the constitutional/legal taxing power of each level (*e.g.* potential for differentiation power with respect to tax rates and basis).

Another basic feature of fiscal settings is the vertical distribution of tasks among levels of government. Once again, knowing who does what, *i.e.* which competencies are attributed to which level of government, is not easy. In fact, many competencies are shared among them. We sub-divide these tasks under various headings ('regalian' functions, health, education, economic development, etc.). Then we turn to the traditional study of fiscal powers regarding revenues and expenditures. Beside this, as for the European examples presented in Chapters 2 and 3, we focus on fiscal inter-governmental interactions related to questions of autonomy, solidarity and stability.

Our third and final dimension is in fact a set of socio-economic variables, which constitute a number of control variables. This includes the size (as proxied by population), the wealth, the macroeconomic performance, and what can be labelled as the potential for conflict in each country, as measured by our cohesion index. Correspondingly it is difficult to identify the precise nature of selected variables as being either explanatory variables of a given decentralisation trend or setting, or even features of the fiscal setting itself. We give clear-cut answers later on.

This gives an accurate and comprehensive picture of twenty-five fiscal settings in the EU. Still embryonic and perfectible, the results presented in the next sections are promising. We hope that further studies on this path will improve this comprehensive comparative evaluation framework of the various fiscal settings (including the actual degree of 'fiscal' decentralisation) in EU countries.

5.2. European Experiences at a Glance

As mentioned above, we consider three different dimensions of analysis in order to understand the various ways in which inter-governmental relationships are actually organised in European countries. In the rest of the chapter, we concentrate on the comparison of different Member States on institutional, political, fiscal and socio-economic grounds. Including political variables, once again we stress their importance to understand a fiscal setting because, as shown in the previous chapters of this work, they happen to be very important when, in reality, policy-makers choose among various 'fiscal setting options'.

In this section our aim is to highlight whether factors like different national traditions, past political regimes (see ex-communist countries), regional differentiation (*e.g.* north/south economic divides, ethnic groups) or institutional background (unitary vs. federal states) have some influence upon centralisation and decentralisation trends.

5.2.1. Institutions and Politics: Measuring Political Decentralisation and Interactions

Tables 5.1 and 5.2 below present two dimensions of European fiscal settings. In table 5.1, in order to evaluate the level of political decentralisation, we comprise the main politico-institutional features of European (fiscal settings) Member States: the type of country (unitary or federal), the existence of special status region (yes/no), the number of vertical layers of government (from 2 to 5), the administrative tradition (weak, medium or strong Weberian, according to Hooghe, 2001), and the strongest sub-central level of government (either local, regional or equal power).

Table 5.2 refers to institutional cooperation. Indeed, the degree of interaction (inter/independence) of vertical layers of government is likely to have an impact on the working of a fiscal setting. It is not possible to understand their current framework if one does not remember that in the past they have been organised as centrally planned economies. The criteria used to assess whether a country exhibits a high degree of political interaction are the rights, given by law, for various levels of government to interfere in other levels of action. The most representative examples of such interactions are: i) the existence of a far-reaching organ of representation of the central level at the sub-national level, such as the *Préfecture* in France; ii) the right of regions to take part in the elaboration/formulation of national policies, which is, for instance, given by federal constitutions; iii) the organ of implementation of national policies; iv) the level of interdependence of taxation powers.

Table 5.1: Political Decentralisation in European Countries

	Type of country	Existence of special region status	Number of levels of government	Administrative tradition	Strongest sublevel in political term	PDI
Belgium	Federal	Capital	5	WW	R	9
Denmark	Unitary	Greenland and *Faroe* Islands	3	MW	L	7
Germany	Federal	3 'city States' Lander: Berlin, Hamburg, Bremen	4	MW	R	7
Greece	Unitary	NO	4	WW	L[d]	5
Spain	Unitary	17 Autonomous Communities 2 Autonomous Towns	3	MW	R	6
France	Unitary	Corsica, New Caledonia and Overseas Departments	4	SW	=	5
Ireland	Unitary	NO	3	SW	L[a]	2
Italy	Unitary	5 special statute regions and 2 self-governing provinces	4	WW	R[b]	6
Luxem-bourg	Unitary	Capital	2	WW	L[a]	4
Netherlands	Unitary	NO	2	MW	L	4
Austria	Federal	9 Lander + Vienna which is 'hybrid', both a Land and a local authority	4	WW	R	8
Portugal	Unitary	Autonomous regions of the Azores and of Madeira	4	MW	R	5
Finland	Unitary	Autonomous province of *Aaland*	2	WW	L	7
Sweden	Unitary	*Gotland* is a municipality with county status	3	MW	L	6
UK	Unitary	Devolution Wales, Scotland	2/4	SW	L for England R for NI, W, S	5/7
Average EU(15)	0.6	1.4	1.93	1.2	0.8	5.9/6

	Unitary	Capital	3	PS	=	4
Estonia	Unitary	NO	2	PS	L^d	2
Cyprus	Unitary	NO	2	PS	L^c	2
Latvia	Unitary	7 Republic Cities with dual region/local authority status	2	PS	L^e	3
Lithuania	Unitary	NO	2	PS	L^c	2
Hungary	Unitary	Capital	3	PS	L^c	4
Malta	Unitary	NO	2	PS	L^f	1
Poland	Unitary	Capital	4	PS	L^d	4
Slovenia	Unitary	NO	2	PS	L	3
Slovakia	Unitary	8 self-governing territorial units (*samospravne kraje*)	3	PS	=	4
Average CEECs	0	0.5	2.1	0	1	3.6
Average EU(25)	0.36	0.96	1.88	0.72	0.96	4.68

Source: authors' own compilation and calculation (*cf.* Appendix)

<u>NB</u>: for Column 2: we consider level of government only governments that are directly voted according to COR (2004).

For Column 4: R means that the strongest sub-national level is the region, L that is the local one and = that both levels have more or less the same power. However, difficulties arise from the absence of regional bodies (such as in Ireland, in the Netherlands and in Luxembourg) or from their national status, *i.e.* some regional bodies have significant power but are not elected and as the representative of the Central government in the region are not independent neither. Please refer to the following for details on the status of regional bodies and to appendix for the discussion of the value given to the corresponding indicator.

(a) no regional body/elected government

(b) after last reform of Titolo 5 of Italian Constitution

(c) regions only implement central policies

(d) the chief of the region is the representative of the State or the region is a sub-division of the central administration

(e) regional power is made up by heads of municipalities

(f) regions are only territorial? (or statistical?) entities

For Czech Republic: recent change not yet a specific law, for Slovenia, region is a voluntary possibility not yet taken.

Table 5.2: Interactions between Levels of Government

	Organ of representation of the central level at the sub-central level	Right of region to take part to the national policy formulation/ elaboration	Level implementing national policies	Fiscal and tax cooperation
Belgium	*Gouverneur de la province*	YES	R-C	1
Denmark	Prefects	NO	L-C	1
Germany	*Regierungspräsident*	YES	R	3
Greece	Prefects and Secretary-general of the region	NO	C	1
Spain	*Delegado del gobierno*	NO	C-R	1
France	Prefects	Advisory	C	1
Ireland	Local government Heritage	NO	C	0
Italy	Prefects	Advisory	C-R	2
Luxembourg	District Commissioner, College of Mayor and *aldermen*	NO	C	0
Netherlands	Queens' commissioner	Advisory By Local authorities	C-L	0
Austria	*Bezirkhauptmannschaft*	YES	nd	1
Portugal	Civil Governor	NO	C	0
Finland	Provincial state offices	NO	C-L	2
Sweden	County Governor	NO	C-L	0
UK	Secretaries of State for Wales, Scotland and Northern Ireland	NO	C-R	2
EU 15				1
Cz. Republic	No	0	C	1
Estonia	County governor	NO	C	1
Cyprus	District officer	NO	C	2
Latvia	Ministry of regional development and local governments	NO	C	0
Lithuania	County governor	NO	C	0
Hungary	Public administration offices	NO	C	1
Malta	Government's local council departments	NO	C	0

Poland	*Vovoid* (governor or prefect)	NO	C	0
Slovenia	No	NO	C	0
Slovakia	District principal	NO	C	1
CEECs				0.7

Source: authors

The analysis of institutional and political indicators leads to the identification of a first category of states regrouping Finland, Denmark and Sweden. They share all of the politico-institutional characteristics included in political and institutional indicators, except for slight differences in the administrative tradition and for the absence of autonomous regions in Sweden. Note that even though the three countries are all unitary states, with an organ of representation of the central level at the sub-central level, lower levels are not merely subordinate to the highest (central) one. In Sweden, the Constitution itself establishes the principle of local self-government and the right of local authorities to levy taxes and determine tax rates. For Denmark, the Constitution establishes the principle that 'the right of local authorities to govern independently under the supervision of the State must be laid down by law'. This means local authorities are free to adopt their own local politics within a broad framework of national laws (OECD, 2002). Scandinavian countries have the most powerful local powers in the EU and exhibit a high level of political decentralisation.

It is well-known, federal states 'leave', by definition, extensive political freedom to regions. Hence, another group, constituted by Germany, Austria, Belgium, to which one can easily add Spain (which is not formally a federation, but which shares most of its features), exhibits a high degree of political decentralisation for the benefit of regions. In fact, in Germany and Austria there is a Chamber to represent them, which, as for the German *Bundesrat*, has a veto power on all legislation affecting the *Länder*. In Austria, the *Landtag* (regional Parliament) has legislative power for areas of relevance to the *Land* (COR, 2004). In Germany, the *Länder* are responsible for administering all federal legislation in areas of concurrent jurisdiction and in Belgium, regions may issue regional decrees, which hold the power of law. In all cases, there is no 'hierarchical' relationship between the regions and the federal authority. Regions are granted either independence or autonomy on most economic grounds. These states have at least four layers of government, and none of its administration follows a strong Weberian model. Furthermore, regions' active role is reinforced by their participation in the formulation of national policies. Nevertheless, such an organisation is by no way straightforward on all grounds. First, the local level of government seems to be relatively weak in political terms, especially when compared to the previous group of countries, as if it suffered from the swallowing of sub-central competencies by the region. Second, there seems to be numerous conflicting situations, but it is difficult to identify whether the reasons are cultural or economic. For instance, in Belgium it is difficult to know whether the real problem is one of cultural and linguistic differences, one of (bad) central management of the north (Flanders) – south (Wallonia) economic divide (as highlighted also by the presence of strong separatist parties, *i.e. Vlaams Belang* and *Volksunie*), or one of constitutional imbalance proceeding from the recent and *de facto* power asymmetry.[2] In Germany (see Chapter 4), conflicts between the rich *Länder* and the Federal State arise from the horizontal problem of inter-regional inequalities, *i.e.* the high economic differences between the western and eastern *Länder* and the issue of who pays for its reduction, still at hand after more than a decade of unification. In Spain too, the violent separatist movement of ETA has been generating turmoil for a long time. Third, although the political decentralisation is among the highest in the EU, countries differ with respect to the level of interaction between different levels of government. For example, Germany follows a long-lasting tradition of Cooperative federalism (see Chapter 4), whereas the low level of interaction seems inversely proportional to the desire for further emancipation for some Spanish regions.

Going on, we can note similarities between Italy and France, regarding their politico-institutional characteristics, as confirmed through the index values we have calculated. These are unitary states, with the presence of Prefects to represent the central state at the lower levels of government, *i.e.* in each of the constituent territories.[3] There are four levels of government in both countries; we find regions, provinces

---

[2] The Constitutional arrangement in Belgium is very complicated, as two different kinds of government co-exist at the same level (*i.e.* what would be called a 'region' in a normal fiscal setting) but rule over different territories (one based on an economic rationale and one based on a linguistic rationale). Although competencies are neatly shared among these 'two levels at the same level' (for instance, Communities are responsible for education, whereas regions for industrial agricultural or industrial policies), asymmetry arises from the *de facto* merger of the Region and Community in Flanders.

[3] In France, each region overheads (without ruling) two or more *départements*. Next to the sub-national elected body (*Conseil Régional* for the region, and *Conseil Général* for the *département*), there is a representative of the State in each *département*. One of the Prefects of *départements* is also the prefect of the region, which gives him more prerogatives than the 'normal prefects', including responsibility for the management of European Regional Funds.

(*départements* for France) and municipalities, being the sub-central components of the 'governmental structure'. Other features approach the two countries, such as the presence of special status regions, one of these for France is Corsica, which has been showing separatist tendencies for many years. In fact, among the separatist parties in France, one of certain magnitude is *Corsica Nazione*. Similar secessionist tendencies are present in Italy too, represented by the Northern League Party,[4] even if they have been showing themselves only since the beginning of the 1990s and if their constitutive rationale is different. Note that in both countries, the outcome of a recent decentralisation reform is still unclear.

The local government in the Netherlands and most of the United Kingdom have an intermediate position between the strong autonomy of these latter in Scandinavian EU countries and their relative weakness in Greece, Ireland, Luxemburg and Portugal (OECD, 2002). Both countries are unitary States, where regions are relatively weak. In the Netherlands, there are two sub-national levels of government, provinces and municipalities, whose powers and responsibilities are established by national laws and furthermore the central government plays a major part in policy implementation at the local level. The UK is however a case in point. Regarding the UK, the unitary state is very centrally biased with a strong Weberian administrative tradition, and with a very weak regional level. However, the British model is the most differentiated model in Europe: in three of the four constituent kingdoms (England, Scotland, Wales and Northern Ireland), the regions, even if with a different structure among them, have very extensive political self-determination power.[5] The exercise of their power is nevertheless strongly restricted to those expressly transferred to them by law and constrained by their limited fiscal autonomy (OECD, 2002).

Greece, Ireland, Luxembourg and Portugal are very politically centralised unitary countries, characterised by relatively weak sub-national levels of government. In fact, the Central state implements national policy and regions do not take part in it. In Greece and Ireland regions have no power to fix tax rates and basis. In Greece and Portugal's distribution of competencies, the central level is the sole responsible for a large part and co-responsible in the majority of the remaining. In most sectors of public intervention, the Central level, thus, keeps the final say.

---

[4] Separatist parties can be distinguished according to their nature. *Corsica Nazione* mimics the ETA and IRA, whereas in Italy (or even in Belgium) the separatist party always used political and institutional means.

[5] The UK is, thus, an asymmetric country in that England remains highly centralised, while Scotland and Wales have a high degree of autonomy.

Finally, a straightforward group, constituted by the ten new entrants, can be underlined. On both dimensions, CEECs tend to share similar politico-institutional features. They are all unitary countries, with few levels of government (except for Poland which has four levels) and with the same post-soviet administrative tradition. Concerning the politico-institutional organisation, the only sizeable difference relates to the existence of special status regions, in this case, mainly capital cities, but nothing like the huge differences encountered in the EU(15). Their similarities from this side of the analysis is confirmed through the calculation of the political decentralisation index (PDI), on average 3 while EU(15) average is 6. Moreover, national policy are mostly shaped and implemented by the central level. Note that it is hard to find precise data about the right of regions to take part in the national policy formulation, as many reforms tending to guarantee more local autonomy are still operating. Finally, in general, regions of the CEECs have no or very marginal power to fix tax rates or its basis. These countries tend to exhibit very low degrees of political decentralisation and interaction. Few differences are however significant: the presence of the central state representation at sub-national levels (*i.e* Prefects in Poland and Ministry of regional development and local governments in Latvia), the existence of separatist parties or strong ethnic conflicts (*Kashubia* in Poland and *de facto* state of Northern Cyprus), the special status and autonomy of the capital region in Hungary, Poland and the Czech Republic. But, all in all, they are unitary states, with three levels of government (national, regional and local) and a predominance of the central one, this latter shaping and implementing national policies, being present in the carrying out of almost all competencies including taxation setting.

To conclude, one can observe that the EU(25) is made up of different groups of countries, whose similar characteristics also stem from their common past history (*e.g.* for many CEECs the same past Communist regime). Countries in each category are often contiguous, but this is not always the case. We have pointed out some groups. A first one is made up of New Member States (NMS), here the power is mainly/highly concentrated at the central level (with the only considerable exceptions of the Czech Republic and Poland whose distribution of competencies indexes, in fact, are 0.63 and 0.71 – meaning that they are highly decentralised states (according to our classification in the next section) and the index of political decentralisation is relatively low (2 or 3, max 4).

A second one is made up of Northern EU countries, where, despite not being federal but unitary countries, local levels of government actually hold their own responsibilities and a high degree of autonomy, set in the Constitution itself.

A third one can be identified as EU federal states and Spain, with regions being of consequence. For two of them, Belgium and Germany, it can be said that their competence allocation is highly decentralised, as pointed out by the corresponding index in table 5.4, whose values are respectively 0.66 and 0.72.

A fourth one is represented by Greece, Ireland and Portugal with very low values of political decentralisation and interaction indexes; they are within the OMS the traditionally less developed and smallest in geographic magnitude.

A fifth group is composed by the Netherlands, Luxembourg and the UK, all traditionally very centralised and administering small territories, although the UK presents a peculiar characteristics being both highly centralised in England and mediumly-highly decentralised in Scotland.

Finally, a sixth category can be identified as the central-southern MS, which have a 'Napoleonic' structure with provinces and prefects and whose values of both indexes of political decentralisation and of competence distribution are very similar.

Table 5.3: Cooperation and Decentralisation in the EU

	Weak Political Decentralisation	Medium Political Decentralisation	Strong Political Decentralisation
Weak Cooperation	England Estonia Malta Ireland Lithuania Cyprus Portugal	Latvia Hungary Czech Republic Luxembourg Slovenia Slovakia Greece Poland	
Medium Cooperation		France Italy Netherlands	Austria Spain Denmark UK (excl. England) Sweden
Strong Cooperation			Belgium Germany Finland

Source: authors

5.2.2. *Repartition of Competencies among Vertical Layers of Government*

After having identified the variety of politico-institutional configurations in the 25 Member States, we can turn our attention to the economic issues involved in the exercise of the sharing of public authority. To understand a given fiscal setting, it is not sufficient to comment on one indicator of public spending. Typically, most studies take as a summary figure (and often as the essence) of a given setting the level of sub-central spending on total taxation. Tables 5.4 and 5.5 in the following pages defend the underlying idea that fiscal settings are unfortunately a bit more complicated than this. To analyse a given setting we consider more variables, precisely we identified the following: basic formal competencies, fiscal power and fiscal interaction.

There are two ways to analyse the distribution of competencies among layers of government. The first one consists in identifying which level generally endorses a given competence in European countries (read table 5.4 line by line). The second one focuses on the way all public prerogatives are distributed in a given country (read table 5.4 column by column).

Analysing the distribution of one competence according to the way it is assigned among government tiers in the various countries reveals the following lessons. For example, defence is a central level task in all of the EU(25). The same holds for international relations and foreign affairs (except for Belgium and Slovakia). Another sole central level competence deals with Universities, this happens in 16 countries, whereas environmental measures and public services is a task to which lower tiers of government participate: in 22 countries such competencies are assigned either to the regional or to the local level or are mixed.

The competence which is most often shared in the highest number of countries, is 'Hospitals and health insurance' (17 states) but also education and social welfare, divided among three or two levels of government in 16 countries. Taxation is a solely central task in 10 states, while in 11 states the competence is mixed. But the central level is anyway present in the sharing of tasks, sometimes with only one, sometimes with both the other tiers of government (regional and local).

In the cases where the sole regional or the sole local level of govern-ment are responsible for certain matters, these are for instance cultural activities, public transport, spatial planning, libraries and sport facilities, building and maintenance of public transport infrastructure. Furthermore, in Hungary, Poland and the Czech Republic, regions have the power to fix tax rates (even if in the Czech Republic it is very low). This demonstrates that Hungary, Poland and the Czech Republic, that are also among the richest new countries, exhibit similar trends.

Analysing the way competencies are distributed in a given country also leads to highlighting diversities. In most NMS (except for the Czech Republic and Poland), the central level is present in almost the whole carrying out of competencies: even when the local level is awarded a given task, this competence is only partially delegated, as the central level always remains involved. This confirms the relatively low decentralisation previously noted on politico-institutional grounds. Note that Malta and Cyprus have similar features: they are the two smallest CEECs, they are islands and the central level is involved in all tasks.

Another group of countries is made up of the northern states of the EU (Sweden, Denmark and Finland), which have most competencies assigned to a particular tier of government and only some of them, like social welfare or spatial planning, are shared among the three levels of government.

We can also analyse the federal states from the distribution of competencies point of view. In Germany, like in Belgium, many are mixed. On the contrary Austria, which in terms of the structure of the state is similar to Germany (*i.e. Länder, Bundesrat*), has few mixed competencies, *i.e.* most of them are assigned to a specific level of government.

In the case of Italy and France, many tasks are shared and the other ones assigned to the central level. Lower levels are generally involved with all the others or at least with another one. Competencies are evenly distributed in both states in nine cases and the other competencies tend to be allocated in a very similar fashion. Nevertheless, overall, Italy seems a bit more decentralised than France.

Table 5.4: Distribution of Tasks among Levels of Government: Formal Competencies

	Bel	Cz	Dk	Ger	Est	Gr	Sp	F	Ir	It	Cy	La	Li	Lux	Hu	Ma	Nl	Aus	Pol	Por	Slov	Sk	Fin	Sw	UK
1 Police, defence and public order																									
A Defence	C	C	C	C	C	C	C	C	C	C	C	C	C	C	C	C	C	C	C	C	C	C	C	C	C
B Police	C	C	C	MC/R	C	C	MR/L	MC/L	C	MC/L	C	MC/L	C	C	C	C	MC/R	C	MR/L	C	C	M	C	C	MCR
C Maintenance of public order	L	M	L	R	MC/L	C	MR/L	C	L	C	MC/R	MC/L	C	C	L	MC/L	MC/L	L	C	C	C	MR/L	C	C	MCR
2/D International relations, foreign affairs, development aid	MC/R	C	C	C	C	C	C	C	C	C	C	C	C	C	C	C	C	C	C	C	C	MC/R	C	C	C
3 Education																									
E Education (education vocational training and research&development)	R	M	MC/R	MR/L	C	C	R	C	M	MC/RL	MC/R	MC/R	MC/RL	MC/L	L	MC/L	MC/L	R	MR/L	MC/L	MCL	MC/R	L	M/CRL	MRL
F Libraries, sports facilities	L	L	L	L	L	L	R	MC/L	L	MC/RL		MC/L	MC/L	MC/L	L	MC/L	MC/L	L		MC/L	MCL	MR/L	L	L	MRL
G Universities	R	L	C	R	C	C	R	C	C	C	C	C	C	C	C	C	C	C	R	C	C	C	MC/RL	C	C
4 Culture																									
H Cultural activities	R	MC/L	M	MR/L	L	L	R	MC/RL	L	MC/RL	MC/R	MC/L	MC/RL	MC/L	L	C	MC/L	R		MC/L	M/CL	MR/L	L	MC/RL	R
I Media and communication, broadcasting and television	R		C	R			MC/R	C		MC/R	C	C	C	C		C	C	C		C	C		C	C	C
5 Health and social welfare																									
J Social welfare *	C	L	M	MC	C	C	R	M	M	MC	MC	MC	MC	M	C	C	M	MCR	MR	MC	M	M	MC	M	C

K	Hospital and health insurance	MC R	L	R	R MC RL	L	C	M	C	M	RL MC R	R M	L MC RL	RL MC RL	M CL	C	MC L	C	M	L MR L	L MC L	CL L MC CL	M	L L	L MC R	MRL
6	**Transport and planning**																									
L	Public transport	MC R	MC L	R	L	C	MC L	MC R	MC RL	MC L	R	MC L	C	MC L	L	MCL	L	M	L	R	MRL
M	Building and maintenance of public transport/road infrastructure	MRL	L	MC L MC RL	MC RL	L	R	MC RL	C	MC L	MC L	MC L	MC L	M	C	M	M	L	R	MRL
N	Spatial planning	MRL	L	MR L	L	MR L	L	R	M	MC RL R	MC L CRL	C	M	C	R	C	M CL	L	MR L RL	L
7/O	**Trade, industry, economic activities**	MC R	C	MC R	M	MC R	C	MC R	M	MC RL	C	C	C	C	C	MR MR L L	C	C
8/P	**Job placement and employment scheme**	MC R	L	MC R	R	MC R	C	MC RL	C	C	C	MC L	C	MC L	L	C	C
9/Q	environment or emergency services	M RL	L	C MR L	MR L	L	M	MC RL	MR L	MR RL	C	MC L	MC R	MR L	MC MCL L	MCL	M	R	L	MRL
10/R	**Agriculture**	MC R L	MC R	MC R	M C	M	M C	MC R	C	C	C MCL	C	MCL R	R	C	C
11/S	**Taxation**	M	M	MC RL	M	M	C	MC R MC R	C	C	C	C	M	C	C	C	MC L	C	MCR
	SUMMARY SCORE	0.66 0.63	0.53 0.72	0.41 0.38	0.74 0.32	0.42 0.53	0.37 0.39	0.29 0.18	0.48 0.13	0.32 0.42	0.71 0.24	0.24 0.62	0.62 0.38	0.50

* social security and welfare, sick leave, child benefit and old age pensions, social assistance, care of mentally and physically disabled people, unemployment insurance and labour inspection

Source: authors

To capture the level of task decentralisation, one may use an unusual indicator (summary score, last line of Table 5.4). Indeed, as one important aim of this study is to compare European fiscal settings, it is worth having a single value, which summarises the way a given country divides its tasks among tiers of government. Note that in such a comparative perspective, it may be wrong to say that, a higher score (for details on calculation methods, see appendix) for a country means more decentralisation, as our indicator is not a weighted average.[6] Still, it provides useful information about the operation of European fiscal settings. A zero value means full centralisation, and a one value means full decentralisation, without any mixed competencies. Our indicator ranges from 0.18 for Malta to 0.74 for Spain. In between, the highest scores are for Belgium, Germany, Finland, Poland (*sic*), the Czech Republic, and Slovakia.[7] The high score of the two latter countries may however originate from data collection and methodological problems. The lowest scores are for Luxembourg, Portugal, Slovenia and France.

According to the index of competence distribution, three NMS (Malta, Slovenia and Lithuania) out of 10 are highly centralised (with a competence index ranging from 0.13 to 0.28), three are only moderately decentralised (Estonia, Cyprus and Latvia, Competence Index ranging from 0.28 to 0.43). Only the Czech Republic and Poland exhibit high indexes, meaning they can be considered decentralised from the sharing of competence point of view.

5.2.3. Fiscal Variables

Traditionally, Fiscal Federalism comparative studies focus on the following variables, without taking into account the previous political and institutional dimension. The study of such variables is compulsory for one wishing to know what various layers of government do. However, there are various ways to observe the problem. This subsection, thus, builds an indicator composed of the most important dimensions of the fiscal allocation of functions.

---

[6] To get a true and accurate decentralisation index, a fully weighted average should be created. In each country, a weight should be assigned to each competence (for instance for the police competence: share of total police spending over total public spending). But comparison of national accounts is very difficult and no data set was available (and is unlikely to be in the near future). Later we account for these main methodological flaws, keeping in mind our indicators is an approximation by transforming the data in rough categories ranging from 0 to 3.

[7] Note that in Table 5.5 below, the 'boundary marks' are the following: From 0.13 to 0.28: 0, *i.e.* highly centralised; from 0.28 to 0.43: 1, *i.e.* moderately decentralised; from 0.43 to 0.58: 2, *i.e.* decentralised; from 0.58 to 0.74: 3, *i.e.* highly decentralised.

Fiscal Powers

In order to evaluate the fiscal power different levels of government really enjoy, it is essential to have access to specific sub-national statistics on spending and revenue capacity. Unfortunately not every Member States has developed such statistics and it is consequently next to impossible to gather this data for all of the 25 EU Member States. This explains the missing data, but this does not invalidate our analyses. In fact a first observation can be made: the missing data comes from specific NMS (traditionally centralised and with a scarce experience of decentralisation, although recently a so-called Fiscal Decentralisation Initiative, FDI, tries to introduce decentralisation elements) and from specific Old Member States such as Ireland, the UK and Denmark.[8] The lack of data is not 'absolute' but derives also from the fact that it was impossible to find all of the data for all MS from the same source. In order to avoid methodological confusions, we opted for not including all data for certain countries: our results are therefore perhaps less complete but gain in coherence.

We start to analyse fiscal settings, in particular total spending and revenues of the EU(25). Graph 5.1 gives us a picture of the total spending of MS as a percentage of the GDP: it is easily comparable as it gives the level of spending for central, regional and local governments. An important variable in spending levels is marked by social security but this is not taken into account in our analysis.

At a first glance, an important feature stands out: the level of spending is not uniform in Europe but it varies between 35 and 65 per cent of the GDP (on average 47.6); it is extremely high in the Czech Republic (65 per cent) and in Sweden (58.3 per cent) and in total only for 8 countries the share exceeds the 50 per cent mark. This indicates that the presence of the 'state' is not so pervasive as is often claimed (Brennan and Buchanan, 1980; Friedman, 1977; and Niskanen, 1971).

Surprisingly, the lowest rates are in evidence in Lithuania (34.1 per cent) and in Latvia (35.4 per cent). This shows that these Baltic republics have undertaken a massive programme of privatisation of the previously centralised economy.

We then move on to analyse the impact of spending on each level of government (we follow the traditional division of the central, regional and local level). Regional data are available only for traditional

---

[8]   The Fiscal Decentralisation Initiative (FDI) is a joint initiative of the OECD, the World Bank, the Council of Europe, the Open Society Institute (Budapest), the UNDP, USAID and some OECD member countries to assist transition economies in Central and Eastern Europe in carrying out intergovernmental reforms.

regionalised or federal states such as Belgium, Spain, Germany and Austria but the share does not show a very significant role of regions in the spending scheme, their share ranging from 10 to 14 per cent of the GDP. The Central state still retains the majority of the spending power. This holds for all MS although only the Czech Republic, Greece, Cyprus and Malta exhibit high figures, above the 35 per cent threshold. Local governments enjoy on average less than 10 per cent of the GDP, but huge differences appear. For example, Sweden (26 per cent), Finland (19.5 per cent), the Netherlands (17.1 per cent) and Italy (15.4 per cent) local governments spend much more than German (7.1 per cent), Austrian (8.6 per cent) and Belgian (6.7 per cent) local entities. Only Greece, Malta and the Slovak Republic show figures beneath 5 per cent of the GPD. This shows that Federalism is often synonymous with lower fiscal responsibilities for local governments, and does not always mean more responsibilities for sub-central governments taken as a whole.

On the revenue side, total public revenues shares of the GDP range between 30 and 60 per cent. The highest shares can be seen in Belgium, the Czech Republic, France, Denmark, Finland and Sweden, while the smallest in Latvia and Lithuania. Central state shares vary generally between 12.9 (Germany) and 39.1 (Malta) per cent of the GDP. Analysing this section for the CEECs, we notice different characteristics. However, from a fiscal power point of view (*cf.* 5.1 and 5.2) fiscal settings are not so similar.

Graph 5.1: Total Public Spending as a Share of GDP

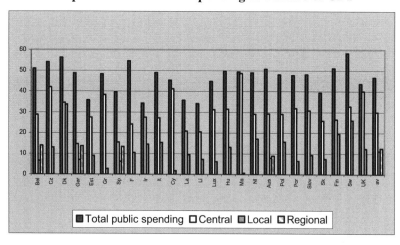

Source: authors

Graph 5.2: Total Public Revenues as a Share of GDP

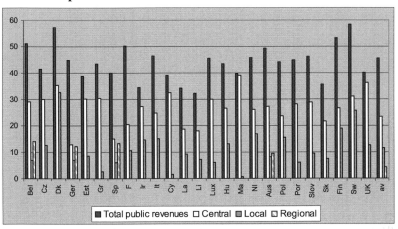

Source: authors

Fiscal Interactions

To understand fiscal interaction and fiscal autonomy, we now consider the level of taxation in central and local governments as a share of total taxation: this lets us infer on how much autonomy local governments enjoy. It appears immediately that in terms of fiscal autonomy, the only MS that does not share its tax is Malta (100 per cent), while nine other MS show figures above the average (60 per cent): the Czech Republic (75.3 per cent), Denmark (61.8 per cent), Estonia (72.2 per cent), Greece (65.5 per cent), Ireland (83.5 per cent), Cyprus (77 per cent), Luxembourg (66.5 per cent), Portugal (60.9 per cent) and the UK (94.3 per cent).

On the other hand, only three MS central governments collect less than 40 per cent of total taxation: Belgium (33.2), Germany (28.4 per cent) and Spain (37 per cent); it is worth noticing that these are traditional federal states. European Central governments enjoy less than 40 per cent of total taxation: Denmark (34.5 per cent), Sweden (32 per cent), and Finland (21.4 per cent), while thirteen MS perform less than 10 per cent (an important observation is the average, being 10.8 per cent) and, among them, six perform less than 5 per cent (Belgium, 4.8 per cent, Greece, 0.9 per cent, Ireland 2.3 per cent, Cyprus 1.3 per cent, the Netherlands 3.7 per cent and UK, 4.4 per cent).

A similar picture derives from the analysis of the share of taxation by level of government as a share of the GDP (*cf.* Graph 5.4). In terms of wealth, local taxation represents on average only 4.4 per cent of national GDP, a very small part of the national product is, hence, at the disposal of local entities. Only in Denmark, Italy, Latvia, Austria, Finland and Sweden the percentage is above 5 per cent and extremely low figures are present in Greece (0.3 per cent), Ireland (0.6 per cent) and Cyprus (0.4 per cent). This comparative analysis shows that Ireland and Cyprus are the most centralised from a fiscal capacity perspective and Denmark, Finland and Sweden are the most decentralised.

These data are among the most controversial in our analysis. The right assignment of tax to each level of government depends on the definition of own taxes, the choice of the tax base and on the importance of shared taxes (even here it is sometimes difficult to distinguish between shared yields or shared rates). We chose the approach of the European Commission (2004) where taxes are assigned to central and local tiers, to social security and to foreign transfers (such as percentage of VAT assigned at EU budget level).

Graph 5.3: Taxation by Level of Governments as a Share of Total Taxation[9]

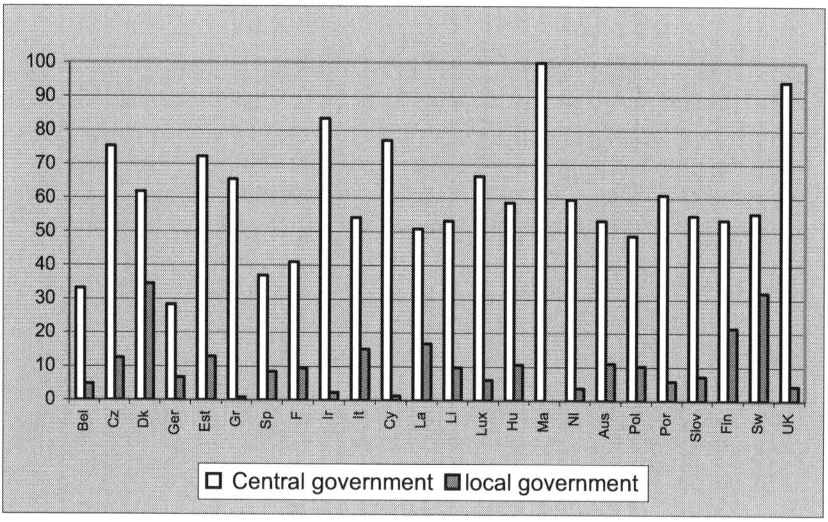

Source: authors based on EC data

---

[9] Total taxation involves not only central and local (including regional) taxes but also, social security funds, transfers to EC institutions, but also, shared taxes, summing all these components we get the 100 per cent as from EC (2004a).

Graph 5.4: Taxation by Level of Governments
as a Share of GDP

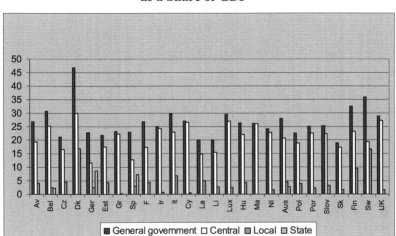

Moving on to the relevance of fiscal power enjoyed by the lower tiers of governments, Graph 5.5 considers as a measure of fiscal independence the so-called indicator of 'vertical imbalance' between tiers. The higher the vertical imbalance, the more centralised (in terms of expenditure autonomy) one MS. Indeed, this indicator equals the transfers received by the sub-central levels from the national government over total sub-national expenditure. In other words, the vertical imbalance is the degree to which sub-national governments rely on central government revenues to support their expenditures (it is also a measure of intergovernmental transfers as a share of sub-national expenditures). In Ireland, the Netherlands, the UK, Italy, Spain, Belgium and Hungary (Greece, Malta, Cyprus, for which data is missing probably have a high level of vertical imbalance) the lower tiers of government depends much on the central level. In Slovakia, Sweden, Germany, Slovenia, the Czech Republic, Estonia, Finland and Latvia, lower tiers of government seem relatively independent from Central revenues. In between, countries like France, Denmark, Luxembourg, Austria, Poland and Portugal have a medium degree of vertical imbalance.

Graph 5.5: Vertical Imbalance

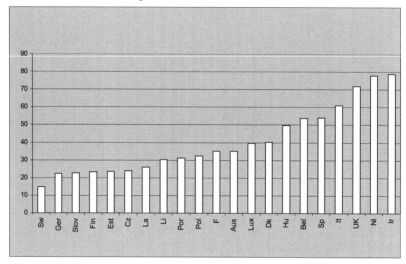

Source: authors based on IMF data

Concluding Remarks on European Fiscal Settings

To sum up what has been discussed in this subsection, a useful indication is the Fiscal Decentralisation Indicator (FDI) in table 5.5. There we find a decentralisation indicator built on the fiscal competence index, global spending index, sub-national spending index, degree of taxation autonomy local governments enjoy and vertical imbalance index. This indicator ranges between 0 to 9 with the lowest figure indicating very low local autonomy (or almost no local autonomy), and the maximum a high level of autonomy.

According to our indicators Denmark, Sweden, Finland, Germany, the Czech Republic and Poland (9-8.5), are the most fiscally decentralised countries, while traditionally federal states – Belgium and Austria – with an index respectively of 6 and 6.5 have a lower degree of decentralisation than certain MS considered unitary states such as Italy with 7.5 and the Slovak Republic with 7. Among the federal states, Belgium results as the less decentralised with an index of 6. We also remark that Malta is the EU(25) most centralised MS, with an index of 1. Apart from Malta, the less decentralised MS are Greece, Ireland, Cyprus and Slovenia, all with an index of 2, followed by Luxembourg, the Netherlands and Portugal with an index of 3.

This indicator lets us infer that the usual contraposition between OMS and NMS does not hold in this specific case and that under the definition of federal states we don't always find that such countries are more decentralised than traditionally unitary countries.

Table 5.5: Fiscal Decentralisation Index

	Fiscal competencies index	Global spending index	Sub-national spending index	Tax autonomy index	Vertical imbalance index	Fiscal decentralisation index
Belgium	3	1	0	1	1	6
Cz. Rep	3	2	1	0.5	2	8.5
Denmark	2	2	2	1	2	9
Germany	3	1	2	1	2	9
Estonia	1	0	1	0.5	2	4.5
Greece	1	1	0	0	0	2
Spain	3	0	2	1	1	7
France	1	1	0	0	2	4
Ireland	1	0	1	0	0	2
Italy	2	1	1	0.5	3	7.5
Cyprus	1	1	0	0	0	2
Latvia	1	0	1	0.5	2	4.5
Lithuania	1	0	1	0	2	4
Lux.	0	1	0	0	2	3
Hungary	2	1	1	0.5	1	5.5
Malta	0	1	0	0	0	1
Nl.	1	1	1	0	0	3
Austria	1	1	2	0.5	2	6.5
Poland	3	1	2	0.5	2	8.5
Portugal	0	1	0	0	2	3
Slovenia	0	1	0	0	2	2
Slovakia	3	1	0	0	3	7
Finland	3	1	2	0.5	2	8.5
Sweden	1	2	2	1	3	9
UK	2	1	1	0	0	4
EU(25) average	1.8	0.92	0.92	0.36	1.52	5.24

Source: authors

5.2.4. The Diversity of Socio-economic Situations

Wealth and Population

Before turning to the potential relationship between the two previous dimensions (politico-institutional and fiscal), it is necessary to widen our analysis of the European fiscal settings to encompass a broad set of socio-economic features. Indeed, the degree of political and fiscal centralisation/decentralisation may depend on other variables usually called control variables. As we will see in section 5.3.2, some of these variables happen to play a role in the composition of the internal inter-governmental organisation of EU Member States.

This section of our empirical analysis gives details about socio-economic variables in the new EU. The macro-economic framework of the EU(25) resulting from our analysis emphasises in particular three variables: the GDP per inhabitant, macro-economic situations (including growth, unemployment and inflation rates), and population.

Graph 5.6 below shows the high level of heterogeneity of Member States with respect to their wealth (income) levels, as approximately measured by their GDP per inhabitant with respect to the EU average. The ratio between the richest (Luxembourg) and the poorest (Latvia) EU countries exceeds 5. Even if one excludes the extremes, the ratio still exceeds 3, *i.e.* Ireland is three times richer than the Baltic countries or Poland. Most countries have a GDP per inhabitant in PPS ranging from 60 to 130 per cent of the European average (accounting for differences in population). This graph presents a symmetric EU: there are as many 'rich' Member States as there are poor Member States. This second group is composed of all of the new member states and the so-called 'cohesion countries', traditionally poor Mediterranean countries. Such a result opens up new interesting challenges on how cohesion policy will work in the coming years.

Regarding population, EU countries are once again very heterogeneous, ranging from small countries with less than 10 million inhabitants to very highly populated countries with more than 30 million inhabitants. Germany with its 82.5 millions is twice as big as Spain (40.8) and Poland (38.2) and eight times larger than most of the other MS. France, Italy and the UK (61.5, 58.1, 59.4 millions respectively) are also up to six times bigger than the remaining countries. All new Member States, apart from Poland, have less than 10 million inhabitants. The dimension is an important issue with respect to the future political impact that every MS will enjoy in the decision-mechanism at EU level. With the replacement of the unanimity voting rule with the qualified majority voting (QMV), the European Constitution sets that, within the

European Council and the Council of Ministers "a qualified majority shall be defined as at least 55 per cent of the members of the Council, comprising at least fifteen of them and representing Member States comprising at least 65 per cent of the population of the Union" (Art. I-25). If it is relinquished, the Nice Treaty will prevail, over-representing some MS such as Spain and Poland.

Graph 5.6: Disparities in the EU,
GDP per Inhabitant in PPS (Basis 100 = Average)

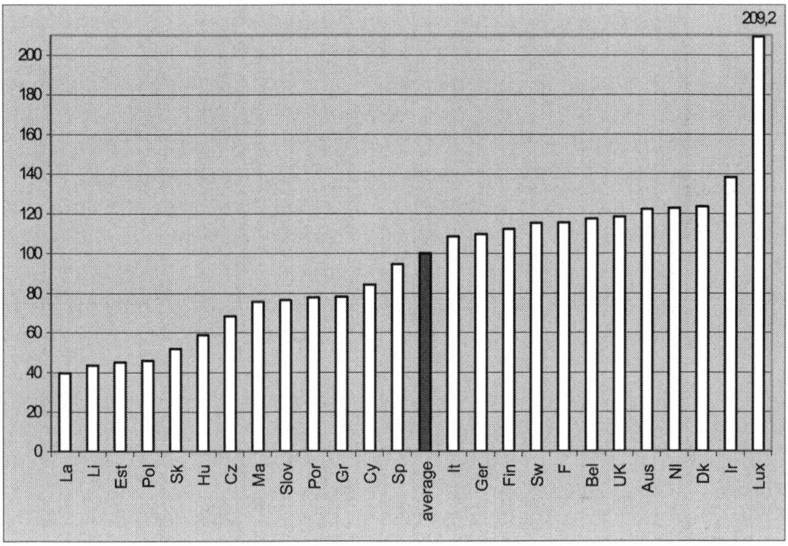

Source: authors based on EC (2004)

This new asset changes the power OMS possessed, and creates the possibilities of new voting coalitions.

Macro-economic Framework

Table 5.6 at the end of this section presents the most scrutinised macro-economic indicators: growth, inflation and unemployment rates, for the last available year (see appendix). Generally, all countries present an unemployment level inferior to 10 per cent. Only Spain, Latvia, Lithuania, Poland and the Slovak Republic exceed this threshold, the last two dramatically so (19.2 per cent and 17.1 per cent respectively). In five countries (Ireland, Cyprus, Luxembourg, the Netherlands and Austria), the unemployment rate is lower than 5 per cent. The best performance is, unsurprisingly, exhibited by Luxembourg, the richest MS. Although new Member States tend to cumulate problems, it is worth noting that some of them perform relatively well with respect to unemployment. Indeed, exceeding the EU(25) average (8.25 per cent), stand some of the richest economies of the continent (Germany, Italy, France) while some new Member States like the Czech Republic, Cyprus, Slovenia and Hungary have relatively low unemployment rates. Unemployment seems higher in the most populated Member States.

Concerning inflation indicators, only eight countries exceed the 3 per cent threshold and, surprisingly, some NMS even exhibit a negative inflation rate (Lithuania, -1.1 and the Czech Republic, -0.1 per cent). On the opposite extreme, we also find eastern countries (the Slovak Republic, 8.5 per cent, Slovenia 5.7 per cent and Hungary 4.7 per cent). EMU countries present a diversified situation, with Germany having the lowest inflation rate (1 per cent) and Ireland having the highest one (4 per cent). Inflation rates give us a different picture in which it is difficult to identify a precise trend, all 25 MS behaving very differently. It is difficult to construct groups of MS exhibiting similar rates, even though OMS present a tiny variance in the inflation rate as a result of their regrouping under a Monetary Union.

An important feature for the growth and the development of the EU(25) area is indeed the existence of a stable economic environment. For the euro area, the SGP fixes rules on how national governments, in charge of national public finance, should behave, while for the 'out' countries (the 13 countries not yet participating to/included in the euro-area), the Maastricht Treaty, through Convergence Programmes, monitors the performance of the public sector.

A first criterion in order to obtain stability is the level (deficit or surplus) of national budgets. EU recommendations require a balanced budget or a budget in surplus (see Chapter 3 for a detailed discussion on this topic). The forecasts of the Commission for 2004 draw a complex picture. Only five countries meet this criterion: Finland (2 per cent), Denmark (1.1 per cent), Estonia (0.7 per cent), Spain (0.4 per cent) and Sweden (0.2 per cent). The remaining countries all exhibit deficits: in some cases very slight (Belgium 0.5 per cent, Ireland 0.8 per cent and Austria 1.1 per cent). Latvia and the Slovak Republic are behaving comparatively well with respect to the other NMS, which are the ones, performing worse: Poland (6 per cent), the Czech Republic (5.9 per cent), Malta (5.9 per cent). These negative values can be understood under a broader view in that these countries are facing enormous challenges in the conversion of their market economy. Relatively better positioned are the majority of states belonging to the euro area but still at the very limit of the SGP criteria: Germany (3.6 per cent), France (3.7 per cent), Italy (3.2 per cent), the Netherlands (3.5 per cent) and Portugal (3.4 per cent).

This picture can be better understood if we consider that the previous variable considers the performance at all levels of government while the SGP rules only constrains the central one, that is usually responsible for the comprehensive fiscal situation. Germany and Italy present a clear example of this situation: although the central government is making big efforts to respect the SGP (some may not agree, but such a discussion is not the purpose of this chapter), sub-national entities are less careful with regards to the discipline of public finance because they are usually not forced to do so. To prevent the so-called free-riding problem, MS have adopted certain fiscal frameworks and enforcement mechanisms to ensure overall budget discipline. Many countries (8) use fiscal rules and borrowing limits to ensure discipline, others use cooperative approach and borrowing limits (5) whereas others use limited fiscal autonomy at sub-national levels and borrowing limits (4) while the remaining, mainly all the NMS, do not yet present such frameworks. A valid explanation could be that sub-national levels were not able to enjoy much discretion and were not previously constrained by EU treaties. In order to enforce the discipline, several mechanisms are possible: market discipline, peer pressure, financial sanctions and administrative procedures, but it is difficult to extract a common feature and trend with this respect.

Graph 5.7: Budget Balance in Percentage of GDP

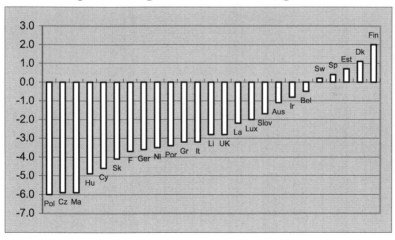

Source: authors, EC data 2004

To fully understand how an economy performs, it is important to consider its growth rate, that measures (imperfectly) the evolution of a country's wealth for international and temporal comparisons. It takes into consideration how the diffusion of technological and organisational innovation can impact on productivity, on product/process quality and on costs (thus potentially on added-value). Capital accumulation and the increase of labour quality and motivation are important ingredients for a growing economy. In the EU, there is a big variance between this indicator (from 0.8 to 6.9) signifying that the dynamics of each country are different. We can easily see that OMS (except the UK and Greece) have a low growth rate (under the EU level), while the NMS (except Malta and the Czech Republic) have rates well above the average. Portugal, the Netherlands, Italy, Germany, France and Austria are the less dynamic economies while the three Baltic Republics are the most dynamic ones.

Table 5.6: The Diversity of European Socio-economic and Macroeconomic Situations

| | Population | Wealth | Macroeconomic Situation | | | |
	in million of inhabitants	GDP per inhabitant in PPS (EU average =100)	Unemployment rate	Inflation rate	Misery index	Growth rate
Belgium	10.4	117.3	8.1	1.5	9.6	2.0
Czech Republic	10.2	68.3	7.8	-0.1	7.7	2.9
Denmark	5.4	123.7	5.6	2.0	7.6	2.1
Germany	82.5	109.7	9.6	1.0	10.6	1.5
Estonia	1.4	45.2	10.1	1.4	11.5	5.4
Greece	11.0	78.1	9.3	3.4	12.7	4.0
Spain	40.8	94.8	11.3	3.1	14.4	2.8
France	61.5	115.6	9.4	2.2	11.6	1.7
Ireland	4.0	138.2	4.6	4.0	8.6	3.7
Italy	58.1	108.5	8.6	2.8	11.4	1.2
Cyprus	0.7	84.3	4.4	4.0	8.4	3.4
Latvia	2.3	39.8	10.5	2.9	13.4	6.2
Lithuania	3.5	43.6	12.7	-1.1	11.6	6.9
Luxembourg	0.5	209.2	3.7	2.5	6.2	2.4
Hungary	10.1	58.8	5.8	4.7	10.5	3.2
Malta	0.4	75.8	8.2	1.9	10.1	1.4
Netherlands	16.2	122.8	3.8	2.2	6.0	1.0
Austria	8.1	122.2	4.1	1.3	5.4	1.8
Poland	38.2	45.9	19.2	0.7	19.9	4.6
Portugal	10.4	77.8	6.3	3.3	9.6	0.8
Slovenia	2.0	76.6	6.5	5.7	12.2	3.2
Slovakia	5.4	51.9	17.1	8.5	25.6	4.0
Finland	5.2	112.2	9.0	1.3	10.3	2.6
Sweden	9.0	115.4	5.6	2.3	7.9	2.3
UK	59.4	118.4	5.0	1.4	6.4	3.0
Average	18.3	100.0	8.252	2.516	10.768	2.964

Other information	Total 456.7	Average level of GDP per inhabitant in euros	Weighted average	Weighted average	Weighted average	Weighted average

Source: authors, based on various sources (*cf.* appendix)

Socio-economic Cohesion

From a socio-economic point of view, many national countries have to deal with strong minorities. Half of the Member States have minorities within their territory (representing more than 10 per cent of the national population) in some cases protected thanks to special laws and a certain degree of autonomy, in others only linguistic acknowledgement is guaranteed. Particular cases are Belgium and Latvia with respectively 40 per cent of Walloon (French-speaking) and 30 per cent of Russian.

To evaluate the cohesion of a MS, it is essential to have an indicator based on history, based on the age of the country, date of independence, and age of the current Constitution. Quite reasonably, 17 MS perform a high or medium level of historical cohesion (represented by the traditional bulk of national states: France, Spain, the UK, Germany, Italy, Poland, Hungary, and Sweden). The remaining, performing a low and very low degree, are states recently formed mainly in eastern Europe after the fall of the communist regimes. They arise from the division of previously artificially created countries. The Czech Republic and the Slovak Republic together with the Baltic Republics (Estonia, Latvia, Lithuania) are the results of such a process.

Another component of cohesion is the level of inequality prevailing in the country. Indeed, the higher the level of inequality, the higher the potential for change, reform and conflicts. It is, however, necessary to distinguish between territorial inequality based on the level of economic disparities among regions in the same MS and the degree of inter-individual inequality.

The first indicator is based on the GDP per habitant of the richest region over the GDP per habitant of the poorest one at NUTS 2 level.[10] Among the best performing (most equal) countries, one finds Austria, the Netherlands, Finland, Ireland, Sweden and Portugal with an indicator under 2 or under the average (2.1). The remaining MS are between 2 and 3. Slovakia is the most territorially unequal country, on the contrary it is surprising that such an advanced economy as France (2.8) perform the same indicator as the Czech Republic. Anyway, it is

---

[10]   Except Ireland, Czech Republic, Hungary, Poland, and Slovakia: NUTS 3.

important to keep in mind that this represents the dispersion of wealth among regions.

Graph 5.8: Internal Degree of Territorial Inequality
and Interindividual Inequality

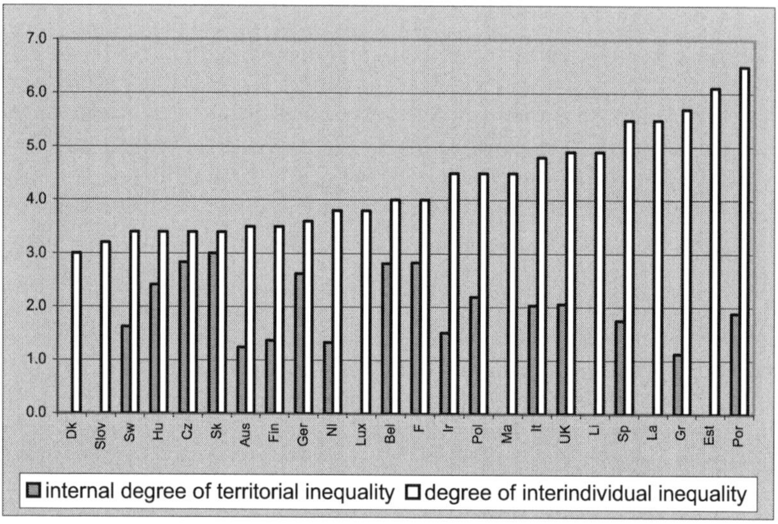

Source: authors

Graph 5.8 gives a more complete description of the inequality among individuals that differs from inequality in geographic distribution of wealth. The indicator is built based on the wealth of the richest 20 per cent over the wealth of the poorest 20 per cent and with a width comprised between 1 and 7 (low inequality to highest inequality). Once again, a complex picture arises. Broadly speaking, the highest concentrations of indicator are between 3 and 5 (a medium level of inequality). The MS above the 5 are two from the NMS (Estonia and Latvia) and three from the OMS (Greece, Spain, Portugal).

This means that, although extremely poor, certain countries share at a significant level their wealth between their inhabitants (see for example Lithuania, Poland or Portugal).

Graph 5.9: Cohesion Index

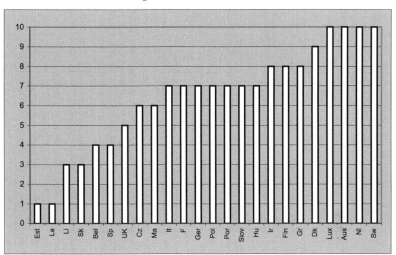

Source: authors

We build a cohesion index made up of several variables (existence of strong minorities, interregional inequalities, historical cohesion and inter-individual inequality) the lower the index the less cohesive one MS is. Denmark, Greece, Ireland, Luxembourg, Hungary, the Netherlands, Austria, Poland, Portugal, Slovenia, Finland, and Sweden are medium/ highly cohesive. While, Belgium, Spain, Latvia, Lithuania, and the Slovak republic are extremely non-cohesive with an index around 3.

Table 5.7: The Components of Socio-economic Cohesion

	Existence of strong minorities	Level of inter-regional inequalities	Degree of historical cohesion	Degree of inter-individual inequality	Cohesion Index
Belgium	Yes, Walloon 40%	2.8	M	4	4
Czech Republic	No, but Moravian 13.2%	2.8	L	3.4	6
Denmark	No	nd-M	H	3	9
Germany	No	2.6	M	3.6	7
Estonia	Yes, Russian 28%	nd-L	VL	6.1	1
Greece	No	1.1	H	5.7	8
Spain	Yes, 17%, Gal: 7%, Bas: 2%	1.7	M	5.5	4
France	No, marginal	2.8	H	4	7
Ireland	No	1.5	M	4.5	8
Italy	No, but numerous small linguistic minorities	2.0	M	4.8	7
Cyprus	Yes, Turkish 17%	nd-H	L	nd	nd
Latvia	Yes, Russian 30%	nd-L	VL	5.5	1
Lithuania	No, but Russian: 8.7%, Pol: 7%	nd-M	VL	4.9	3
Luxembourg	No, but cosmopolite	nd-L	H	3.8	10
Hungary	No	2.4	M	3.4	7
Malta	No	nd-M	L	4.5	6
Netherlands	No	1.3	H	3.8	10
Austria	No, but small linguistic minorities	1.2	H	3.5	10
Poland	No	2.2	M	4.5	7
Portugal	No	1.9	H	6.5	7
Slovenia	No	nd-M	L	3.2	7
Slovakia	Yes, Hung: 10.6%	3.0	VL	3.4	3
Finland	No, but strong Swed. minority 6%	1.4	M	3.5	8
Sweden	No	1.6	H	3.4	9
UK	Yes, Scots: 10%, Irish: 4.2%, Gael: 2%	2.1	H	4.9	5
Average	Yes, small	2	M-H	4.3	6.4

Source: Authors' compilation based on various sources (*cf.* appendix)

5.3. Summary: Ideal-types, Diversity and Causal Links

The previous section has captured the 25 European fiscal settings on two broad dimensions: a politico-institutional one, and an economic-fiscal one. It identified politico-institutional ideal-types, on the one hand, and fiscal decentralisation ideal-types, on the other hand. Moreover, it also underlined the great European heterogeneity among Member States with respect to their macro-economic situation, wealth, population and cohesion.

It is interesting to see what kind of relation there may be between the two former dimensions. Note that this analysis is indirectly rooted on our definition of what a 'fiscal setting' may be. We decided to infer it from reality, opposing it to traditional Fiscal Federalism theory, and putting more emphasis on history, culture, tradition and institutions than only to tax transfer or bare tax assignments.

The purpose of this section is to gather the evidence collected in the previous section to get a clear and comprehensive picture of European fiscal settings. Although it is tempting to build comprehensive ideal-types by regrouping the countries featuring similar trends, we insist on the relative diversity of European models.

Most of this section concentrates on a bi-dimensional analysis of the previous variables, trying to show correlations among important dimensions. Once again, this provides evidence, which can improve the vision of traditional Fiscal Federalism theory and the working of prevailing fiscal settings.

5.3.1. European Fiscal Settings: Similar Trends, Great Diversity

Trying to sum up all of the findings of the previous paragraphs, a first observation concerns new Member States. In fact they probably constitute a specific group of countries with regards to some politico-institutional and socio-economic indicators: they are similar (with rare exceptions) as far as main characteristics are concerned: type of country, number of levels of government, lower wealth, higher levels of unemployment than in EU(15) and so on. Furthermore, they all show low (or very low) indexes of political decentralisation; which range from 1 to a maximum of 4, that is, under the average of 6 calculated for the EU(15). This can be explained by their relatively small dimensions (as for Cyprus and Malta) or, as for Eastern European countries, by their long common history under communist regimes, still too recent to find a real level of political decentralisation in such states.

On the contrary, when one observes other features, such as inflation for instance, as shown in table 5.6, some of them even exhibit a negative inflation (Lithuania and the Czech Republic), while some others have high inflation (Slovakia, Slovenia and Hungary). Moreover, fiscal power indicators like level of spending sometimes differ with respect to one another (*i.e.* the level of spending in the Czech Republic is 65 per cent of the GDP while in Latvia and Lithuania, respectively 35.4 per cent and 34.1 per cent). Considering the revenue side, again some CEECs show very high values of total public revenue as a share of the GDP, in line with those of NMS (*i.e.*, Hungary 43.4 per cent and the Czech Republic 51.3 per cent), while some others exhibit very low figures (*i.e.* the three Baltic Republics from 34 to 36 per cent).

Differences among performances of NMS from a fiscal point of view are also confirmed through the calculation of the fiscal decentralisation index (FDI), which in fact shows, on the one hand, very low values for some NMS and, on the other hand, high values for the Czech Republic and Poland for instance. Estonia, Latvia and Lithuania have also similar percentages of the GDP as total public spending and revenue.

So, the CEECs can be defined as an ideal-type from a general point of view but keeping in mind that one must also consider each state as specific and not comparable in terms of all features.

States, which form another ideal-type, are Denmark, Finland, and Sweden. They have the highest values of total public revenue as a share of GDP (over 50 per cent). The part of the national product at disposal of local entities is well above the EU average. They exhibit high or medium figures of political decentralisation indexes (respectively 7, 7 and 6 which are all (well) above the EU(25) average) and highest values of FDI, even if they are not federal but unitary states. They also share the way to distribute competencies, with most of them assigned to a particular level of government and only a few being mixed.

In European federal countries, our previous analysis points out the considerable importance held by regions. For two of them, Belgium and Germany, we can say their competence allocation is highly decentralised, as pointed out by the corresponding index, respectively 0.66 and 0.72, as calculated in our empirical table 5.4. A slight difference is in sight in Austria where this value is 0.42 and also comes from the interaction index in table 2 which is smaller. We remarked previously that, in Germany and Belgium, many competencies are mixed but always with the participation of lower tiers of government, in particular that of regions. Even if it is not a traditional federal state, Spain exhibits similar trends to this group with a high degree of fiscal interaction, a high fiscal competence index, a high political decentralisation index.

In Spain, like in Italy and France, regional governments enjoy a varying degree of independence and responsibility. In two of them (Italy, especially after the 2001 Constitutional reform, and Spain) regional authorities exercise in some areas legislative powers comparable with those of regions or States in federal countries (OECD, 2002). As for Italy and France, they approximate one another in terms of the organisation of the state (notably the number of levels of government, Prefects, or the existence of special status regions) and with regards to the distribution of competencies. Nevertheless, both the PDI and the FDI are higher in Italy than in France. This is an indication of the deep decentralisation process taking place in Italy.

As for the UK, it is made up of four nations (England, Scotland, Wales and Northern Ireland). In Scotland and Wales at present the Scottish Parliament and the Welsh National Assembly exercise important responsibilities such as health or relations with local authorities. In Northern Ireland there is a sharing of power between the main communities. The UK is an asymmetric country, because Scotland in particular enjoys a high degree of autonomy while England remains centralised (even if signs of regional governments have recently emerged and the long time government's aim is to establish in England elected regional governments). Note that the same holds in Belgium, but for different reasons. Another group is made up by the Netherlands, Ireland, Greece, and Portugal with a low level of decentralisation.

Finally, the smallest EU Member States are very similar. Malta and Cyprus approximate one another in size and in the prominence of the central government in the carrying out of every task. With regards to Malta and Luxembourg, note the lack of a regional tier of government – in Malta, regions are purely administrative territorial entities grouping a number of local districts (COR, 2004). An embryonic regional presence is present instead in Cyprus, even if only in the form of districts whose District Officers are responsible for applying government policy at this level.

5.3.2. Decentralisation Analysis

The analysis above tried to find, on the basis of different variables, a bit of order in the jungle of European fiscal settings. The purpose of this section is to establish whether these variables are correlated with one another. This will allow to evaluate whether traditional relationships tied to decentralisation still hold or if new relationships can be identified. A significant reference is the so-called Oates-Tiebout hypothesis and fiscal decentralisation studies by the IMF and World Bank: we will use them as guiding references in order to evaluate the 'validity' of our decentralisation analysis. The traditional economics of decentralisation of the public sector assumes, first, that the higher the level of per capita income in a state, the more centralised should be its public sector, as a result of a higher level of involvement in redistributive programmes. Second, the larger the population of the state, the less centralised should be its public sector. Third, the larger the size of a state in terms of land area, the less centralised should be its public sector. Fourth, the more unequal the distribution of income, the less centralised should be the state and local sector. Fifth, more 'diverse' states (as measured by socio-economic indicators) should tend to have a more decentralised public sector. These briefly represent some of the underlying hypothesis of the Fiscal Federalism Theory used in empirical analysis. Most of these empirical works are based on Wallis and Oates (1988).

In order to study these correlations, we investigate the links between the various dimensions of our fiscal settings, and between the latter and our 'control variables': political decentralisation indicators, fiscal decentralisation indicators, wealth (GDP), and population.

Decentralisation and Fiscal Discipline

Often, it is claimed that fiscal discipline is stronger when the central government is predominant and conversely weaker when lower tiers of governments enjoy a deep autonomy. A wide literature on hard budget constraints asks for more discipline in sub-national governments as a pre-condition for economic stability. See among others von Hagen and Harden (1994) and Alesina and Tabellini (1990). Moving on to observe whether decentralisation has some influence on economic stability, we notice that the relation between fiscal decentralisation and the balance of the budget is slightly positive (the more decentralised the more stable), contradicting the previous assumption.

Generally, we can say that at least in Europe, there is not a clear relationship between budget balancing and decentralisation. A possible explanation is that the EU fiscal framework already puts strong pressure on all levels of governments so that no-one can act 'irresponsibly' in respect to fiscal discipline.

Graph 5.10: Budget Balance and Fiscal Decentralisation

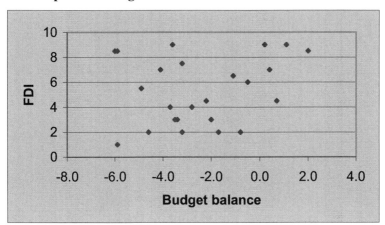

Source: authors

Wealth and Decentralisation: the Uncertain Link

Graph 5.11 below shows that the link between fiscal decentralisation and the wealth level is far from being straightforward. Indeed, our data, concerning relatively rich countries (on a World basis), and encompassing many different aspects of fiscal decentralisation, tends to suggest that there is no direct link between decentralisation and wealth. Obviously, this empirical analysis is loose. However, as our fiscal decentralisation indicator is comprehensive, it is striking to see such a lack of relationship. Note that excluding CEECs, the countries for which data are of a weaker quality still reveals the same picture. This contradicts all the pro-decentralisation arguments, which tend to argue that decentralisation *per se* brings more efficiency, in redistribution and allocation of resources. For instance: one of the theoretical rationales for fiscal decentralisation is heterogeneity of preferences and cost conditions. The smaller the country, the smaller the number of people living there, the more homogeneous the preferences and cost conditions and the lower the potential benefit of decentralisation. However, in fact, our correlation analysis does not confirm the Fiscal Federalism theory.

Graph 5.11: Wealth and Fiscal Decentralisation

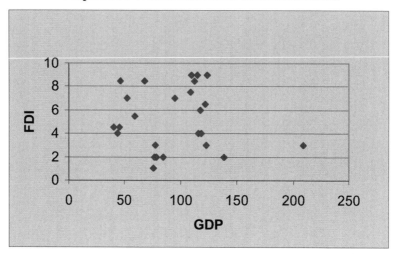

Source: Authors

It is also worth testing whether the distribution of wealth in a given country has some influence on the degree of political decentralisation. Fiscal Federalism predicts that 'the higher the level of per capita income in a state, the more centralised, other things equal, should be its public sector, as a result of a higher level of involvement in redistributive programmes'.[11]

It is important to remark that the income level has two effects on decentralisation that work in opposite directions. The first effect is linked to the observation that developing countries have more centralised public sectors than richer countries (Oates, 1985). Higher income countries tend to have a much stronger tendency toward decentralisation due to the fact that decentralisation is expensive (Wheare, 1964) or possibly as suggested by Martin and Lewis (1956) centralisation is needed in the early stages of development in order to maximise economies of scale in administrative practices. Therefore, this negative relationship between per capita income and decentralisation seems to be unimportant in rich countries like the UE. On the contrary, the level of wealth can influence the level of fiscal decentralisation in view that the propensity to engage in redistribution has a high income elasticity. Local governments are likely to be less efficient in redistributing income because of the mobility of resources across jurisdictions, hence redistribution is centralised.

---

[11] See the hypothesis described by Wallis and Oates (1988).

According to this reasoning, we should find a negative relation between levels of per capita income and decentralisation. As seen previously, it is possible that decentralisation increases economic growth and hence GDP, the regressor being as consequently endogenously biased. Taking as an explanatory variable, the GDP per inhabitant based on PPS (with EU average=100), we build a scatter diagram (results are presented in Graph 5.12). A positive relation can be evidenced meaning that with the growth of the GDP the level of political decentralisation could increase, rendering more evanescent Fiscal Federalism theory explained in Chapter 1 and the above hypothesis. In fact, in Chapter 2, analysing European Cohesion Policy, we conclude similarly. An explanatory reason could be the political power of certain areas thanks to lobbying pressure on the central government and the tendency of richer regions to participate more actively in national redistribution policy in order not to 'lose' the income produced there, hampering the redistribution policies of the central government.

Graph 5.12: Political Decentralisation and Wealth

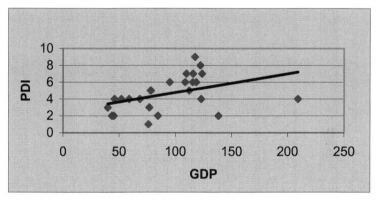

Source: authors

The Bigger the Country, the Higher the Need
for Decentralisation?

An important option for explaining the degree of decentralisation or the degree of sophistication a given fiscal setting exhibits is as simple as the size of a country and/or the size of its population. Indeed, the bigger the population, the higher the need for a complex organisation. According to Fiscal Federalism, this could come from many sources: for instance the heterogeneity of preferences may increase with the number of inhabitants. One of Oates's hypotheses asserts that "the larger the population of a state, other things equal, the less centralised should be its public sector" (Wallis and Oates, 1988). Our analysis supports such a hypothesis: Graph 5.13 indicates a positive relationship between the population and fiscal decentralisation. If we take as a control variable political decentralisation, the result is much more significant. Hence, decentralisation depends much on political and institutional variables, as often claimed in previous chapters. This is an important result that witnesses that in order to fully understand decentralisation, political and institutional factors have to be taken into account.

Graph 5.13: Population and Fiscal Decentralisation

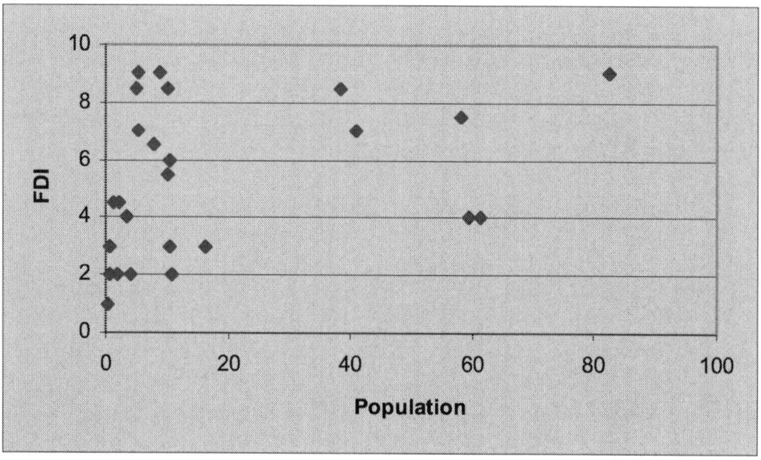

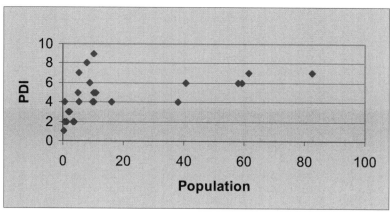

Source: authors

Graph 5.14: Population and Political Decentralisation

Source: authors

According to Graph 5.14, the population level seems to have some influence on political decentralisation.

Another simple hypothesis, barely tested by the Fiscal Federalism theory, is to see whether the number of levels of government present in a given country depends on its population. The answer is positive, as seen in Graph 5.15 below. This relationship between the two seems both strong and significant. One reason can be that when the population of a country is abundant, there is a higher probability that different classes/ layers of people expect a certain representation of their territory which has to be nearer the land where they live than the central state. Another simple argument relates to easy management issues. A simple way to understand it is to refer to the way companies are managed in the private sector. Indeed, the bigger (or the most dispersed in space) the company, the higher the number of executives needed to manage it. It is not necessary to have many layers of government in smaller countries, where the central government/locus of power is automatically closer to citizens.

Graph 5.15: Population and Levels of Government

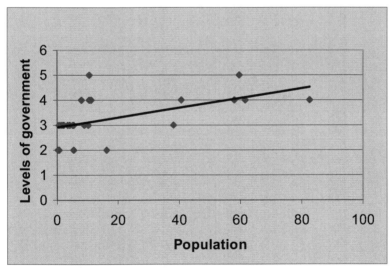

Source: authors

Cohesion and Decentralisation

Our cohesion index made-up of several variables (history, economic and territorial inequalities) leads to contradict FF theory according to which 'the more unequal the distribution of income, the less centralised,

179

should be the state and local sector'. Graph 5.16 shows that there is a negative relation between these two variables, hence that the more cohesive, the more centralised. Once again, the validity of our hypothesis is stronger if we consider political rather than fiscal decentralisation. Another possible interpretation of our cohesion index (see appendix) is that it could be an indicator of preference heterogeneity. In this case, the traditional outcome that the more heterogeneous (homogeneous) the preferences, the higher the need for more decentralisation (centralisation) would not prevail. This result however paves the way for many different interpretations.

Graph 5.16: Cohesion and Decentralisation

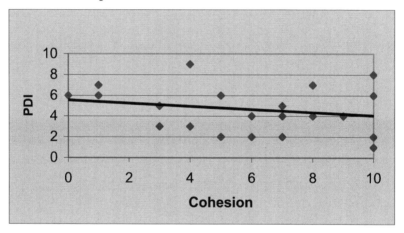

Source: authors

The links between political and fiscal decentralisation: pleonasm, correlation or causality?

As shown in Graph 5.17 there seems to be a deep link between political and fiscal decentralisation. As the latter is more likely to originate from the former than the opposite, this gives evidence of the fact that political decentralisation is one of the main factors of fiscal decentralisation.

Note also that all our scatter diagrams happened to be much more significant by using the PDI than the FDI. This may simply mean that political decentralisation determines fiscal decentralisation. For sure, this means that political and institutional factors play a central role in the 'contours' of national fiscal settings. Still, the descriptive nature of our result does not allow to determine the direction of the causality between politics and fiscal and taxation systems.

The demand for fiscal decentralisation either comes from the benefiting political entities (asking for more powers and self-determination capabilities), from the heterogeneity of preferences (which is deeply political too), or from representatives of the Central government ideologically or politically committed to decentralisation (*e.g.* France). Central planner concerns about efficiency and fiscal federalist type arguments are either secondary or *ad hoc* justifications of already decided measures. Demands for higher political decentralisation (being local politicians nearer to citizens' will) generally trigger and precede demand for fiscal decentralisation.

Eventually, although it would seem too strong to conclude on the definite nature of the correlation between the various dimensions of European fiscal settings, such links at least induce that studying them in isolation (as does the traditional normative theory of Fiscal Federalism) is not relevant.

Graph 5.17: Political and Fiscal Decentralisation

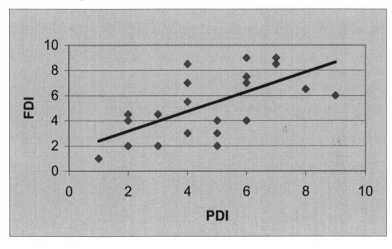

Source: authors

5.4. Conclusion: The Need for Political Realism

The analysis carried out in this chapter aimed to clarify the relationship between theories and facts highlighted many times in this book, in order to determine lessons from national experiences for the EU (dimension 1 of our problematic) and for the theory of Fiscal Federalism (dimension 2). In line with this positive perspective, which presupposes the plurality of dimensions constituting existing fiscal settings (defined as the numerous 'Fiscal Federalism' practices encountered in reality), the main features of most European countries were captured by using various indexes. The identification of 'ideal-types' of states sharing similar features can, it was argued, provide interesting lessons for the EU as a whole. Next to this, Chapter 5 also provided more insights about the interactions between political decentralisation, fiscal decentralisation and socio-economic variables. The important dimensions of any fiscal setting are mainly political, institutional, fiscal and socio-economic. In particular, and in contrast with most fiscal federalist studies, the originality of this chapter comes from that it did not only concentrate on the analysis of tax and fiscal decentralisation (*e.g.* tax autonomy, total spending and revenue, etc.), but it also involved politico-institutional and socio-economic variables. It is worth noting that the inclusion of politico-institutional indicators allows to stress once more one of the main ideas developed in previous chapters of this contribution: *one cannot leave aside political factors when studying national fiscal settings because they also have a strong influence on decisions regarding the latter.* Our perspective thus tries to avoid a major flaw of Fiscal Federalism theory, that disregards political factors, which happen to be very important when, in reality, policy-makers choose among various 'fiscal setting options'.

First, we identified, on the basis of the calculation of various indexes, a *series of ideal-types.*

Federal (Austria, Germany, Belgium) and quasi-federal (Spain) countries are highly decentralised under most dimensions. This decentralisation, which benefits regional governments, is also synonymous to less political and fiscal powers for local governments, as if the regional level was swallowing most of the sub-central powers.

Scandinavian countries also exhibit very high degrees of decentralisation, but this decentralisation mostly benefits local governments. Regional governments are either powerless or non-existent. In both cases, power is 'swallowed' by one sub-central level of government.

Other countries, traditionally very centralised (like France or Italy), diffuse political, fiscal and taxation powers more evenly among vertical levels of government. Current reforms, still under way, may however change the current institutional equilibrium.

Still among OMS, southern countries, such as Portugal or Greece, or northern countries such as the Netherlands, the UK and Ireland, to which one can add Luxembourg (and its small size) are characterised by heavy centralisation. It can be noted, however that the UK is a dual model, as it has handed large amounts of political power to Scotland or Wales, but not to English regions in England. However, regional autonomy, from a fiscal and taxation perspective is still rather limited in the entire of the United Kingdom. Moreover, these countries are very centralised in the sense that elected sub-central governments are either rare or powerless. Nevertheless, this does not necessarily mean that the bulk of fiscal, economic and political decisions are taken in the capital city. Indeed, the lack of political decentralisation is generally partially compensated by the existence of State or administration representatives at a lower scale, very similar to the Napoleonic model of territorial organisation known as the *Préfectures*. The extent to which the latter agencies know local cost conditions, preferences and to which they take them into account is still indeterminate and may vary from one country to the other (especially there could be a further ideal-type differentiating northern and southern centralised countries).

Eventually, the CEECs seem to share similar features, with heavy centralisation, both political and fiscal. For the last fifteen years, the concern has been related more to 'destatalisation'/privatisation than to the vertical reorganisation of the State. It must not be forgotten, however, that some countries are undergoing massive reforms.

Second, *inside similar ideal-types, a huge variety still prevails*. For instance, the Belgian federation, which exhibits similar inequality levels as in Germany, deviates from other European Federations in that it is very asymmetrical (with the merger of the Flanders region and community). Similarly, countries like France and Italy, which used to share similar vertical structures of government, are likely to take different paths, with Italy being more and more regionalised whereas France seems keen to keep a balance between different levels of government. The same holds if one analyses the ten new MS. Conversely, some countries belonging to different ideal-types resemble one another as they share one or more important features. For example, France and the UK, Italy and Belgium, or Luxembourg and Malta. For instance, a variable as trivial as the size of the country (the very imperfect proxy being the population) seems closely linked to the extent of political decentralisation and/or the number of levels of government (in our framework, the former is one dimension of the latter).

The only inferences one may draw from this huge diversity of fiscal settings are the following. In each country the degree and modalities of fiscal decentralisation seem to come from political features (and not the reverse). Those in turn, may be explained through history, as the belonging to one ideal-type often goes hand in hand with a common history (Scandinavian countries, Germany and Austria, Southern countries and the Napoleonic model, CEECs, etc.). However, once this is said, it seems that each country has developed its own mode of vertical organisation of the public sector. In federations, regions swallow power, whereas localities do so in Scandinavian countries. In countries like France or Italy, the balance seems more respected. Thus, the need to manage effectively one's public sector is everywhere salient, but the responses given to this need differs among countries.

Furthermore, the existing models of organisation do not correspond to a heroic decentralisation/centralisation spectrum (where centralisation means that decisions are taken far-away from the citizens, in the capital city), as most countries exhibit significant levels of political or administrative *déconcentration*/decentralisation. In the same vein, it is a mistake to suppose that political Federalism is necessarily synonymous to more decentralisation or to better economic outcomes. For instance, countries like Germany or Belgium more or less exhibit the same levels of political and fiscal decentralisation as Scandinavian countries.[12] The construction of 'ideal-types' confirms that it is just not true to think that federal states are automatically more decentralised; in fact, this chapter pointed out that Denmark, Finland and Sweden have strong features of decentralisation. This contradicts the implicit Fiscal Federalism assumption, which presupposes implicitly that mature parliamentary Federations are the ideal kind of states to which its prescriptions should lead to (dimension 5 of the problematic). Actually, we have seen that their lower levels of government are not merely subordinate to the highest; for example, in Sweden and Denmark, the right to self-determination of local self-government is set in the Constitution and in Sweden local authorities can levy taxes and determine tax rates. These unitary countries can be defined as decentralised both from the political side, showing high or medium values of political decentralisation index, and from the fiscal side. Italy, Spain and France, which look very similar in terms of structure (*i.e.* same kind of levels of government, presence of Prefects), perform (already high) levels of PDI and FDI that are higher in Italy and Spain than in France, showing that the former have undergone a consistent process of decentralisation.

All in all, the variety of fiscal settings encountered in the European reality shows that, even though there is not just one model of internal organisation of the public sector, these various settings all share a common point: there are various ways to manage effectively the public sector. Ready-to-wear decentralisation recipes are, thus, likely to fail if they do not take into account historical and institutional specificities,

---

[12] Among European federal states, Germany stands out showing high degrees of all indexes. Already in Chapter 4, we highlighted the importance of the German case: here again, Germany has been able to reach an high degree of political and fiscal decentralisation, of cooperation and cohesion, which the EU as a whole could take into consideration as a way of realising the same aims at the Union's level (dimension 1 of the problematic). More realistically though, the EU could at least use the example of such a mature fiscal setting in order to avoid the same mistakes.

which, in practice matter the most. Each country has generally found its own way to organise its public sector among vertical layers of government. The various configurations of competence distribution, sub-central spending powers or autonomy, next to the improbable link between fiscal decentralisation and wealth, do not allow to identify a 'superior' or 'optimal model'. We have seen that 'no relationship' is already an important finding. The lack of correlation between fiscal decentralisation and wealth means that decentralisation may not be such a panacea, or that it may not be seen as a major cause of economic development. Its benefits may be more political than economical, thus contradicting the indicative 'optimal' decomposition of functions supposed to give full economic justifications to decentralisation. The idea here, is not to claim that decentralisation is not 'good', or that it cannot bring economic benefits. It is more to say that the normative fiscal federalist perspective is not exempted from ideological biases. If this analysis does not seek to contradict other findings or theoretical insights of traditional Fiscal Federalism theory, it brings, at least, a set of presumptions,[13] which are momentous for the future understanding of both national countries and the EU. To put it simply, in the EU countries, there is no clear-cut correlation between the level of GDP per inhabitant and fiscal decentralisation as the theory of Fiscal Federalism would predict.

The main lessons from national fiscal settings for the European Union are straightforward. Looking for such things as a superior fiscal setting or an optimal degree of fiscal decentralisation is misleading. It gives the impression that decentralisation (of the allocation function) or the centralisation (of the redistribution and stabilisation functions) is firstly best regardless of the political features of the polity in which the fiscal setting operates. In reality, fiscal settings are shaped to fit the politico-institutional reality in order to make the public sector function effectively. Reforms can either be motivated by political factors (calls from the regions or localities to be granted more tasks) or by real-world development already analysed by Fiscal Federalism (for example, inter-jurisdictional competition or fiscal equity), but at the end, political features determine fiscal ones and not the reverse. Thus, providing an indicative yardstick of an *a priori* superior model of Fiscal Federalism is an *'exercice de style'*, which may be useless as such for European decision-makers. Note that as our fiscal decentralisation indicator and our political decentralisation indicator are deeply intertwined, it is not

---

[13]   Advanced readers could object that we did not provide 'hard' econometric evidence. However, data collection and other methodological problems let us think that the production of such kind of empirical test is unlikely to be possible (or relevant) in the near future.

easy to identify hard causalities. The contention that fiscal settings are complex systems of interactions in which non fiscal variables play a pre-eminent role may be contradicted. Still, this points to the necessity to take simultaneously into account these two dimensions to understand and reform a given fiscal setting.

In other words, if one wants to improve the EU fiscal setting (without any reference to an *ad hoc* optimal), it has to find a setting, which is compatible with the prevailing political features (modes of decision, political nature and objectives) of the EU. If not, any reform is likely to fail. The next chapter returns to this issue at length.

CHAPTER 6

Concluding about European Fiscal Federalism

A Political Economy Perspective

Clément Vaneecloo, Margherita Fornasini and
Augusta Badriotti

At the centre of most debates about the European Union, one can find its current and future fiscal setting. Indeed, the evolutionary and hybrid nature of the EU makes any decision regarding the allocation of competencies to Brussels or its financing look 'quasi-constitutional'. Any change in the fiscal and/or political organisation, even incremental, may thus constitute an infinite source of conflicts. Indeed, reforms of the fiscal setting are implicitly linked to a wider set of questions, to which it is impossible to provide comprehensive answers here: What *is* the EU? What *does it do*? What *could* the EU be/do? What *should* the EU be/do? The theory of Fiscal Federalism mainly provides answers to the first, second and fourth questions. Later, we shall partly answer to these questions, with a special emphasis on the third question.

As we have seen, if one assumes that the EU is a traditional State – with the EU being the central level, and the national Member States, their regions and localities constituting the sub-central levels – the normative theory of Fiscal Federalism prescribes a given distribution of functions among these vertical layers of government. This '*ideal*' distribution does not hold in practice. In the EU, if the allocation function is in the hand of the sub-central levels of government, this is not the case for most components of the redistribution (fiscal redistribution and social security being cases in point) and of the stabilisation functions.

While observing the gap between normative prescriptions and the actual decomposition of functions, one temptation would be to apply blindly this broad framework and argue for a Europeanisation of redistribution and stabilisation, which in practice would imply signifi-cant 'upward devolution' of some of the economic functions of Member States (and the related finances) to Brussels (together with a boom of the European budget). Two interrelated reasons may lead us to think this would be the wrong route to follow. First, as we argued many times, the normative theory of Fiscal Federalism, as such, seems to be an inadequate indicative framework for the EU. Second, any (proposal of) change has to 'owe respect' to the real situation, including the deeply political nature of the EU and of the integration process. This is both a matter of 'scientific honesty' and a *sine qua non* condition for the success of any reform.

If this is true, what can the theory offer for the comprehension and reform of the EU fiscal setting? This chapter seeks to show that *a* fiscal federalist perspective still retains some relevance regarding *i)* the identification of some potentially unsustainable states of affairs and of some potential solutions, *ii)* the identification of the actual incoherence in the European fiscal setting, *iii)* the clarification of the various sets of politico-fiscal organisations among which EU decision-makers could currently choose from. This validity is however conditioned to an appropriate incorporation of the politico-institutional features (some label it as governance) of the European Union.

This last chapter thus provides an assessment of the current European fiscal setting by insisting on the general political dynamics of the budget, still largely unacknowledged by most economists. The first two sections summarise briefly the 'EU fiscal setting' by answering two questions: what does the EU do? With what means? Section 6.3 points out the main problems caused by the current political and fiscal organisation. Section 6.4 criticises the relevance of the normative theory of Fiscal Federalism and proposes to go 'beyond theoretical confusions'. It also provides a political economy point of view of the EU fiscal setting. The ambition is prospective as it seeks to clarify (with a special focus on political and budget-related issues) the different paths the EU could actually take.

6.1. What Does the EU Do? Tasks and Policies

What does the EU fiscal setting look like? What is the EU supposed to do and is it successful in doing so? This section, which summarises and complements Chapters 2 and 3, considers the EU as a fiscal setting in its own right: the central level becomes the EU, the sub-central levels being composed of the national, regional and local levels of government. However, this setting is particular. The tasks undertaken are quite extensive and to some extent are subject to constant re-interpretations. European competencies are numerous compared to the relatively limited means (*cf.* section 6.2) devoted to them: the EU is incredibly weak in budgetary terms both compared to what it is supposed to do and to other Federations of the same size. To some extent, thus, this section underlines the wide competencies already held by the EU.

6.1.1. *'European Tasks' and Instruments*

The competencies assumed by the European Union are defined in the Treaties, and re-affirmed at the beginning, in part I, title 3, from Article I-11 to Article I-18 of the European Constitution (Article I-11 explains the principles of competence allocation: subsidiarity and proportionality).[1] Each competence allocated to the EU already gives rise to a prolific economic literature, to which it is not possible to owe respect hereafter.[2] Nevertheless, it seems unavoidable to present them briefly. Table 6.1 gives a rough idea of the policies assumed by the EU. The criteria for assessing the real importance of a given competence are numerous. For instance, as in table 6.1, it can be the degree of exclusiveness to which the EU assumes a given task. The EU assumes full responsibility for a number of policies, such as the Competition policy or the Trade policy. Other policies are shared with the sub-central levels of government and their impact are clearly related to the implementation of other national policies (*e.g.* environment policy, transport policy, research policy, etc.), if not partially (*e.g.* Cohesion policy) or fully (*e.g.* the SGP) dependent on Member States 'good will' regarding implementation.

---

[1]　When we started writing this book, the Constitution had just been adopted by the Council and was set to be ratified through referendum or parliamentary ratification. In June 2005, after the result of referendum in France and Holland, where the "no" to the EU Constitution won, the EU integration process is once again under (temporary) stress. European Councils of June and December 2005 did not solve anything. The constitution is available *via* the EU website or on eur-Lex. See website references at the end of the book.

[2]　See for instance Breuss and Eller (2003) for a recent empirical and theoretical survey, with an emphasis on the Fiscal Federalism perspectives. See also Buti (2003) or Boyer and Dehove (2003).

Table 6.1: EU Policies at a Glance

DEGREE OF EXCLUSIVENESS	POLICY	Constitutional Basis
HIGH 'areas of *exclusive* competencies'	– Customs union – Establishing of competition rule necessary for the functioning of the internal market – Monetary policy (euro MS only) – Conservation of marine biological resources under the common fisheries policy	Article I-13
MEDIUM 'areas of *shared* competencies'	– Internal market – Social policy [a] – Economic, social and territorial cohesion – Agriculture and fisheries (exc. *Supra*) – Environment – Consumer protection – Transport – Trans-European networks – Energy – Area of freedom, security and justice – Common safety/ public health [a] – Research – Development cooperation and humanitarian aid – Coordination of employment and economic policies	Article I-14
	– Common commercial policy – Common foreign and security policy	Article I-15 Article I-16
LOW 'areas of *supporting, coordinating or complementary action'*	– Protection and improvement of human health – Industry – Culture – Tourism – Education, youth, sport, vocational training – Civil protection – Administrative cooperation	Article I-17

(a) on precise aspects only, defined in Part III of the Constitution

Source: Treaty establishing a Constitution for Europe

A second criterion is the sharing of a given policy in the total European budget (*cf.* section 6.2). Indeed, each of these responsibilities has a more or less big impact on the working of the European Union economy. For instance, the Agriculture policy, which has historically been the first expenditure of the European budget (*cf. infra*), is not solely undertaken by the EU level. Indeed, national levels of government, and even sometimes sub-national ones (like Belgian regions) also have their own agricultural policy. But EU regulations, and its leading role in shaping the face of European agriculture, *via* its policy instruments, have completely determined the evolution of agriculture on the European territory. This is currently exemplified by the role played by the EU on the reshaping of CEECs primary sectors. On the contrary, some exclusive competencies of the EU, which are 'costless' in budgetary terms, have a big impact on European economies (*e.g.* Competition policy, Monetary policy for the euro area). To be consistent with our definition of what a Fiscal Setting is (Chapter 1), it is important to keep in mind the decomposition of the numerous 'non-European competencies' among 'sub-central' levels of government, inside national Member States (*cf.* Chapter 5).

Nevertheless, EU decisions often have a wide and deep impact, which is reinforced by the primacy of EU law over national laws. It is commonly estimated that more than half of national laws originate from EU laws. In other terms, the EU mostly uses two major instruments of policy delivery. First, the EU, or its institutional triangle (Commission, Council, Parliament), uses the regulation tool extensively, trusting the European Court of Justice (ECJ) and national judiciary systems for the enforcement of all legislation (directives, regulations, etc.) under the EU field of competencies.[3] As argued by Majone (1993), the EU thus provides a large amount of regulation without using the fiscal tool. But the EU also uses its budget to undertake its own policies, such as Cohesion Policy, external policy (development aid) or its research policy. The following goes back to two instances of policies, which, in practice, involve many different levels of government but take rather different political forms.

6.1.2. Solidarity and Cohesion in the EU

Chapter 2 analysed in depth the Cohesion Policy, one of the most – if not the most since the last enlargement – important 'on the ground' European policies. Interesting lessons were drawn under each of the dimensions presented in Chapter 1, clearly showing the interactions between the theory of Fiscal Federalism and the reality of this major element of the European fiscal setting.

First, regarding dimension 4, we highlighted the main lessons from Fiscal Federalism for the Cohesion Policy. Chapter 2 has argued that the 'vicious' circle between mobility and differentiated redistribution policies could lead to the failure of national redistribution systems, thus providing important theoretical justifications allowing traditional theory of Fiscal Federalism to advocate for the 'centralisation' of the redistribution function at the European level. With more realistic assumption about the EU and the actual status and working of the Cohesion Policy, the theory of Fiscal Federalism, *via* its analysis of grants, also helps to draw useful lessons. On top of giving solid justifications to the latter, the

---

[3] The Constitution states in Article I-11 the Fundamental principles of the Competence attribution.

normative view also allows to infer the likely comparative effect of different types of intergovernmental grants. Consequently, the type of grant/inter-territorial distribution (the form of the Cohesion Policy) matters and should be chosen according to the purpose it wants to serve. The additionality principle of the Cohesion Policy is hence justified as a means to avoid the flypaper effect.

Secondly, however, the overwhelming focus on the fiscal components of redistribution and the ignorance of other politico-economic modalities accompanying these financial transfers lead us to think that the analysis from the traditional normative Fiscal Federalism perspective was to be taken with great caution. Indeed, the latter, as such, is not so much relevant for the Cohesion Policy as the functional decomposition which is used as a yardstick tends to lose its accuracy in the EU context. Even though cautiousness in the way the Fiscal Federalism perspective is used allows to reach interesting findings about the likely future of distributive and social Europe, this traditional perspective seems to be a suit, which does not fit the Cohesion Policy very well.

Thirdly, it is possible to reverse the previous point of view to highlight the lessons of the Cohesion Policy for the theoretical paradigm (dimension 3). For instance, it seems that distribution in a fiscal setting can be inter-jurisidictional and still represents a first-best. Moreover, it was claimed, the EU is very innovative. The application of the partnership and subsidiarity principles, which are a mix of centralisation and decentralisation, can lead to higher welfare gains than either of both alternatives. The traditional perspective of Fiscal Federalism could incorporate this singular setting as a way to achieve higher public sector effectiveness. Last but not least, cohesion policy also exemplifies the fact that political factors are to be taken into account if one wants to assess the effectiveness of any policy and the results or impact of any fiscal setting. We go back to this last point in the next section.

6.1.3. Stability in the EU: Fiscal Rule (mis)Definition, (mis)Cooperation and (mis)Enforcement

Next to the Cohesion policy, a second important element of the European fiscal setting is the degree to which it helps to stabilise the EU economy. More accurately, it is the weak degree of stabilisation provided at the EU level. According to the traditional Fiscal Federalist view, drawing on the Musgravian decomposition of state functions, macroeconomic stabilisation should be centralised (dimension 4). In practice, however, the stabilisation function is not centralised as there is no representative, European-wide, authoritative body taking decisions on the macro-management of the EU or of the euro area. Despite recurrent calls for cooperation among national fiscal policies, and the setting-up of new bodies like the Ecofin, Member States still do whatever they think is good without taking into account the situation in their neighbouring countries.

Note that stabilisation refers to something very broad as it encompasses all of the actions a given government can undertake in order to attenuate the variations of economic cycles. Since the 1970s, Europe has to deal with rising unemployment and steady but capricious growth (such as in 1993 or since 2001), which have been the main focus of most macroeconomists ever since. The main economic and social problem of our time is, thus, to employ the European working force, which is overwhelmingly correlated to the growth rate.

Since the irrevocable fixing of bilateral nominal exchange rates of former European currencies in 1999, and the birth of the euro two years later, economic debates essentially focused on the functioning, objectives and credibility of the European Central Bank and on the Stability and Growth Pact. The current debate mainly insists on two questions: i) once most EU(15) European countries share one currency, should there be a set of rules constraining their fiscal behaviour, ii) if yes, what should these rules be, and in particular, are current rules the good ones. Closely linked to these debates are the issues of the efficiency of fiscal policies and, to a lesser extent, the capacity to implement a Policy-Mix at the European level. The majority of the economic literature suggests that the answer to the first question is positive. However, the consensus explodes when it comes to define precise rules. Particularly, the rules of the Stability and Growth Pact are criticised as being either ill-defined or unenforceable. The practice seems to confirm this criticism as the mechanism adopted in the European Union in order to guarantee stability in the Economic and Monetary Union, the SGP, has been effective during the first years of its application (although several criticisms arose almost immediately) but has encountered enormous problems when the Member States started facing economic difficulties. Chapter 3 proposed improvements, which could actually be applied to the EU stabilisation policy: the proposals are numerous but the will to change is still limping.

Anyway, several arguments call for a more extensive fiscal setting, mainly in the form of a bigger budget. Above all Fiscal Federalism improves the absorption of (demand) asymmetric shocks in that it triggers an interregional redistribution mechanism similar to fiscal stabilisers. The state or the region victim of the shock sees its tax falling and hence its contribution to the federal budget but at the same time the contributions (social expenditures or unemployment benefits) from the federal budget grow. The federal budget can finance public expenditures in a context of discretionary policies such as grants in aid to economic reconversion (which is already put in practice in Objective 2 regions). In particular, Fiscal Federalism is more effective when asymmetric shocks are important and this depends on the degree of diversification of national economies in that less specialised economies are less subject to regional shocks.

The question asked here is the following. With a 'centralised' monetary policy, how much fiscal policy coordination is needed among countries that have already fully centralised their monetary policy? Common macroeconomic shocks may require a coordinated response. According to the Maastricht Treaty, countries are free to pursue any mix of spending and taxing policies, provided that budget deficits are roughly balanced. Constraints on the size of the budget inside a monetary union are backboned by credibility arguments (Obstfeld, 1997). Countries with high public debts may have incentives to 'inflate the debt away' by reducing the interest burden. In a monetary union, a free-rider problem makes this credibility problem more accurate: national public debts are likely to be relatively good substitutes, since being free of exchange risk. The expectation of bail-out creates a moral hazard problem and weakens the incentives to pursue a balanced budget in the EMU. The current configuration of the EMU implies a response to macroeconomic shocks with the use of fiscal policy instruments at the European level, thereby leading to stronger demands for a bigger EU budget and possibly for EU deficit-spending. In any case, even the simple respect of the current balanced budget rule by national governments requires additional enforcement powers at supranational level which in turn requires a higher legitimacy of supranational institutions, hence reinforcing the old call for political reforms.[4]

The striking difference between the European Cohesion and Stabilisation policies does not relate to their justifications as both of them can be justified on economic grounds. It neither relates to their importance as the former seeks an even distribution of growth across the EU territory by reducing inter-regional inequalities, while the latter seeks theoretically to promote growth on the entire European territory. Neither does it relate to the degree to which they are contested, nor to the level of implication of sub-central (either national or regional) authorities (maximum in both cases).

---

[4] Ten years ago, Persson *et al.* (1996, p. 15), among many others, already stated that: "this illustrates the role of complementarity between various policy dimensions, so far neglected in the theory of Fiscal Federalism. [...] There are no examples in history of large and political powerful countries that have completely delegated their monetary policy to an independent supranational agency, while at the same time retaining their political autonomy."

The most significant difference between the two policies is that stabilisation policy is based on a not-credible, not-enforceable agreement,
without clear leadership, whereas the Cohesion Policy is a credible, self-
enforced agreement where, once decided the envelope for each country
and region, the Commission plays a supervisory and controlling role.
This does not represent a call for a transposition of Cohesion Policy
governance to the SGP. This just suggests that a condition for any
cooperation in stabilisation at the European level is the true commitment
of national governments to common objectives. This commitment, to be
enforceable, needs to be credible and suited to European countries. The
main difference has to do with the fact that political factors are pre-
eminent and cannot be figured out after an optimal situation is sketched
by the normative theory of Fiscal Federalism. The theory has to take for
granted the political dynamics at the European level, as theoretically
superior designs, whatever there are, explode in the face of real difficulties. The SGP illustrates it perfectly. Although it was supposed to be a
superior theoretical cooperation framework, its practical application
only produced dissatisfaction so far. The failure of the March 2004
discussions on the SGP, and its eventually soft reform, in March 2005,
are unsatisfactory as they do not achieve their theoretical duties for
obvious political reasons.

6.2. With What Means? Budgetary Issues and Alternative Modes of Cooperation

The second element of the EU fiscal setting is the budget: one of the
two tools, next to regulation, at its disposal for undertaking its tasks. The
European budget tends to focalise attention and crystallise conflicts.
Proponents of further integration argue for its extension, whereas oppo-
nents of further integration call for its containment. This, in return, tends
to slow down its expansion under the unanimity rule. However, despite
its smallness, it is sufficient to undertake some ambitious policies.
Moreover, it uses an 'alternative way', instrumentalising the Cohesion
Policy in the context of Financial Perspectives, to reach significant
agreements about the wider integration process. Once again, this indicates that the political dynamics of a particular nature is pre-eminent in
the process of economic integration.

6.2.1. Revenues, Expenditures and Budget Negotiation

Although it is still limited in real terms (*cf.* next sub-section), the
European budget now amounts to more than 110 billion euros annually.
On the financing side, the European Union budget is financed mainly by
'own resources', meaning by resources made available to it by Member

States. The Council decides about its level by unanimity and with the ratification of national parliaments. Therefore, the process is slow and new resources have to pass through the ratification of each Member State. Own resources can be classified according to four types. The first is made up of levies on imports on agricultural products from non-member countries and of sugar levies, the second is represented by customs duties. In the aftermath of the first enlargements, these two types were not sufficient to finance the budget; new resources were, thus, introduced. Since 1979, the third type of resources comes from the application of a uniform rate to Member States' VAT bases. Finally, the fourth resource is an 'additional' resource, because it is calculated in order to cover the part of total expenditure not covered by the other resources. It results from the application of a uniform rate to Member States' GNP. This last resource amounts for around half of Community revenues, as opposed to around 30-35 per cent for the VAT resource.

On the spending side, the European budget is divided among different categories. Graph 6.1 presents the evolution of these categories over time as a share of total spending. The last column of table 6.2 presents actual expenditures for 2004. In the early days of the Community, most resources were devoted to the CECA, the CEAA and administration. Since the late 1960s, the Common agricultural policy (CAP) has been the most resource-consuming Community policy. Its main objectives are the increase in agricultural competitiveness, the stability of markets and prices and a particular attention, in recent years, to the environmental situation in which agricultural activities are performed. The budget is also used to promote the economic and social cohesion of the European Union (Chapter 2), in order to reduce inequalities in wealth distribution, improve employment or protect the environment. The remaining part of the EU budget is assigned to finance programs related to trans-European (transport) networks, communication technologies, research and bio-technologies, health, development of new sources of energy and to promote student mobility. However, these last categories do not exceed 5 per cent of the budget. As for the external policy, the action of the EU is mainly devoted to development and humanitarian aid, in particular through the European Development Fund or the European Community Humanitarian Office, which acts in regions suffering from natural disasters or coming out of war (*e.g.* Kosovo after 1999).

Graph 6.1: Evolution of the Main Spending Categories of the European Budget from 1957 to 2000

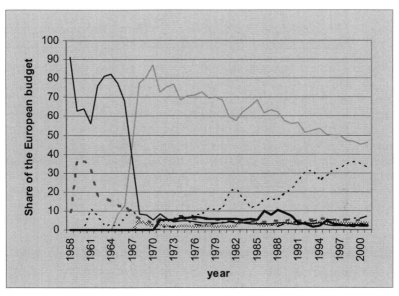

———	Research
———	CAP-EAGGF (European Agricultural Guidance and Guarantee Fund)
··············	Cohesion Policy – Structural Actions
▬▬	Reimbursement and other
··········	External Action
———	CECA+CEEA+EDF
– – – –	Administration

Source: authors, based on EC (2000) data

Furthermore, Articles 268 to 280 of the EC Treaty set the various rules and principles of the European budget.[5] Article 268 states the principle of balance, that revenue must be equal to expenditure so that the budget cannot be in deficit. Although the budget is passed annually (under an inter-institutional agreement and with a pre-eminent role of the Parliament), it has been since 1988 completely constrained by the financial perspectives negotiated every five to seven years among national governments. This new system of mid-term budgetary planning allowed to end the budgetary conflicts of the early 1980s between the

---

[5] The main ones are the principles of unity, universality, specialty, annuality and balance; see EC (2000), page 6 for the description of these principles and pages 7 to 11 for details on the annual procedure. Few changes have been made in the Constitution.

Parliament and the Council. Moreover, it has played a certain role in European integration by offering alternative modes of cooperation through the budget.

6.2.2. The Financial Perspectives: An Alternative and Original Mode of Cooperation through the Budget?

Since 1988, Financial perspectives (FPs) set the overall budget ceiling, and the shares of the budget to be spent on each of the above-mentioned categories. Political in nature, as they set the maximum ambition in each policy field for the next couple of years, they constrain the annual budget, without determining it fully. National governments gather in the Council under the unanimity rule and agree on a 'Policy package'. The Commission proposal (see EC, 2004 a and b), one to two years before, can be interpreted as being the basis for the negotiations (maximum budget). The climax of the negotiation occurs in Summits, where national heads of government tend to 'trade' their vote on a given issue against another's voting support on another issue (see Laffan and Shackleton, 2003 and Allen, 2003). So far, the EU has adopted three financial perspectives,[6] which have been modified at each enlargement.

Recently, at the 2005 Brussels Summit under the UK Presidency, a big step towards the fourth Financial Perspective Agreement has been made. The 25 Member States agreed on a 862 billion euros budget for the 2006-2013 period (between 121 and 127 billion euros yearly). The fact that the Parliament refused the agreement at the beginning of 2006 is unlikely to modify it significantly, but it will probably increase it a bit. What is certain however is that Cohesion Policy, under the 'sustainable growth heading', will account for at least 380 billion euros (2004 prices) within the period, 44 per cent of the budget, and nearly 0.5 per cent of the EU GDP. The CAP will gradually decrease, with direct payments and market intervention accounting for less than a third of the budget. In many ways, however, this budget seems very low. It clashes with the important structural needs of new MS and seems unlikely to allow to match-up to the Lisbon ambition. Moreover, both appropriation for payment and commitment are planned to decrease gradually. In 2013, they will respectively account for only 1 per cent and 0.94 per cent of the EU(25) GNI. The only positive point is that a complete re-organisation of the budget has also been scheduled. The Commission will make a new proposal in 2008-2009.

---

[6] *Delors I*, agreed in Brussels in 1988 for the 1988-1992 period, *Delors II* agreed in Copenhagen in 1992 for the 1993-1999 period, and *Agenda 2000*, agreed in Berlin in 1999 for the 2000-2007 period.

Table 6.2 presents the current financial perspectives as modified by the Copenhagen Summit in 2002. This Summit re-negotiated Financial Perspectives to take into account enlargement. The table compares these 'predicted or capped expenditures' to actual budgetary data in 2004. The budget for the EU(25) exceeds 111 billion euros in appropriation for commitment and approximates 100 billion euros in appropriation for payment (0.98 per cent of the EU(25) GNI).

Table 6.2: Financial Perspectives: EU(25), in Million Euros at 1999 Prices (Appropriations for Commitment)

	2000	2001	2002	2003	2004	2005	2006	2004 FP-share of the budget	2004 actual App. for Com.
1. Agriculture	40920	42800	43900	43770	44657	45677	45807	43.4%	42.0%
2. Structural Actions	32045	31455	30865	30285	36665	36502	37940	35.6%	35.9%
Inc. Structural Funds	*29430*	*28840*	*28250*	*27670*	*30533*	*31835*	*32608*	*29.6%*	*31.8%*
Inc. Cohesion Funds	*2615*	*2615*	*2615*	*2615*	*5132*	*4667*	*5332*	*5.0%*	*5.1%*
3. Internal Actions	5930	6040	6150	6260	7877	8098	8212	7.6%	7.8%
4. External Actions	4550	4560	4570	4580	4590	4600	4610	4.5%	4.7%
5. Administration	4560	4600	4700	4800	5403	5558	5712	5.2%	5.4%
6. Reserves	900	900	650	400	400	400	400	0.4%	0.4%
7. Pre-adhesion Funds	3120	3120	3120	3120	3120	3120	3120	3.0%	1.6%
Inc. agriculture	*520*	*520*	*520*	*520*	*0*	*0*	*0*	*0.0*	
Inc. Ispa	*1040*	*1040*	*1040*	*1040*	*0*	*0*	*0*	*0.0*	
Inc.Phare	*1560*	*1560*	*1560*	*1560*	*0*	*0*	*0*	*0.0*	
8. Compensations					1273	1173	940	1.2%	1.3%
Total credits: appropriation for commitment	92025	93475	93955	93215	102985	105128	106741	100%	100%
Total credits: appropriation for payment	89600	91110	94220	94880	100800	101600	103840		
Appropriation for payment in % of GNI	1.07	1.08	1.11	1.1	1.08	1.06	1.06	1.08%	0.98%
Margins in % of GNI	0.17	0.16	0.13	0.14	0.16	0.18	0.18	0.16%	0.26%
Own Resource Ceiling in % of GNI	1.24	1.24	1.24	1.24	1.24	1.24	1.24		

Source: own compilation from EC data

In reality, Financial Perspectives achieve more than setting very loosely EU ambitions in various Policy areas in the medium term; they put strong constraints on the annual budget. The table shows that the 2004 budget respects Financial Perspectives almost perfectly. As often is the case, the only sizeable difference relates to Agriculture and Structural Actions expenditures, as Financial Perspectives constitute/set a maximum for the former and a spending objective for the latter. As pre-adhesion funds and compensations are mainly targeted towards relatively poor newcomers, if one adds them to the structural action category, Cohesion Policy nearly equals 39 per cent of the total budget. Thus, despite the appearance of decreasing monies for cohesion compared to the previous FPs, this Policy still grows in Financial terms. This steady growth will continue during the 2007-2013 period.

There is significant evidence that the Cohesion Policy has been used to solve a difficult equation: how to make the integration process go forward without increasing significantly the overall budget? Obviously, this is not the only use of this policy. It has its own rationale, its own objectives, and its own problems. But this policy is itself an instrument of European Integration at its first stage of policy-making (budgeting). The central role of the Cohesion Policy comes from its flexible nature and from the fact that it is, by definition, targeted to the poor. Indeed, the latter has been used as an instrument of integration at its first policy stage: budgeting in the framework of FPs. It has participated to breaking deals in the Council about such things as deepening (*e.g.* the SEA, the Maastricht Treaty) and enlargements (to the South in 1986, the North in 1995 and the East in 2004). It would take too long to present the full set of available evidence here.[7] One can notably refer to Tardschys (2003) or Allen (2000) for political science descriptive accounts of the pork-barrel political dynamic of Council negotiations on Financial Perspectives.

Still, Graph 6.1 shows that the share of the budget devoted to the CAP has been negatively correlated to the share devoted to the Cohesion Policy.[8] The latter has increased whereas the former has gradually decreased in real terms (not in nominal terms though). One could explain this by the growing concern for inter-regional solidarity. However, the correspondence between shifts in Cohesion Policy and shifts in integration is too obvious not to be noted. Graph 6.2 presents the evolution of the Cohesion envelope with respect to the European

---

[7]   Wallace, in 1977 already showed that this underlying logic is nothing but new. A more comprehensive, thus convincing, contribution can be found in the author's PhD Thesis (chapter 3).

[8]   The correlation between the two variables as measured by the r-square equals 0.96.

GDP. The most striking thing is the correspondence between years of growth in the Cohesion Policy and the dates where important 'history-making' decisions were reached among national governments.

Graph 6.2: Evolution of Cohesion Policy Spending (in per cent of GDP) (1960-2001)

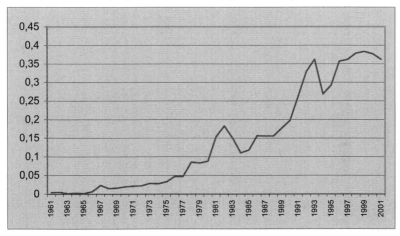

Source: own Compilation from EC data

Examples are numerous. To cite the most obvious ones, the very creation of the European Regional Development Funds (ERDF) in 1975 was a way to compensate newcomers (Denmark, the UK and Ireland) and Italy for the bias of the CAP with respect to older or more prosperous Member States. Structural Funds doubled a first time and temporarily for the benefit of Greece to accept the arrival of Spain and Portugal. Doublings of the Structural Funds in the aftermath of the Single Act (1986) and the Maastricht Treaty instituting the EMU (1993) benefited Southern countries (notably Spain) which were scared to lose from these new integration steps. Even the Northern enlargement in 1995, which included rich countries to the EU, was marked by a rise in Cohesion Policy expenditure thanks to the creation of the under-populated area objective and the European Economic Area (EEA) extra-financing. The bonus 'won' by Poland in 2002 follows the same logic.

Such an account of European integration gives a 'gloomy' image of opportunistic Member States seeking side-payments. It tends to blur the noble appearance of the European adventure. Still, some things are noteworthy. First, it would be a mistake to deduce from the previous analysis that such use of the Cohesion Policy has the one and only cause of the acceleration of the integration process for the last twenty years. It is definitely an original and efficient tool (a 'facilitator') of integration, but the *cause première* of history-making decisions ultimately comes from the political will of European Heads of Governments. Second, 'bribers' accepting to give more money to Structural Actions also benefited from these Financial Perspectives on other grounds. Indeed, France benefited from the CAP, the UK from its rebate, Germany from the EMU, Belgium and Luxembourg from Administration, etc. Nevertheless, this tool proved useful in making national perceptions and positions on European integration converge: without this largely implicit and unofficial mode of 'deal-breaking' cooperation, integration would probably have been slower.[9]

6.3. The Limits of the Current EU Fiscal Setting

The European fiscal setting is currently under stress after the recent enlargement and deepening of the European Union. The limits of the EU fiscal setting mainly relate to the intrinsic incoherence of the (size of the) European budget and its inadequate organisational form. Both problems suggest that the past model and ambitions of integration will come to an end ... unless one solves them.

6.3.1. The Limits of the Current Budgetary Arrangements: Big Aims, but Small Monies, a Fiscal Dwarf Full of Ambition

Increasing the budget? This question has been at the centre of European integration for the last thirty years, dating back from the Werner (1970), McDougall (1977) and Padoa-Schioppa (1987) Reports, to recent debates related to the SGP, the last enlargement or the negotiation of the 2007-2013 financial perspectives. However, the recurrent calls for a bigger budget have not been followed with facts. Graph 6.3 shows that, since the late 1970s, the budget has stagnated both as a percentage of GDP and as a share of total public spending.

The analysis at the end of the previous section gives a potential reason for the low increase, not to say the stagnation, of the budget as a percentage of the GDP: as alternative modes of cooperation existed and allowed to deepen integration without touching the budget, Member States preferred it to engaging in a politically costly/difficult boom of the European budget. Here, we provide evidence that the EU budget has definitively become too small. Possible 'escape routes' from this dead-end will be analysed in the next sections.

---

[9] 'Probably' here refers to the fact that certainty is not possible as it is impossible for researchers in such matters to have access to the alternative: what would have happened if the Cohesion Policy had not existed?

Graph 6.3: Evolution of the European Budget between 1960 and 2001

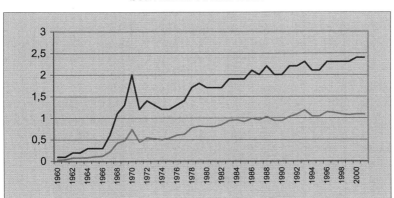

upper line: Community Spending in per cent of total public spending of Member States
lower line: Community Spending in per cent of Community GDP

Source: authors based on EC (2000) data.

The question one has to ask with respect to the limited dimensions of the current budget is the question of the comparative: If the budget is too small, compared to what is it too small? One could for instance refer to existing States such as the US, where the Federal budget, which approximates 20 per cent of the Growth National Income (GNI), is more than eighteen times bigger than the European one. Chapter 5 showed that national budgets of European countries are even more important. But such a comparison is not meaningful when one takes into account the real *sui generis* political nature of the EU, which does not aim to replace existing states.[10] Still, there exist sufficient arguments to justify a bigger budget. They all refer to the official ambitions of the EU.

First, the budget seems too small with respect to the possibility of macro-economic management in the EMU. This is particularly true when one considers that i) the European Central Bank (ECB) remains committed primarily to an inflation containment objective (as opposed to the Federal Reserve – FED – which also/mainly promotes growth), ii) the SGP 'constrains' Member States without providing any adequate stabilisation coordinating body, neither for the EU as a whole, the euro area, nor for depressed regions. The small size of the budget (ceiling) does not leave any effective power neither to the Commission nor to the Council to manage stabilisation policy, that is to use instruments of fiscal and/or monetary policy to correct macroeconomic imbalances

---

[10] The '*Unity in diversity*' device in the Preamble of the Constitution makes this point sufficiently clear.

such as low growth, unemployment, etc. This role is still in the hands of national governments, which themselves rule over increasingly per-meable and (inter)dependent economies. The Commission (or the eurogroup) only promotes coordination of the Member States fiscal policies, but this coordination is not pro-active (taking political decisions necessary to implement fiscal policies takes too much time, which is also true in national context) or so unenforceable that, in reality, the Central level (the EU, either the Commission or the Council) has no effective stabilising power. To make the EU able to perform a stabilisation policy, either the size of the budget should increase and/or deep changes in the EU institutions are necessary. The EU could be granted a real spending capacity, which could for instance be accom-panied by the introduction of majority voting and joint decision-making of the European Parliament and the Council of Ministers as for both revenues and spending.[11]

Secondly, the budget seems too small to reduce the huge level of disparities induced by the arrival of CEECs. Note that, ironically enough, economic, social and territorial cohesion still appears central in the new constitution without any new means devoted to it. One can simply wonder how long it would take to make the poorest countries converge towards economies which are three times richer, with a yearly budget approximating 0.5 per cent of the EU GDP! Although economic integration may, *per se*, imply net gains for new entrants, it is unlikely to reduce dramatically economic disparities in a foreseeable future.

Thirdly, and perhaps most importantly, given that most part of the budget is absorbed by the CAP and by cohesion/redistribution, only marginal resources are left for new policies (the environment, R&D, industry, trans-European networks, not to mention a Common or even harmonised Social Policy). These subjects are particularly important both economically and politically. In a context of growing globalisation, these policies are less and less 'manageable' at the national level, as acknowledged by the Lisbon Agenda. As shown by recent developments in economic theory (such as the new growth theory), tomorrow's growth depends on the amounts spent today on R&D or communication and

---

[11]   An option to finance the increase in the community budget could be a European surtax, levied on top of the income taxes collected by the Member States (Majocchi, 2003). Revenues of this surtax would be distributed to Member States on the basis of each state's GDP share of total community GDP. The coefficient which determines each state's contribution to the community budget would be based on the ratio between the country's per capita income and the average per capita income of the community, so that richer countries' contribution would be higher than weaker countries'. Through this scheme, citizens could realise the real burden in community financing. Furthermore, yields of such a surtax could be redistributed among different areas of community intervention.

transport networks, which are still too low in many countries such as France or the UK. One can then wonder, referring to the Lisbon objectives, how the EU can possibly manage to transform itself into the most social, research oriented and competitive economy of the planet by 2010 with the current budget? In short, the budget, regarding real and positive objectives, should indeed increase significantly.

6.3.2. An Inadequate Organisational Form?

We have shown in the previous section that, for the past twenty years and despite a stagnating budget, Cohesion Policy has been used recurrently in the context of inter-governmental bargaining to reach agreements on wider (non budgetary) aspects of European integration. However, some recent developments may limit the possibility to use such a logic to 'backbone' integration in the future. For instance, Cohesion has reached a critical size. Its size is now more or less similar to a CAP which, since the European Council of Brussels (October 2002) is set to decline gradually in real terms until 2012. Moreover, enlargement automatically widens the list of Cohesion countries from 3 to 10-13, *i.e.* from one fifth to half of European countries. These two factors imply that it will probably prove more difficult to use Cohesion expenditures as side-payments. The change of categories in the Commission's proposal for the 2007-2013 Financial Perspectives is symptomatic of this changing logic.[12] The 'Letter of the Six', addressed to Romano Prodi in December 2003, also illustrates the unwillingness to pay (above 1 per cent of the EU GNI) of richer 'old' countries. The failure of the June 2005 negotiation and the low budget reached by the December 2005 deal, which occurred after the draft completion of this book, seem to confirm it.

Unanimity is still required for Fiscal matters, either for budget setting in the FPs or for tax harmonisation. This holds both under the EC Treaty and under the currently applied Nice Treaty. It is also interesting to note that this would have been (will be?) the case too if the European Constitution had been passed. According to the Constitution, the unanimity of voting within the Council is still a rule in various matters, some of them concern taxation, for example concerning indirect tax measures, Art. III-171 sets that:

> A European law or framework law of the Council shall establish measures for the harmonisation of legislation concerning turnover taxes, excise duties and other forms of indirect taxation provided that such harmonisation is necessary for the establishment or the functioning of the internal market and

---

12 Structural Actions, Agriculture and Research are now sub-categories of wider sustainable growth and sustainable development (including environment) categories.

to avoid distortion of competition. The Council shall act unanimously after consulting the European Parliament and the Economic and Social Committee.

Furthermore, unanimity in the Council is necessary for example for environmental taxes (Art. III-234.2) and for fiscal measures in the field of energy (Art. III-256.3).

Qualified Majority Voting (QMV) on issues not directly related to taxation or fiscal matters renders it difficult to reach agreements with more negotiators at the table, even though the European tradition of Consensus could still prevail. Possibilities for enhanced cooperation are also deeply constrained (Art. I-44).

The same holds for another important clause introduced in the Constitution with regards to specific matters: the bridging (or *passerelle*) clause means that where unanimity voting applies in a policy field, a unanimous decision can be taken in the European Council or in the Council of Ministers to change voting rules to QMV for that field. Art. IV-444 states *"Where part III provides for the Council to act by unanimity in a given area or case, the European Council may adopt a European decision authorising the Council to act by a qualified majority in that area or in that case"*. In this way, there is the possibility of modifying the voting rules without recourse to the usual Treaty revision process followed by national ratifications. To put an example forward, Art. III-234.2 provides that *"The Council, on a proposal from the Commission, may unanimously adopt a European decision making the ordinary legislative procedure applicable to the matters referred to in the first subparagraph"*, in this subparagraph there are also fiscal measures concerning environment. Therefore, the bridging clause can be applied to environmental taxes.

Yet, there is the possibility, for Member States, to block this process, if any Parliament objects to it within six months (Art. IV-444.3). This is a right of veto of Member States on the *passerelle* clause. The horizontal bridging clause allows to bring under QMV arrangement policies of Part III of the Constitution normally subject to unanimity, except on military and defence issues (Art. IV-444.1), while no measures in Parts I or IV can be amended using this provision. Thus, there is a 'double lock' safeguard mechanism preventing any haste to change existing rules, made up of the MS right of veto and of the limitation in the application of the clause to policies of Part III. But moreover, what has to be remarked is that such application is subject to unanimity in the European Council (Art. IV-444.3) and unanimity is always the difficult issue.

Article I-44 provides that Member States can establish an enhanced cooperation between themselves *"to further the objectives of the Union, to protect its interests and reinforce its integration process*". An aspect of enhanced cooperation is especially important: Art. III-422 gives the possibility to the countries, which take part in an enhanced cooperation initiative to amend the voting rules within that enhanced cooperation arrangement. For example, if a group of countries uses enhanced cooperation in tax fields, it is possible to introduce QMV within this arrangement. Nevertheless, enhanced cooperation is not simple to establish not only because of the fairly long process to be followed to establish it but also because unanimity is required once more, given that Art. III-419 sets "*Authorisation to proceed with enhanced cooperation shall be granted by a European decision of the Council acting unanimously*".

6.3.3. The Limits of the Past Model of Integration

The EU is currently at a crossroads. It has developed so far a *sui generis* model, based on a mixture of inter-governmentalism and supranationalism, which political scientists have difficulties to capture (see Puchala, 1972; Moravscik, 1998; Marks and Hooghe, 2001; or Rosamond, 2000). Indirectly, the last steps of enlargement and of the Constitution may make any European-wide agreement more difficult to obtain, both on economic and political grounds.[13] Notably, any significant increase in the budget, which is justified on the basis of a literal lecture (*cf. supra*) of the EU official ambitions, is unlikely within the current context. Where does one go from there and how does it relate to a criticism of the Fiscal Federalist perspective? The first question is open indeed and will be tackled at the end of this chapter. The second one can be given a more straightforward answer.

This last point, perhaps the most important one, deals with high politics. Political factors explain most of the discrepancies between the Fiscal Federalism guidelines and the European Fiscal setting. If the EU does not assume such extensive competencies as the theory prescribes, it is simply because national governments did not find it necessary to do so (so far). This can be explained by the fact that reality is not as spectacular as theory foresees. For instance, keeping redistribution or stabilisation decentralised (at the sub-central/national level) may not imply obvious short-term explosion of social systems (*cf.* Chapter 2) or deep recessions (*cf.* Chapter 3). Theories generally over-simplify,

---

[13] There may well be a *Marble effect*. Indeed, the Constitution includes precise indications about economic policies. Any change may become more difficult than before, when touching Treaties only implied an erasure on the paper. The Constitution tag may be used or perceived by some actors as being a threat to Fundamental Principles of the European agreement, thus implying buoyant debates, delays, and ultimately hinder the ability to change it.

highlighting potential threats, which in practice only concretise themselves in the medium or long-term. If national systems had exploded in the aftermath of the EMU, Heads of Government of Member States would have been forced to address the situation in emergency. The given response would have been one of the following ones: to increase the budget, to put enforceable credible pressures on MS deficits, or to abolish the euro. Practical political time thus differs from theoretical economic time. This, in turn, induces that the latter should not be blindly adapted to the normative theory of Fiscal Federalism or only at the condition that this comes from a demand from national governments (which can neither be seen as benevolent central planners nor as Leviathan). In contrast, Fiscal Federalism should take the political nature of the EU into account. It should admit that traditional assumptions do not hold in the European case and that the traditional – largely implicit – political assumptions correspond to mature Federations. If not, this theoretical perspective will have to relinquish its universalistic ambitions (*i.e.* applying to all types of countries, or authority dispersed, entities).

6.4. Towards a Reconstruction of Fiscal Federalism(s)

This book has already presented the main results stemming from Fiscal Federalism theory for the EU. We now turn the argument upside down and argue that the theoretical normative framework has to be enriched if it is to provide a wide theoretical framework from which lessons could be drawn for the EU. The underlying argument is that Fiscal Federalism is ill-suited as such, *i.e.* that it disregards the main features of the EU fiscal setting, which itself comes from the political peculiarities of the EU. This is backboned by the fact that, as highlighted in Chapter 5, political organisation is more likely to be the explanatory rather than the explained variable (*i.e.* it explains much of national fiscal settings). Our aim is to go beyond theoretical confusions.

If something does not work, the reform should be justified on practical grounds and the reform recipe should be itself applicable. If not, the reform may imply waste and delays. To improve something, which does not work, one has to forget about an ideal/optimal fiscal organisation to undertake the less ambitious objective of a 'better fiscal organisation'. Thus, the questions then become the following: i) what are the various possibilities to improve the existing EU fiscal setting and what are their main relative advantages/drawbacks? ii) to which political ambitions does each of these reform options correspond to?, iii) what are the various political conditions required to transform each of the above-mentioned possibilities into reality? The choice between the various possibilities, it is argued, is a question of political will. To illustrate this argument, we remind the main flaws of the normative view, before undertaking a joint analysis of the budget and of the economic tasks that are/could/should be transferred to the EU.

6.4.1. The Inadequacy of the Normative Theory of Fiscal Federalism

The traditional theory of Fiscal Federalism is a heroic theoretical framework. Its agenda is central to the comprehension of most problems arising on the EU scene. However, it is too *naive* in the sense that its framework is shaped to enlighten existing or mature States. Two problems seem particularly significant: i) the scale, function and tool problem, and ii) the neglect of political factors.

Short Reminder

The five previous chapters recurrently evaluated the potential useful-ness of a theoretical framework focusing on intergovernmental relation-ships. The question of whether the theory of Fiscal Federalism was a suitable indicative theoretical framework for the EU provided a miti-gated answer indeed. Our way to reason was to decompose traditional themes tackled by the literature and to identify five original dimensions in which our problematic was split into. In previous parts of this contri-bution we dealt with, on the one hand, the way the theory of Fiscal Federalism could enlighten the EU reality, and on the other hand, the lessons the EU could draw from national fiscal settings.

Chapter 1 has made it clear that Fiscal Fedefalism is not a single the-ory. It is a perspective, which welcomes different views, the common feature of which is to study multi-level polities in economic terms, such as the EU. A broad consensus arises in the literature for an optimal assignment of functions, which should be taken as a flexible guideline. According to the traditional/dominant view, stabilisation and redistribu-tion should be centralised, whereas allocation should be divided among the different levels, with a presumption in favour of decentralisation. This perspective mirrors the most debated economic issues in the EU, where conflicts among levels of government are a daily concern. How-ever, it was noted, this still leaves some place for sharp criticisms of this literature. The contested relevance of the Fiscal Federalism perspective should not make one throw the baby with the bath water. We thus presented a new framework, which, in our sense, could guide Fiscal Federalism theorists specialised in EU studies.

The analysis of some real-world components/elements of various fis-cal settings prevailing either in the EU (Chapters 2 and 3) or in Euro-pean countries (Chapters 4 and 5) proved to be decisive. A theory is a way to ordinate the world. As such, it is, by definition, a simplification.

However, it is argued, too much simplification may limit the relevance of a theory. A description of the traditional theory (in the line of Musgrave, Tiebout and Oates), its underlying argument, and its ontological position, helped us understanding its main flaws. This justified the idea that changing it in order to encompass the political modalities/factors which accompany/determine a given fiscal setting would be a major positive breakdown. The fiscal setting of the EU, *i.e.* the way the public sector is organised, vertically, horizontally, and using various means either budgetary or regulatory, is still misperceived. Despite the springing of recent contributions on this literature trying to understand the EU, the EMU, Enlargement, Cohesion Policy and macroeconomic stabilisation under a political economy perspective, the normative view still constitutes a recurrent yardstick. Future research within this framework should try to apply the following reform recipe: an 'empirics-based' study, which takes into account the specific political, historical and institutional features of both the EU and its countries, with an emphasis on policy-making in specific areas rather than with extensive references to a heroic decomposition of functions.

Incorporation of Territory Scales, Economic Functions and Tools

One of the most obvious problems of the theory is that it is applied in a more or less similar way regardless to the scale of analysis. Some researchers can, by using the same framework, say opposite things according to what they consider to be the various vertical levels of government. For instance, a researcher focusing on, say Germany, would conclude that stabilisation should be assumed by the federal State, whereas a researcher focusing on the EU as a whole would argue, by referring to the same theory, that stabilisation should be a task of the European level. These contradicting prescriptions only come from the fact that the supposedly central level of government changes from one analysis to the other. There is, thus, a lack of clarity regarding the definition of what a central level of government is, and regarding the definition of the sub-central territories to which it corresponds.

Another problem refers to the definition of functions, which are too 'ideal'. One hardly encounters purely redistribution measures, or purely allocative ones, and so on and so forth. In contrast, the policy-maker, and especially the European policy-maker, has to make prosaic choices about down-to-earth policies, which, taken in isolation, involve a mix of all functions. The Cohesion Policy for instance includes dimensions of allocation, stabilisation and redistribution. So, should it be left to the European level or should it be re-nationalised, as recurrently argued by net contributors to the European budget? Moreover, some economic roles of the government are undertaken by non-financial tools. The EU is a perfect example of a political entity achieving many economic tasks of the public sector by extensively using regulation.

The Pre-eminence of Politics

The power delegation problem can be stated as follows. In the EU, national governments gradually delegate some of their supremacy (their participation to a new prerogative is also subject to their good will) to the EU level. In contrast, Fiscal Federalism is a guideline, which was built to fit to well-established states. For instance, when the former French Prime Minister Jean-Pierre Raffarin, the Italian president of the Council (*e.g.* Berlusconi) or its coalition members (*e.g.* Northern League) or the American President (*e.g.* Bush or Reagan) argue for more decentralisation by using fiscal federalist arguments, reforms, which are often directed towards more decentralisation, are quite easy to implement. Indeed, the decision-maker in power just has to 'give' some of its prerogatives to its constituent territories, which generally accept it, given the latter also benefit from extra-corresponding finances. In the EU, the logic of power devolution is reversed and implies an opposite political dynamic. Sub-central (national) governments relinquish power to the central level, and the more they transfer power, the higher the risk to 'lose' in the inter-governmental institutional balance.

The cooperation issue is actually related to this neglect of political factors. Once more, we insist on the fact that centralisation and cooperation are not equivalent. This may be so in a context of mature states (*e.g.* Belgium, *cf.* Chapter 3), where central states devolve some of their power to sub-central levels. However, this is not the case in the EU. And this comes from the above-mentioned power delegation problem. The SGP is once again a good example. It was originally aimed to be the first step towards a more integrated 'European macroeconomic policy' but mainly because of strong national opposition it was not possible to design a clear, complete and coherent device to deal with fiscal policy overall in the EMU. In fact stabilisation is the direct outcome of how national states manage their fiscal policy power and it usually reflects national preferences: national countries resisted to losses of control. In order not to hurt national interests, the mechanism found was an economic hybridism.

Neither economic theory in general nor Fiscal Federalism support it. Firstly, if macroeconomic theory calls either for coordination of different policies or the imposition of rules, it suggests different economic variable-targets. Hence, according to economic theory, the SGP is ill-defined and to properly work needs some changes in its formula (golden rule, cyclical adjustment and so on). Secondly, Fiscal Federalism predicts that stabilisation has to be centralised. According to our assumption, (being the EU ruling the biggest territory) fiscal policy should be centralised at the EU level. Now, the framework implicit in the SGP is not centralisation but a weak form of coordination where national governments (sub-central in our terminology) agreed on 'maintaining' the budget balanced but with complete autonomy on how to reach it (hence even the application of harmful practices for neighbour MS). This is clearly in contrast with the task of the coordination emphasised by Fiscal Federalism where coordination is mainly reached through the means of a complex system of grants.

It is doubtless that the actual framework has to be improved, but how? Fiscal Federalism is one means but encompasses several flaws namely political (factor of vital importance when dealing with sovereign countries and the possibility to redesign sovereign and enforceability powers among them). Fiscal Federalism does not distinguish properly between centralisation of a given function (stabilisation) and coordination because it focuses on various types of grants and does not consider (enough) the valid instruments that regulations, fiscal coordination or a bigger budget could be in a decentralised context. In short, the way the EU works does not correspond to Fiscal Federalism implicit assumptions.

As shown by Chapter 5, there is no such thing as a 'superior' fiscal setting. European countries exhibit at the same time great diversity and high degrees of political determinism. This carries the following implications. It is impossible to understand, reform or prescribe a fiscal setting without taking into account its political mode of operation. The fact that the fiscal structure of the public sector is so overwhelmingly politically determined means that any decision on the latter has to take into account/include political organisation/variables. There seems to be evidence that the political organisation explains the fiscal organisation more than the opposite. Economic factors are less important, not to say marginal, in the way competencies are actually shared. This also means that the EU should find its own way and that any reform of the fiscal setting should take into account the peculiar political features underlined above. The desirable nature of a reform is not enough, it should first be politically acceptable. The latter depends, for each State, on the set of political, fiscal and socio-economic particularities analysed in Chapter 5. Put differently, national ideotypes may determine national positions at the EU level. In turn, the EU fiscal setting is, by definition, a compromise, as it has to fit to all national fiscal settings and political features. For instance, it comes with no surprise that the unitary and centralised UK, which has been engaged in major conflicts with Wales, Scotland and Northern Ireland in the past, is also one of the most euro-sceptical countries (at least regarding all the symbols of sovereignty: currency, fiscal prerogatives, social regulations, security, etc). The same holds for Scandinavian countries (except Finland), which have always been politically aware of keeping decision-making as close as possible to citizens. National ideal-types may in fact help to reveal preferences.

All in all, the traditional theory of Fiscal Federalism suffers from a biased ontological view, which hinders its ability to propose reforms or raises doubts on the applicability of these reforms.

6.4.2. Conclusion: Europe, Once Again at a Turning Point

Once again, Europe seems to be at a turning point. This situation is not new as such, as it approximately occurs once every decade, as in 1957, in 1966, in 1975, in 1986, and in 1993. The choices among which to choose, in 2006, with a European Union composed of 25 Member States, are known: either the Constitutional Treaty, the Nice Treaty, or some third option opened to time-consuming re-negotiation. What is new, however, is the fact that this choice, for the first time, is in the hands of European citizens in countries as diverse as Spain, France, the UK, Denmark or Poland. The recent results of May 2005 referendum in France and the Netherlands, rejecting the EU Constitution, have attracted public and media attention to the current crossroads at which the EU seems to be. It is like a group of 25 persons, stuck at a given point because they know they all have to follow the same path but disagree on the path (among many possible paths) to follow.

The Actual, the Likely, the Possible and the Desirable

A simple way to understand the European dilemma and the challenge it offers to the economic theoretical perspective of Fiscal Federalism is to make distinctions between 'the actual, the possible, the likely and the desirable'. The *actual* refers to sections 6.1 and 6.2, namely what does the EU do and how does it work. The *desirable* refers either to the normative traditional FF theory (Chapter 1 and section 6.4.1) and to the intrinsic incoherence of the current fiscal setting regarding Treaty provisions or to EU ambitions (section 6.3), namely what should the EU do. The two views are different in scope. The first one refers to theoretical problems and gives theoretical answers based on Welfare Economics, without taking into account the actual (political) functioning of its object of analysis. The second one refers to theoretical obligations induced by real-world decisions, and does not seek to put value judgement about the way the EU operates. The *likely* refers to the probable future of the European setting regarding current evolutions such as change in the number of countries involved in decision-making. It is one of the *possible* future of the EU: the *could* question. However, it has to take into account only feasible situation. For instance, a full devolution of national powers to the EU does not enter into this category in the near future. This comes from the fact that the political dynamics is very unlikely to deliver such a dramatic change, given political and institutional factors.

These questions are often confused. That is why there is a huge difference between the fiscal federalist prescriptive yardstick and the reality of the EU. The traditional conclusion is to assert that this gap means there are efficiency losses. In our opinion, this is a misleading conclusion. Conversely, primacy should be given to reality and this (political) reality should be explicitly included in the FF theory, to allow it to keep it relevance and fulfil its potential for useful analysis. While the validity of the Fiscal Federalist agenda seems undisputable (Chapter 1 and 6.1.2), it seems necessary to depart from *the dominant normative theory of Fiscal Federalism to change the EU Fiscal setting or reform it.*[14] It is, thus, important to go beyond theoretical confusion. The following 'proposal' does not seek to answer to the normative question of the desirability of various fiscal settings compared to heroic/ideal theoretical frameworks. The following 'proposal' only seeks to improve the match between the actual fiscal setting of the EU and its official ambitions (the second should question, *cf.* above). Primacy is given to the political dynamics, in the sense that the latter is 'given', *i.e.* taken as the first exogenous data in any analysis of European integration. Our 'proposal', thus, respects a straightforward applicability condition: it has to enter in the set of the possible options. This means that a positive answer to our 'should' question is conditioned to (requires) a positive answer to the 'could' question.

'Proposals' regarding the EU Budget, Fiscal Setting and Political Organisation

This sub-section readdresses some of the issues highlighted in section 6.3 above at the light of the previous criticism of the theory of Fiscal Federalism. It provides an analysis of the EU budget and fiscal setting taking into account the two main types of European Integration steps: deepening and enlargement. This discussion is deeply intertwined with all the questions asked in this chapter's introduction. What is the EU? It is neither/less than a State nor/but more than an international organization. However, it is a polity as a whole, featured by a fiscal

---

[14] There is a growing economic literature branch that seeks to study the influence of political agents. Forerunners, or at least excellent synthesis-makers of this "political economy" approach are Persson and Tabellini (2000) and Drazen (2000). However, the normative approach has to be discarded for being unrealistic (*cf.* Généreux, 1996 and Dixit, 1995). The positive approach seems to pay too little attention to the EU governance and fiscal setting *yet.*

setting which is particular with respect to many aspects: it currently works with a very low budget; it uses regulatory powers, consensus and bargains, as a way to overcome their self-allocated veto power; its organisational form is an inverse hierarchy, which gives 'power to do' to the college of sub-central authorities and 'power not to do' to each of them taken individually; the way policies are implemented is also particular as it largely depends on the goodwill of national governments (*e.g.* the SGP).

The EU already faces major problems (6.3), which are likely to be unsolved in the context of the current political and fiscal setting. Clearly, there is a gap between what the EU officially wants to do, and what it now does or can do in facts. The budget is too small compared to all the things the EU has to do in order to reach the Lisbon's goals. The proposal of the Commission (which can be regarded as a maximum) regarding the next Financial Perspectives was symptomatic of such a discrepancy. Next to the present size of the budget, the Constitution does not include any major change about the political organisation of decision-making. This mixed effect of the current political and budget-ary organisation makes integration likely to slow down dramatically in the near future. It will be more difficult to reach decisions with the growing number of members and the unanimity rule for fiscal matters. This will also be worsened by the probable subsequent disappearance of the alternative mode of decision-making through FPs (*cf.* section 6.2). Clearly, the main – and legitimate – concern from national governments is to gain/not to suffer from integration. The past model of integration, where this concern was overcome by the above-mentioned recipe based on a politico-fiscal mix of ingredients, has come to an end: the provi-sions in the Constitution are *caeteris paribus* insufficient to overcome national fears.

The question, then, arises of what should be done to 'fill the gap'? Even more than the opinion of most observers (fiscal federalists, the Commission, even some national decision-makers), real-world develop-ments (EU ambitions, Lisbon, constitution, enlargement) call, on econo-mic grounds, for an extension of both the competencies and the means granted to the EU. The precise modalities of such an extension (how could the EU do it) remain unclear. What is clear, however, is that a *status quo* on the budget and the political organisation will, after the enlargement and the Constitution, at most produce a *status quo* on European integration. In other words, it will slow it down.

If one still wants the integration process to go ahead, the EU needs some reforms on economic and political grounds. The shift to an extensive European Fiscal setting, supported from many parts, implies a growing common European budget, to a much more important weight than the current one of 1.24 per cent of the GNI of the whole EU area. More prosaically, the growth of the EU budget is a *sine qua non* condition for pursuing its ambitions; if not, Lisbon and Treaty goals will not be achieved in a foreseeable future.

The trade-off between deepening and enlargement only becomes absolute if one considers the political framework to be unchangeable. If one also changes the way things are decided, this trade-off disappears. Can the EU do it? The potential for reforms is difficult to estimate. However, the probability one can assign to the realisation of this reform outcome, is an open question, which, for sure, depends on political factors. Among them, ultimately, political will (preferences) is the most important one. As in the case of German unification, the means devoted to the development and convergence of a bigger or more ambitious EU depends on the strength of political will of Member States. Any appeal for a bigger budget based on Fiscal Federalism and more generally on economic theory is vain if it does not take into account the political dynamics of the European integration process. The finding of a sustainable economic solution depends, in the EU more than anywhere else, of it being also a political equilibrium.

Whether such a change in political decision-making is likely to occur is uncertain. Currently, many European net contributors are opposed to a rise in the European budget or to the additional upwards devolution of power. From the 'Letter of the Six' to the low budget adopted by the Council in December 2005, it seems clear that EU members have exhibited a clear lack of political will. On political grounds, the possibility to strengthen EU institutions and policies cannot be achieved without replacing unanimity with qualified majority voting. This does not mean such a replacement would automatically lead to this desirable outcome, as what will effectively be done will then become what a majority of European governments perceive as what should be done. This could trigger desirable changes on fiscal grounds mentioned above, giving the EU a real tax and spending capacity. But this could also lead Europe to *a status quo* if the majority of governments were against it. As EU countries seem to have lost a chance to match their means to their ambitions in December 2005, the European citizen seeking more political and economical coherence has to wait for the Commission's proposal on the budget re-foundation in 2008.

The Constitution is likely to equal *status quo*, as is the Nice Treaty. How can an EU shaped by the most traditionally euro-sceptic countries be avoided? Pessimism aside, it is also necessary to respect the future and accept that the evolution of the political dynamics is as uncertain as it is specific. European governments have already shown their capacity, in the past, to identify and to find solutions to dead-ends linked to integration. If Europe is at a crossroads, once again, impatience, political will, or economic pragmatism is likely to make one or more of the group's 25 members propose 'cutting corners'.

References

Chapter 1

Ackrill, R. (1998), "The European Union Budget, the Importance of the Balanced Budget Rule, the Future of the Rule under Economic and Monetary Union", Centre for European Economic Studies, Department of Economics, University of Leicester, August.

Aubin, C. and J. Léonard (2000), "Fédéralisme Budgétaire: et s'il était urgent d'attendre?", Colloque CEDECE, Poitiers.

Boyer, R. and M. Dehove (2003), "La répartition des Compétences en Europe, le double Éclairage du Droit et de l'Économie", présenté au Journées de l'AFSE, Lille, Mai.

Breuss, F. and M. Eller (2003), "On the Optimal Assignment of Competences in a Multi – Level Governed European Union", *European Integration online papers* (Elop) Vol.7, September.

Brosio, G. (1995), *Equilibri Instabili, Politica ed Economia nell'Evoluzione dei Sistemi Federali*, Laterza, Bari.

Buchanan, J. (1955), "An Economic Theory of Clubs", *Economica*, Vol.32: 1-14, February.

Buti, M. and M. Nava (2003), "Towards a European Budgetary System", *EUI Working paper*, RSC No.2003/08.

Costello, D. (1993), "Intergovernmental Grants: what Role for the European Community?", pp. 101-119, *European Commission reports and studies: The economics of community public finance*, No.5.

Derycke, P.-H. and G. Gilbert (1988), *Économie Publique Locale*, Economica, 308 p.

Dixit, A. (1995), "The Making of economic policy, a transaction-costs politics analysis, Munich Lectures in economics, MIT Press, 192 p.

European Commission (1993), *European Commission Reports and Studies: The Economics of Community Public Finance*, No.5, Brussels.

Gamkhar, S. and W. Oates (1996), "Asymmetries in the Response to Increases and Decreases in Intergovernmental Grants: some Empirical Findings", *National Tax Journal*, 49: 501-12.

Généreux, J. (1996), "L'économie politique, analyse économique des choix publics et de la vie politique", Larousse, Bordas, Paris, 479 p.

Gramlich, E. M. (1987a), "Federalism and Federal Deficit Reduction", *National Tax Journal*, 40: 1174-1185.

Gramlich, E. M. (1987b), "The Economics of Fiscal Federalism and its Reforms", pp. 152-174, in Swarz T. R. and J. E. Peck (eds.), *The Changing Face of Fiscal Federalism*, M E Sharpe Inc, 256 p.

Guihéry, L. (1999), "Fédéralisme Fiscal et Fonction de Redistribution: entre Centralisation et Décentralisation", *Cahiers du CUREI*, No.13, Université de Grenoble.

Inman, R. P. and D. L. Rubinfeld (1997), "The Political Economy of Federalism", pp. 73-105, in D. Mueller, *Perspectives on Public Choice: A Handbook*, Cambridge University Press.

Inman, R. P. and D. L. Rubinfeld (1998), "Subsidiarity and the European Union", in ed. by Peter Newman, *The New Palgrave Dictionary of Economics and the Law*, Vol.2: 545-51.

Inman, R. P. and D. L. Rubinfeld (1999), "Federalism", in Boudewijn Bouchaert and Gerrit De Geest (eds.), *The Encyclopedia of Law and Economics*.

Mundell R.A. (1961), "A Theory of Optimum Currency Areas", *The American Economic Review*, Volume 51, No.4: 657-665, September.

Musgrave, R. A. (1959), *The Theory of Public Finance*, McGraw-Hill, New York.

Musgrave, R. A. and P.B. Musgrave (1984), *Public Finance in Theory and Practice*, second edition, McGraw-Hill, New York.

Oates, W.E. (1972), *Fiscal Federalism*, Harcourt and Brace, Iovanovich Inc., New York.

Oates, W.E. (1991), *Studies in Fiscal Federalism*, Edward Elgar Publishing Ltd., 455 p.

Oates, W.E. (1999), "An Essay on Fiscal Federalism", *Journal of Economic Literature*, Vol. 37, pp. 1120-1149, September.

Oates, W.E. and C. Brown (1987), "Assistance to the Poor in a Federal System", *Journal of Public Economics*, 32: 307-330, April.

Oates, W.E. and R.M. Schwab (1988), "Economic Competition among Jurisdictions: Efficiency-Enhancing or Distortion-Inducing?", *Journal of Public Economics*, 35: 333-54.

Padoa-Schioppa, T. *et al.* (1987), *Efficiency, Stability and Equity*, Oxford University Press, New York.

Pauly, M. (1973), "Income Redistribution as a Local Public Good", *Journal of Public Economics*, 2: 35-58.

Rosamond, B. (2000), *Theories of European Integration*, The European Union Series, Palgrave, 232 p.

Stehn, J. (2002), "Towards a European Constitution: Fiscal Federalism and the Allocation of Economic Competences", Kiel WP, No.1125.

Tabellini, G. (2002), "Principles of Policymaking in the European Union: an Economic Perspective", presented at Munich Economic Summit, June.

Théret B. (2002), "Protection Sociale et Fédéralisme, l'Europe dans le Miroir de l'Amérique du Nord", *PUM*, Montréal, 495 p.

Tiebout, C. (1956), "A Pure Theory of Local Expenditures", *Journal of political economy*, No.5: 416-24, October.

Vaneecloo, C. (2003), "L'Applicabilité du Fédéralisme Fiscal à l'Union Européenne", présentation au séminaire HPE, Université de Lille 1, December.

Walsh, C. (1993), "Fiscal Federalism: An Overview of Issues and a Discussion of their Relevance to the European Community", pp. 25-62, in *European commission reports and studies: the economics of community public finance*, No.5.

Wildasin, D. (1990), "Budgetary Pressures in the EEC: a Fiscal Federalism Perspective", *American Economic Review* 80 (2): 69-74, May.

Chapter 2

Allen, D. (2000), "Cohesion and the Structural Funds, Transfers and Trade-Offs", pp. 243-265, in Wallace H. and W. Wallace, *Policy-Making in the European Union*, Oxford University Press.

Boulding, K. E. and M. Pfaff (1972), *Redistribution to the Rich and the Poors, the Grants, Economics of Income Redistribution*, 390 p., Wadsworth Publishing Company, Belmont, California.

Brueckner, J. (1998), "Welfare Reform and the Race to the Bottom: Theory and Evidence", Institute of Government and Public affairs, University of Illinois, WP 64.

Costello, D. (1993), "Intergovernmental Grants: what Role for the European Community?", pp. 101-119, *European Commission Reports and Studies: The Economics of Community Public Finance*, No.5.

Derycke, P-H. and G. Gilbert (1988), *"Economie Publique Locale"*, Economica, 308 p.

Desjardins, P-M. and L. Guihéry (2001), "La Redistribution Interrégionale 'sous le Feu' des Critiques: Expériences Canadiennes et Allemandes", Forum Européen de Prospective Régionale et Locale, Lille, May.

European Commission (2004), *Third Report on Economic and Social Cohesion*, COM (2004) 107, February, Luxembourg, 248 p. (French Version).

Feldstein, M. and M.V. Wrobel (1998), "Can State Taxes redistribute Income?", *Journal of Public Economics*, 68 (3): 369-397.

Gramlich, E. M. (1987a), "Federalism and Federal Deficit Reduction", *National Tax Journal*, 40: 1174-1185.

Gramlich, E. M. (1987b), "The Economics of Fiscal Federalism and its Reforms", pp. 152-174, in Swarz T. R. and J. E. Peck (eds.), *The Changing Face of Fiscal Federalism*.

Guihéry, L. (1999), "Fédéralisme Fiscal et Fonction de Redistribution: entre Centralisation et Décentralisation", *Cahiers du CUREI*, No.13.

Hooghe, L. and G. Marks (2001), *Multi-Level Governance and European Integration*, Rowman and Littlefield Publishers Inc., 249 p.

Moravcsik, A. (1998), *The Choice for Europe, Social Purpose and State Power Form Messina to Maastricht*, Cornell University Press, 514 p.

Musgrave, R.A. (1959), *The Theory of Public Finance*, New York, McGraw-Hill.

Musgrave, R.A. (1969), "Theories of Fiscal Federalism", *Public Finance*, No 4: 521-532.

Musgrave, R.A. and P.B. Musgrave (1984), *Public Finance in Theory and Practice*, second edition, New York, McGraw-Hill.

Oates, W.E. (1972), *Fiscal Federalism*, Harcourt and Brace, Iovanovich Inc. New York.

Oates, W.E. (1999), "An Essay on Fiscal Federalism", *Journal of Economic Literature*, Vol. 37, pp. 1120-1149, September.

Oates, W.E. and C. Brown (1987), "Assistance to the Poor in a Federal System", *Journal of Public Economics*, 32: 307-330, April.

Pauly, M. (1973), "Income Redistribution as a Local Public Good", *Journal of Public Economics*, 2: 35-58.

Saavedra, L. A. (1998), "A Model of Welfare Competition with Evidence from AFDC", Inst. Gov. and Pub. Affairs, University of Illinois, WP 63.

Spahn, B. (1993), "The Design of Federal Fiscal Constitutions in Theory and in Practice", in *European Commission Reports and Studies: the Economics of Community Public Finance*, No.5.

Vaneecloo, C. (2005), "Economie Politique de la Solidarité Européenne, l'Influence des Facteurs Politiques, Institutionnels et Organisationnels sur la Politique de Cohésion et son Efficacité", Thèse de Doctorat, Université de Lille I, novembre.

Wildasin, D. (1990), "Budgetary Pressures in the EEC: a Fiscal Federalism Perspective", *American Economic Review* 80 (2): 69-74, May.

Wildasin, D. (1995), "Factor Mobility, Risk and Redistribution in the Welfare State", *Scandinavian Journal of Economics*, Vol.97: 527-546.

Chapter 3

Ackrill, R. W. (1998) "Fiscal Federalism and the European Union: The Need for a New Paradigm" *Working Papers in European Economic Studies* No.98/3, Department of Economics, University of Leicester.

Ascari, G. (2003), "Un'Authority per la Politica Fiscale", *La voce*, September 2003, Milan.

Bini Smaghi, L. and G. Tabellini (2003), "How to improve Economic Governance? The Coordination of Macroeconomic Policies in Europe", Aspen European Dialogue "Redesigning Europe", 28 February – 8 March, Rome.

Blinder, A. S. (1997), "Is Government too Political?", *Foreign Affairs* 76 (6): 115-126.

Brunetta, R and G. Tria (2003), "Il Patto di Stabilità e Crescita: Regole Fiscali da cambiare", *Economia Italiana*, 2: 303-350.

Calmfors, L. (2003), "Fiscal Policy to stabilise the Economy in the EMU: which Lessons can be learnt from Monetary Policy?" *CESifo Economic Studies* 49, 3/2003: 319-353.

Carlsen, F. (1998), "Central Regulation of Local Authorities", *Public Finance Review*, 26 (4): 304-326.

Casella A. (1999), "Tradable Deficit Permits: Efficient Implementation of the Stability Pact in the European Monetary Union", *Economic Policy*, 323-361.

Coricelli, F. and V. Ercolani (2002), "Cyclical and Structural Deficits on the Road to Accession: Fiscal Rules for an Enlarged European Union", *CEPR discussion paper* No.3672.

De Grauwe, P. (2003), *Economics of Monetary Union*, Oxford University Press, fifth edition, Oxford.

Dévoluy, M. (2004), *Les Politiques Economiques Européennes*, Enjeux et Défis, Edition du Seuil, Paris.

Eichengreen, B. (1997), "Saving Europe's Automatic Stabilisers", National Institute Economic Review, 159:92-98.

European Commission (2002), "Strengthening the Coordination of Budgetary Policies", COM (2002) 668, November.

Galì, J. and R. Perotti (2003), "Fiscal Policy and Monetary Integration in Europe", *NBER working paper* 9773.

Giavazzi, F., T. Jappelli and M. Pagano (2000), "Searching for non-linear Effects of Fiscal Policy Evidence form industrial and developing Countries", *European Economic Review* 44.

Guihéry, L. (2001), *Economie du Fédéralisme*, L'Harmattan, Paris.

Inmam, R. P. (1996), "Do Balanced Budget Rules work? US Experience and possible Lessons for the EMU", *NBER working papers*, No.5838 November.

International Monetary Fund (1999), *Manual on Fiscal Transparency*, Washington D C.

Oates, W. E. (1977), "Fiscal Federalism in Theory and Practice: Applications to the European Community", in MacDougall D *et al.* (1977), *Report on the Role of Public Finance in European Integration EC Commission*, Volume II: 279-318.

Obstfeld, M. (1997), "Dynamic Seignorage Theory: an Exploration", *Macroeconomic Dynamics*, No.3.

OECD (2003), "Fiscal Relations across Government Levels", *Economics Department Working Papers* No.375, Paris.

Perotti, R. (2003) "Estimating the Effects of Fiscal Policy in OECD Countries", *Economics Working Papers* 15, European Network of Economic Policy Research Institutes.

Persson, T., and G. Tabellini (2003), *The Economic Effects of Constitutions*, The MIT Press.

Persson, T., G. Roland, and G. Tabellini (1996), "The Theory of Fiscal Federalism: what does it mean for Europe?" Paper presented at the Conference "Quo vadis Europe", Kiel, June 1996.

Pisani-Ferry, J. (2002), "Fiscal Discipline and Policy Coordination in the euro zone: Assessment and Proposals", *Report to the Group OF Economic Analysis of the European Commission*, April.

Pisauro, G. (2001), "Intergovernmental Relations and Fiscal Discipline: between Commons and Soft Budget Constraints", *IMF working paper* 01/65.

Poterba, J. and K. Ruben (1999), "Fiscal Rules and State Borrowing Costs: Evidence from California and Other States", Public Policy Institute of California, San Francisco.

Rogoff, K. (1985), "The Optimal Degree of Commitment to intermediate Monetary Target", *Quarterly Journal of Economics*, 100:1169-1189.

Sapir, A. (2003), "An Agenda for a Growing Europe", *Report to the President of the European Commission*, Brussels.

Sutherland, A. (1995), "Fiscal Crisis and Aggregate Demand: can high Public Debt reverse the Effects of Fiscal Policy?" *Journal of Public Economics*, 65 (2), 147-162.

von Haghen, J. (1991), "A Note on the Empirical Effectiveness of Formal Fiscal Restraints", *Journal of Public Economics*, 44:199-210, March.

Wyplosz, C. (1999), "Economic Policy Coordination in EMU: Strategies and Institutions", *ZEI Policy Papers* BI.

Wyplosz, C. (1999), "Towards a More Perfect EMU", *Moneda y Credito* 208: 221-52.

Wyplosz, C. 2002), "Fiscal Policy: Institutions versus Rules", *CEPR Discussion Paper*, No.3238, March.

Chapter 4

Ackrill, R. (1998), "The European Union Budget, the Importance of the Balanced Budget Rule, the Future of the Rule under Economic and Monetary Union", Centre for European Economic Studies, Department of Economics, University of Leicester, August.

Barnevik, P. (2002), "Enlargement: Main Policy Challenges for 2004-2010", European Round Table.

Bchir, H., L. Fontagné, and P. Zanghieri (2003), "The Impact of EU Enlargement on Member States: a CGE Approach", *CEPII Working Paper* No.2003-10, August.

Beierl, O. (2001), "Reforming Intergovernmental Fiscal Relations in Germany: the Bavarian Point of View", Department Financial Policy, Bavarian State Ministry of Finance, September.

Börzel, T. (2003), "What can Federalism teach us about the EU: the German Experience", *Online paper 17/03*, Universität Heidelberg, May.

Busch, U. and C. Müller (2004), "Despite or Because – Lessons of German Unification for EU enlargement", KOF Working Papers No.87 April., Zurich.

Comité des Régions de l'UE (2001), *Les Pouvoirs Régionaux et Locaux en Europe*, Bruxelles

Corrado, M. (2001), "La Costituzione Finanziaria Europea", *Bollettino 11/2001 dell'Osservatorio Costituzionale*, Università Luiss Guido Carli, Roma.

European Commission (2000), "Education and Culture Publications Unit The budget of the European Union: how is your Money spent?", Bruxelles, February.

European Commission (2003), "Qualified Majority Voting on Tax Issues: detailed Arguments and specific Examples by Sector" (http://europa.eu.int/comm/taxation_customs/resources/documents/egs_en.pdf).

European Communities, "Preliminary Draft General Budget of the European Communities for the Financial Year 2004", General Introduction, (www.europa.eu.int).

German Federal Foreign Office "Facts about Germany: Unemployment", (http://www.tatsachen-ueber-deutschland.de)

Groenendijk, N. (2003), "Limited Ambitions. The European Convention and Decisions concerning Taxation in the EU after Enlargement", Paper presented at "Tax Policy in EU Candidate Countries. On the Eve of Enlargement", Centre for European Studies, University of Twente, The Netherlands, September.

Guihéry, L. (2000), "An Economic Assessment of German Fiscal Equalization Schemes since 1970: what Prospects for a Unified Germany?", Institute of Transport Economics, Université Lumière Lyon 2 – France.

Hega, G. (2003), "Between Reformstau und Modernisierung: The Reform of German Federalism since Unification", Department of Political Science, Western Michigan University, October.

Heiland, F. (2004), "Trends in East-West German Migration from 1989 to 2002", *Demographic Research* 11(7): 173-194.

Keuschnigg, C., M. Keuschnigg, and W. Kohler (1999), "Eastern Enlargement to the EU: Economic Costs and Benefits for the EU present Member States: Germany", *Final Report on Study XIX/B1/9801*, September.

Majocchi, A. (2003), "Fiscal Policy Rules and the European Constitution", in *The International Spectator*, 2

Praussello, F. (2003), "How Enlargement will change the EU Economy", Associazione Universitaria di Studi Europei.

Prey, T. (1995), "German Unification and European Integration", International Economics Faculty, The American University of Paris.

Rodden, J. (2000), "Breaking the Golden Rule: Fiscal Behaviour with Rational Bailout Expectations in the German States", Centre for European Studies, Harvard University, November.

Röscheisen, R. (2002), "Federalism in Germany", August (http://www.decentralization.ws/icd2/papers/federalism_germany.htm)

Seitz, H. (2000), "Sub-national Government Bailouts in Germany", in Publication data provided by the Inter-American Development Bank, European University Viadrina, November.

Sinn, H.-W. (2000), "EU Enlargement and the Future of the Welfare State", in *CESIFO Working Paper Series*, Working Paper No.307, June.

Timmins, G. (1996), "European Union Policy towards East-Central Europe: Prospects for Enlargement", University of Huddersfield.

von Hagen, J. and R. Strauch (1999), "Tumbling Giant: Germany's Experience with the Maastricht Fiscal Criteria", Center for European Integration Studies, Rheinische Friedrich-Wilhelms – Universität Bonn, March.

Walter, N. (2002), "Germany at the European Crossroad", Aspen Institute Italia.

Watts, R. L. and P. Hobson, (2000), "Fiscal Federalism in Germany", Institute of Intergovernmental Relations, Queen's University Kingston, Ontario Canada, December.

Werner, J. (2003), "The German Fiscal Federalism in a State of Flux", J. W. Goethe University, Frankfurt on the Main, September.

Chapter 5

Alesina, A., and G. Tabellini (1990), "A Positive Theory of Fiscal Deficits and Governments Debt", *Review of Economic Studies* 57: 403-14.

Brennan, G. and J. M. Buchanan (1980), *The Power to tax: Analytical Foundations of a Fiscal Constitution*, Cambridge, Cambridge University Press.

Committee of the Regions (2004), "Devolution in the European Union and the Candidate Countries", Brussels.

Darby, J., A. Muscatelli, G. Roy (2003), "Fiscal Decentralisation in Europe, a Review of Recent Experiences", University of Glasgow, Working paper, April.

European Commission (2004a), "Structures of the Taxation Systems in the European Union", Office for Official Publications of the European Communities, Luxemburg.

European Commission (2004b), "Spring 2004 Economic Forecasts", Directorate General for Economic and Financial Affairs, April.

Friedman, D. (1977), "A Theory of the Size and Shape of Nations", *Journal of Political Economy* 85: 59-77.

Niskanen, W. A. (1971), *Bureaucracy and Representative Governments*, New York, Aldine-Ahterton.

OECD (2002) "Fiscal Decentralisation in EU Applicant States and Selected Member States", Centre for Tax Policy and Administration, Report prepared for the workshop on "Decentralisation: trends, perspective and issues at the threshold of EU enlargement", October.

von Hagen, J. and I. Harden (1994), "National Budget Process and Fiscal Performance", *European Economic Reports and Studies* 3, EU, Brussels.

Wallis, J. and W. Oates (1988), "Decentralisation in the Public Sector: an Empirical Study of State and Local Government", in H. Rosen (1988), "Fiscal Federalism: Quantitative Studies", NBER.

World Bank (2002), "Concept of Fiscal Decentralisation and Worldwide Overview", edited by Robert D. Ebel and Serdar Yilmaz.

Chapter 6

Allen, D. (2000), "Cohesion and the Structural Funds", Chapter 9, pp. 243-265, in Wallace and Wallace (eds.).

Boyer, R., M. Dehove (2003), "La Répartition des Compétences en Europe, Le double éclairage du Droit et de l'économie", paper presented at the Journées de l'AFSE, Lille, May 2003.

Breuss, F., M. Eller (2003), "Efficiency and Federalism in the European Union, The Optimal Assignments of Policy Tasks to Different Levels of Government", *IEF* Working Paper No.50.

Buti, M., M. Nava (2003), "Towards a European Budgetary System", RSC No.2003/08, Pierre Werner Chair Series, European University Institute Working Papers.

Commission Européenne (2000), "Vade-mecum Budgétaire", office des publications officielles des Communautés Européennes.

Commission Européenne, DG de la politique régionale (2004), "La Cohésion au Tournant de 2007", Fiche d'information, inforegio.

Commission Européenne, DG de la politique régionale (2004) "Troisième Rapport sur la Cohésion Économique et Sociale: un Nouveau Partenariat pour la Cohésion Convergence Compétitivité Coopération".

European Commission (2004a), "Building our Common Future, Policy Challenges and Budgetary Means of the Enlarged Union 2007-2013", Communication from the Commission to the Council and the European Parliament, February.

European Commission (2004b), "Financial Perspectives 2007-2013", Communication from the Commission to the Council and the European Parliament, July.

Drazen, A. (2000), *Political Economy in Macroeconomics*, Princeton, NJ: Princeton University Press.

Hooghe, L., G. Marks (2001) *Multi-Level Governance and European Integration*, Rowman and Littlefield Publishers Inc., 249 p.

Laffan, B., M. Shackleton (2000), "The Budget, who gets what, when and how?", Chapter 8, pp. 211-241, in Wallace and Wallace (eds.).

Leroy, M. (2004), "Quelle Évaluation de la Politique Structurelle Régionale pour l'Élargissement de l'Europe", *Revue du Marché Commun et de l'Union Européenne*, No.477, pp. 215-225, Avril.

Majocchi, A. (2003), "Fiscal Policy Co-ordination in the European Union and the Financing of the Community Budget", *SIEP Working Paper 298*, University of Trento.

Majone, G. (1993), "The European Community, between social protection and social regulation", *Journal of Common Market Studies*, pp. 153-170, Vol.31, No.2.

Moravscik, A. (1998), *The Choice for Europe: Social Purpose and State Power from Messina to Maastricht*, Cornell University Press.

Montagnon, A. (2004), "Le Cadre Financier de l'Union Européenne pour l'après-2006", *Revue du Marché Commun et de l'Union européenne*, No.477, pp. 211-214, April.

Obstfeld, M. (1997), "Dynamic Seignorage Theory: an Exploration", *Macroeconomic Dynamics*, No.3.

Persson, T., G. Roland, and G. Tabellini (1996), "The Theory of Fiscal Federalism: what does it mean for Europe?" Paper presented at the Conference "Quo vadis Europe", Kiel, June 1996.

Persson, T. and G. Tabellini (2000), *Political Economics, explaining Economic Policy*, The MIT Press, Cambridge, London.

Tarschys, D. (2003), "Reinventing Cohesion, the Future of European Structural Policy", Swedish Institute for European Policy Studies, Report No.17, Stockholm, September.

Wallace, H., W. Wallace (eds.) (2000), *Policy-Making in the European Union*, 4th edition, the New EU Series, Oxford, Oxford University Press.

Consulted websites for empirics

http://www.cia.gov/cia/publications/factbook

http://www.constitution.org

http://www.cor.eu.int

http://www.euractiv.com

http://www.europa.eu.int

http://www.europarl.eu.int

http://www.europa.eu.int/comm/eurostat

http://www.imf.org

http://www.oecd.org

http://www.wikipedia.org

Construction and sources
of Indicators in Chapter 5

Tables 5.1, 5.2, 5.4, 5.5, and 5.7 have been elaborated by the authors, using different data from various sources. These data mostly come from Eurostat, the European Commission, the Committee of the regions, the International Monetary Fund, the OECD and the World Bank; others are own elaborations from national accounts. Our aim was to build new indexes more comprehensive and reliable than the ones usually presented in traditional decentralisation literature. We choose four indexes, each of them composed by several variables. As these variables may have different natures, we built 'weighted dummies' in order to obtain comparable values. This sign: '=' stands for: '*was given a value equal to*'.

1. Notes on the Construction and Calculation of the Various Indexes

Table 5.1. Political Decentralisation Index (PDI)

For each variable, a high value means a higher political decentrali-sation. Note that the first and last variables are, by construction, substitutes, so that the actual value range of the PDI is [0; 11].

Type of country
Unitary state '=' 0   centralised
Federal state '=' 3   decentralised

Existence of special status regions
No '=' 0   centralised
Capital and city state '=' 1
Small special status/autonomous regions (population<10%) '=' 2
Big autonomous regions '=' 3   decentralised

Number of levels of elected government (from local to central)

1 to 2 '=' 1 centralised

3 to 4 '=' 2 decentralised

5   '=' 3 very decentralised

Administrative tradition

Weak Weberian (WW)	'=' 2	decentralised
Medium Weberian (MW)	'=' 1	moderately decentralised
Strong Weberian (SW)	'=' 0	highly centralised
Post Sovietic (PS)	'=' 0	highly centralised

Strongest sublevel of government in political terms

Deduction from various sources (see the note below the table) of the most important sublevel in political terms level of government, coded as follows.

$R = L$ [a, f]   '=' 0   regional level politically stronger than the local one

weakly decentralised

$R=L=L$ [c, d, e] '=' 1   local and regional enjoy more or less the same power

moderately decentralised

L   '=' 2   local authorities politically stronger

highly decentralised

Tables 5.2 and 5.3 Interaction Index

We originally calculated an interaction index, which was put aside for reasons of strong interaction between this index and the Fiscal decentralisation index. This was the basis for the classification by line in Table 5.3. For information, the following presents the different values (hence, their weight in the overall index) we originally gave to each component of the interactions between central and sub-central levels of government in each country.

Organ of representation of the central level at the sub-central level

It either takes the value of 0 or 1, with 0 for no (either no data found or no representation) and 1 standing for the existence of a representation body. Note that it is very difficult to find the exact competencies these 'representations' enjoy, so the existence is at least a good sign that central and local have an 'institutional' meeting point in the decentralised unit.

Right of region to take part to the national policy formulation/elaboration

YES	'=' 2	high interaction
Advisory	'=' 1	medium interaction
NO	'=' 0	low interaction

Level implementing national policies

R-C	'=' 2	high interaction
L-C	'=' 2	high interaction
R	'=' 1	low interaction
C	'=' 0	centralised, no interaction

Fiscal and tax cooperation index

No	'=' 0	centralised
Tax rate, only tax rate	'=' 1	decentralised
Yes/Yes very low	'=' 2	highly decentralised

Table 5.4. Distribution of formal competencies among levels of government

Construction of the fiscal competencies indicator

First, we computed, on the basis on the COR 2004 research, the following symbols:

- C, when the competence was *fully*   central,
- R,   regional,
- L,   local,
- MCR, when the competence
was *shared* by the   central and regional levels,
- MCL   central and local levels,
- MRL   regional and local levels,
- MCRL   central, regional and local levels,

231

– M when the competence was mixed but in an uncertain fashion (lack of information, *e.g.* when one level was mentioned without details).

When we had no information at all concerning a competence, we left a blank case. We had 33 blank cases, *i.e.* 1.28 blank case on average out of 19 competencies, in total 33 blanks out of 475 data (approximately 7 per cent of missing data, which seems all right). Then we assigned to each of these symbols a number, which is given below:

– C   '=' 0, when the competence was *fully* central,

– R   '=' 1,   regional,

– L   '=' 1,   local,

– MCR '=' 0.5 when the competence

was *shared* by the   central and regional levels,

– MCL   '=' 0.5   central and local levels,

– MRL   '=' 1   regional and local levels,

– MCRL   '=' 0.75   central, regional, local levels

– M   '=' 0.5 when the competence was mixed but in an uncertain fashion

We then added the number assigned for each competence in each country, to get a kind of overall decentralisation score (does not appear here) which had to be divided by the number of known competencies by country. This allowed to account for the difference in known competencies in each country. For instance, the score of a country like Poland would have been too low compared to the actual case just because five competencies were missing. This methodology may overvalue the actual level of decentralisation.

The 'normalised weighted' average is thus comprised between 0 and 1. 0 would be the case where all competencies belong to the central government and 1 the opposite case, where all competencies belong to the regional AND/OR the local level of government or a mix of the two. We preferred not to differentiate between regions and localities (the latter could have been for instance assigned a bigger score), having a dichotomy centralised/decentralised.

Obviously, the only aim of the study is to compare European fiscal settings. In this comparative perspective, it may not be true to say that a higher score means more decentralisation. To get a true and accurate decentralisation index, a fully weighted average should be created. In each country, a weight should be assigned to each competence (for instance for the police competence: share of total police spending over total public spending). But comparison of national accounts is very difficult and no data set was available. The methodological flaws are numerous, that is why we later transformed the data in rough indicators ranging from 0 to 3.

Table 5.5. Fiscal Decentralisation Index

Fiscal competencies index

From the data above, we coded the 'boundary marks' as follows:

From 0.13 to 0.28:   0   highly centralised
From 0.28 to 0.43:   1   moderately decentralised
From 0.43 to 0.58:   2   decentralised
From 0.58 to 0.74:   3   highly decentralised

A 0 value means full centralisation, and a 1 value means full decentralisation, without any mixed competencies. This indicator ranges from 0.18 for Malta to 0.74 for Spain. In between, the highest scores are for Belgium, Germany, Finland, Poland, Czech Republic, and Slovakia. The high score of the two latter countries may however originate from data collection and methodological problems. The lowest scores are for Luxembourg, Portugal, Slovenia and France.

Global spending index
(total public spending as a share (per cent) GDP)

[0-40['=' 0
[40.1-55['=' 1
[55.1-70['=' 2

Sub-national spending index

It is calculated as a share of total national spending (source WB); the data are mostly for 1999 but the trend is quite similar in previous years.

[0-20['=' 0   weakly decentralised ,
[20-30['=' 1   moderately decentralised
>30   '=' 2   highly decentralised

Tax autonomy index 'taxes by local level as share of total taxation'

Taxes by level of government give an idea on how fiscal tax decentralisation is effectively. Generally, localities may have tax autonomy (either tax rate or tax base) but if they enjoy it on relatively small tax revenues at the end these localities are not so independent.

[0-10[	'=' 0	centralised
[10-25[	'=' 0.5	moderately decentralised
[25.1-40[	'=' 1	decentralised

These data come from "Structures of the taxation systems in the European Union", European commission (2004), appendix a, table b2 page 266 and following, and they refer to 2002. They are made up by central level, local + regional level, social security fund and transfers to the EC institution. The sum is always 100 (+/- 1.5 per cent)

Fiscal autonomy index based on vertical imbalance WB

[0-21[	'=' 3	decentralised
[21-41[	'=' 2	moderately decentralised
[41-61[	'=' 1	centralised
[61-80[	'=' 0	highly centralised

Table 5.7. The Components of Socio-Economic Cohesion

Construction of the cohesion index

The cohesion index is once again a loose indicator, which is supposed to give us a rough idea of the level of cohesion in a given country. Roughly speaking, the lower the cohesion, the higher the probability of trouble (including fiscal struggles, political conflict, secession, wars), and the higher the need to provide for a fiscal setting which smoothes potential tensions inside the country. It potentially ranges from 1 (very low cohesion) to 10 (very high cohesion).

The value judgments underlying our cohesion index should be made explicit. For instance, we have the feeling that cohesion cannot be exclusively captured by micro or macro variables respectively, nor can it be encompassed in exclusively sociological, economic or historical factors. We think that the level of cohesion depends on a mix of all these elements. First, history matters: the maturity of a country is a factor of cohesion. The more one leaves with other nationals in a given constitutional setting, the more cohesion is likely to be high. It can also be seen as an indicator of absence of past conflict, if the setting has been there for a long time. Second, cohesion also depends on linguistic and ethnical homogeneity: the more a country is ethnically homogeneous, the less it is likely to give rise to conflicts concerning the rights of minorities (or the respect and enforcement of these rights), distributional conflicts and the more preferences are homogeneous. When there are big minorities, conflicts tend to be deeper. When there is a small minority only, there tends to be higher devolved autonomy (special status) as a way to solve conflicts and preserve human rights (a European *sine qua non, cf.* Copenhagen). Cohesion can also be measured by economic indicators: the higher the level of inequality, the lower the cohesion. However, inequality is not only interpersonal, it carries a territorial relationship. Indeed, we defend the idea that when inequality is geographically concentrated, the probability of trouble is higher.

Note that we did not take into account the separatist party (which could have been given a negative score: *e.g.* – 1 when it exists, or take it as an indicator of ethnical cohesion per se).

For the numerical values assigned to each of these dimensions of cohesion, see below (*i.e.* socioeconomic indicators). The higher the overall index the higher the cohesion of the country (it ranges from 0 to 10). The lowest values are for Baltic countries and Belgium. The highest ones being for Austria and Nordic countries.

Existence of strong minorities

No	'=' 2
Yes Small minority < 10 per cent	'=' 1
Yes Strong minority > 10 per cent	'=' 0

Internal degree of territorial inequality

This indicator is calculated as the ratio between the richest region and the poorest region at the NUTS 3 or NUTS 2 (when it is the only available data, which is the case in most small countries) levels. The mean equals 2. Sensitively, and based on other information (some small countries can be considered having low degrees of inter-territorial inequalities (*e.g.* Luxembourg), others not (*e.g.* Cyprus)), missing data for inter-territorial inequality were given the following values: Denmark(1), Estonia(0), Cyprus(0), Latvia(0), Lithuania(0), Luxembourg(2), Malta(1), Slovenia(1).

[0; 1.6['=' 2
[1.6; 2.3 ['=' 1
[2.3; 3.1['=' 0

Degree of historical cohesion

This indicator carries a wide range of dimensions, mainly related to the 'age' of the nation or country, the date of independence and the 'age' of current constitution. It excludes the minority problems, already accounted for in a previous indicator.

high (H)   '=' 3
medium (M)   '=' 2
low   (L)   '=' 1
very low (VL)   '=' 0

Interindividual inequality:

The mean equals 4.3 and the median 4, ranging from 3 to 6.5.

[0-4['=' 3   moderately unequal
[4-5.5['=' 2   unequal
[5.5-7['=' 1   highly unequal

2. Main Data Sources

INDICATOR	SOURCE	YEAR
Type of country	Own	2004
Existence of special region status	COR	2004
Number of levels of government	Own based on COR	2004
Administrative tradition	Hooghe	1996
Organ of representation of the central level at the sub-central level	Own	2004
Right of region to take part to the national policy formulation/elaboration	European Parliament	2002
Implementation of national policy	Own	2004
Existence of a strong separatist	Own from constitution.org and	2004

party	wikipedia	
Power of regions to fix tax rates and basis	OECD	1999
Degree of MLG	Hooghe	1996
Cross-representation degree and power/political decentralisation index	Own	2004
Overall decentralisation of responsibilities	COR	2004
Total public spending as a share of GDP	Eurostat	2003
inc. Central	Eurostat	2003
inc. Regional	Eurostat	2003
inc. Local	Eurostat	2003
Social security	Eurostat	2003
Sub-national spending as share of total expenditures	IMF	1999
Total public revenues as a share of GDP	Eurostat	2003
inc. Central	Eurostat	2003
inc. Regional	Eurostat	2003
inc. Local	Eurostat	2003
Social security	Eurostat	2003
Taxes by level of government as % GDP Central government	European Commission	2004
State government	European Commission	2004
Local government	European Commission	2004
Taxes by level of government as % total taxation Central government	European Commission	2004
Local government	European Commission	2004
Vertical imbalance	IMF	1997
Budget balance in % of GDP	Commission spring forecast (spring 2004)	2004
Enforcement mechanisms	Own based on OECD	2003
Fiscal decentralisation indicator	Own	2004
GDP per inhabitant	Eurostat	2002
Unemployment rate	Eurostat	2003
Inflation	Eurostat	2003

Population	Eurostat	2003
Existence of strong minorities	World fact book	2004
Internal degree of territorial inequality (level of economic disparities)	Own, basis third report on cohesion EC (2004)	2001
Degree of historical cohesion (based on age of the country, date of independence and age of current constitution, and excluding the ethnic problems)	Own, from miscellaneous sources	2004
Degree of interindividual inequality	Eurostat	2001

International Financial Relations

The *International Triffin Foundation*, hosted by the Institute for European Studies at the 'Université catholique de Louvain' (Belgium), has the objective of establishing a centre dedicated to the continuation of the scientific work and the intellectual legacy of Robert Triffin (1911-1993) in the field of the international monetary system, and more generally in the areas of economics, finance and the social sciences.

Regular publications in the series *"International Financial Relations"* will ensure promotion of individual or collective works whose main themes are the ones with which Robert Triffin was particularly associated (the European Payments Union, the creation of Special Drawing Rights, the European Monetary System), as well as addressing the new problems which the international monetary system will be confronting at the dawn of the 21st century (external effects of the European Economic and Monetary Union, new tasks for the International Monetary Fund, prevention of financial crises, etc.).

Series editors:
Alexandre Lamfalussy, Bernard Snoy & Michel Dumoulin

Series Titles

No.1 Alexandre Lamfalussy, Bernard Snoy & Jérôme Wilson (eds.), *Fragility of the International Financial System. How Can we Prevent New Crises in Emerging Markets?*, 235 p., 2001.

No.2 Clément Vaneecloo, Augusta Badriotti & Margherita Fornasini, *Fiscal Federalism in the European Union and Its Countries. A Confrontation between Theories and Facts*, 240 p., 2006.

P.I.E. Peter Lang – The website

Discover the general website of the Peter Lang publishing group:

www.peterlang.com